BETWEEN THE RULE OF LAW
AND STATES OF EMERGENCY

BETWEEN THE RULE OF LAW AND STATES OF EMERGENCY

The Fluid Jurisprudence of the Israeli Regime

YOAV MEHOZAY

To Elinor

ILLUSTRATIONS

Figure 1. Diagram: The Co-Constitution of Law and Emergency   17

Figure 2. Output of Emergency Regulations: *Procedures following Changes in Currency Rates and Essential Work Service*s, 1948–2012   115

Table 1. Emergency Legal Mechanisms   55

CONTENTS

	List of Illustrations	ix
	Acknowledgments	xi
	Abbreviations	xiii
1.	Introduction: The Co-Constitution of Law and Emergency	1
2.	Israel's Legal-Political System: A Fluid Structure	27
3.	Fluid Emergency Legal Sources	53
4.	Practicing Fluidity I: The Complementary Relationship between Israel's Emergency Legal Sources	83
5.	Practicing Fluidity II: Emergency Powers for Economic and Financial Ends	103
6.	Conclusion	133
	Notes	145
	Bibliography	169
	Index	187

Cover design by Anat Saacks, A design studio.

Published by State University of New York Press, Albany

© 2016 State University of New York

All rights reserved

Printed in the United States of America

No part of this book may be used or reproduced in any manner whatsoever without written permission. No part of this book may be stored in a retrieval system or transmitted in any form or by any means including electronic, electrostatic, magnetic tape, mechanical, photocopying, recording, or otherwise without the prior permission in writing of the publisher.

For information, contact State University of New York Press, Albany, NY
www.sunypress.edu

Production, Jenn Bennett
Marketing, Kate R. Seburyamo

Library of Congress Cataloging-in-Publication Data

Names: Mehozay, Yoav, 1973- author.
Title: Between the rule of law and states of emergency : the fluid jurisprudence of the Israeli regime / Yoav Mehozay.
Description: Albany : State University of New York Press, 2016. | Includes bibliographical references and index.
Identifiers: LCCN 2016007712 (print) | LCCN 2016007844 (ebook) | ISBN 9781438463391 (hardcover : alk. paper) | ISBN 978-1-4384-6338-4 (pbk : alk. paper) | ISBN 9781438463407 (e-book)
Subjects: LCSH: War and emergency legislation—Israel. | War and emergency legislation—Political aspects—Israel. | Arab-Israeli conflict—Law and legislation—Israel.
Classification: LCC KMK2650 .M44 2016 (print) | LCC KMK2650 (ebook) | DDC 342.5694/062—dc23
LC record available at http://lccn.loc.gov/2016007712

10 9 8 7 6 5 4 3 2 1

ACKNOWLEDGMENTS

Many people have helped to make this book possible. I wish to thank my mentors from the Graduate Faculty of the New School for Social Studies: Andrew Arato, Uri Ram, who spent two years at the New School while I was there, Oz Frankel, and Ann Stoler. Andrew Arato has inspired me with his intellectual enthusiasm; thank you for sharing your brilliance and analytical rigor and for your support throughout the years. Uri Ram was the first person who, for better or worse, made me think about a project related to Israel. My deepest gratitude to Oz Frankel, who has been my biggest supporter at the New School over the years. Oz, I cannot thank you enough for your support and advice. I also wish to thank Ann Stoler, who in conversations over the years has advanced my work.

Chapter 5 and some of the theoretical ideas of the book were developed during my tenure at the the Center for Middle Eastern Studies at Harvard University. I would like to thank Sue Kahn, Roger Owen, Baber Johansen, and the stuff of the Harvard Law Library. An earlier version of chapter 3 was originally published in the *Law & Society Review* in 2012. In recognition of part of the work presented in this book, I won the Association for Israel Studies Baruch Kimmerling Prize. I would like to thank the Prize Committee: Hanna Herzog (chair), Ian Lustick, and Mary Totry, and the AIS president at the time, Gad Barzilai. The final configuration and preparation of the book was done in my current position as a faculty member of the school of criminology at the University of Haifa. I would like to thank my colleagues and the administrative staff of that school. Finally, I wish to give an enormous special thanks to my dear friend Eran Fisher. Thank you for reading and commenting on my work, but much more for always being there for me and encouraging me in my toughest moments throughout this difficult process. The arguments expressed in this book, and any errors of fact or interpretation, are, of course, exclusively mine.

Special thanks to Lauren Horwitz, who accompanied me throughout this project, for her most valuable editorial assistance. A big thank you to my sister, Anat Saacks, who designed the cover of the book. I also want to thank SUNY Press for their support, especially Michael Rinella and Rafael Chaiken. Last, but certainly not least, I would like to thank my lifetime companion, my wife, Elinor Dehan. I cannot begin to express my gratitude; without you this project would have been impossible. This book is dedicated to her and our amazing children, Naomi and Nathan.

ABBREVIATIONS

Guide to General Abbreviations

HCJ High Court of Justice
LAO Law and Administration Ordinance, 1948
OPT Occupied Palestinian Territories
SOE State of Emergency

Guide to Abbreviations of Official Publications of the State of Israel

DK   Protocol of the Knesset Proceedings.
HH   Hatza'ot Hok—Bills Presented to the Knesset.
IR   Iton Rishmi—Official Gazette during the Provisional Council of State (before the Knesset).
KT   Kovetz Ha-Takanot—Regulations Issued by Ministers of the Government.
LSI Law of the State of Israel.
SH   Sefer Hahukim—Statue Book.
YP   Yallkut HaPirsumim—Government Notices.

Guide to Abbreviations of Court Materials

AD   Case Materials, Additional Deliberation.
CA   Case Materials, Civil Appeal.

EA	Case Materials, Election Appeal No.
FH	Further Hearing No.
HC	Case Materials, High Court No.
PD	Piskei Din—Law Reports of the Supreme Court of the State of Israel

1

INTRODUCTION

The Co-Constitution of Law and Emergency

Israel's physical security is a central theme in the evolution of the state's law and society. Indeed, few would dispute that the democratic state's legal systems are intertwined with ensuring the safety and security of citizens.

But students of Israeli history may be surprised to learn that, even when physical security was not threatened, the Israeli authorities have resorted to emergency legal measures to achieve desired political goals. In fact, the state has a long history of using emergency powers to ensure various political and economic outcomes that have no bearing on the state's security. In essence, the state has used emergency powers to achieve desired political outcomes, even when that use of power ran roughshod over democratic rule.

In general, a state of emergency (SOE) is a severe condition that results from a clear and imminent threat to the well-being of the state and its people. With an SOE, traditional law is suspended to address the crisis—often with military means—to ensure safety and security, and then reverts to traditional democratic rule once the immediate crisis has passed. But in the case of Israel and regimes like it, the emergency suspension of laws continues after the precarious moment has passed. In Israel, a legal SOE has been in place since the inception of the state.[1] It was proclaimed amid Israel's war of independence with the expectation that it would be temporary, but it has remained in effect ever since. With emergency declared, the state can suspend regular governance for a variety of weakly justified exceptions. The continual SOE has produced peculiar outcomes.

Consider how it has been used with respect to purely political issues, such as the state's currency valuation. In October 1977, for example, the newly elected government in Israel used emergency measures for a non-security purpose. Headed by the Likud party, the new government was determined to open the foreign exchange market as the first step in liberalizing Israel's economy. Just a few months prior, the state underwent a major political upset, with the right-wing Likud party winning elections for the first time. Israel's liberal party was a faction within Likud, and its members came armed with a ready-made economic plan.

While the new economic strategy was expected, the method of achieving it was not. What is surprising—and practically unacknowledged—is that this "major reform of controls" (Halevi 1986, 244), was executed with emergency powers. But the sole function of these emergency powers should be to address situations that threaten the physical security of the state. Instead, a new economic program, which should have been introduced via primary legislation and which had nothing to do with supporting a population during wartime, was instituted using emergency regulations.

As the events of October 1977 suggest, Israel's emergency powers are so deeply embedded in its governance that normal and exceptional modes of governance become virtually indistinguishable. Israel's political structure also highlights the commonness of exception in its legal system. With its single-house parliamentary system, the government could have used its coalition majority to enact this new policy rather than resort to emergency powers. The evidence presented in this book reveals a reality in which law and emergency make up a co-constitutive mode of governance.

But the events of October 1977 point to an equally important phenomenon that extends the power of emergency laws even further. The implementation of the new foreign exchange policy reveals how by building emergency into the fabric of the law, it is the structural dynamics of the law, and not just the authority of the law, that extends the power of the sovereign: the Israeli authorities. Israel's legal system features several emergency legal mechanisms that exist alongside one another. The authority of these mechanisms is overlapping but also complementary. These multiple legal sources work together to create a fluid structure, enabling authorities to travel easily between different emergency legal sources as justifications for measures, while nonetheless maintaining a degree of legitimacy as a government by law. These dynamics of law grant flexibility in the application of law. As a result, Israeli authorities can capitalize on multiple emergency legal sources to achieve their aims, sometimes by patching laws together for a desired result or moving freely from one legal mechanism to another when the first does not serve desired ends. In what follows, I elaborate on this concept.

Let us examine this strategy in practice: how certain emergency regulations and laws have been interwoven to create this fluidity. In October 1977, the Israeli government applied not one, but two emergency legal mechanisms that stem from two distinct emergency legal sources. On the one hand, the government relied on the Mandatory Emergency (Defence) Regulations, specifically, the Mandatory Defence (Finance) Regulation of 1941,[2] to introduce a new monetary policy to control currency rates. Despite their originating in the British mandate, partly as a means to exert control over the Jewish community, the Mandatory Emergency Regulations are now part of Israeli law. As such, the Israeli government has a ready-made legal source to create emergency measures that do not hinge on declaring an SOE. On the other hand, the Israeli government used an original Israeli emergency mechanism. This alternative emergency legal source empowers the Israeli government to issue emergency regulations at the ministers' discretion, and at any given moment without seeking the Knesset's approval. With this authority, the minister of finance issued, two emergency regulations: the Emergency (Procedures Following Changes in Currency Rates) Regulation[3] and Emergency (Cancelation of the Services Import Tax and the Travel Tax, and Correction of the Value Added Tax Law) Regulation,[4] which blocked any benefit from devaluing the Israeli currency and implemented a new fiscal policy to ease controls on payments for goods and services, respectively.

Thus, the power that emergency authorities grant is based not only on their application beyond the realm of security necessities, but on dynamics of the law. Having a complex legal system that enables the authorities to call on whichever legal mechanism is most politically expedient for the situation is beneficial. It enables the authorities to pivot between legal mechanisms and to call on whatever is most appropriate to achieve a desired political outcome.

But when states of emergency become ever-present modes of governance, the question is whether they have become institutionalized, rather than being aberrations from the norm. And when these states of emergency become governing norms, what is the relationship between states of emergency and the rule of law? This book examines the interplay of emergency and the rule of law and explores whether these modes of governance are less distinct than previously understood. It asks, in fact, whether they are mutually reinforcing and mutually enabling—and how these states of emergency have imparted a particular character to regimes like Israel.

Rule of Law and Emergency Powers

Most scholarship on the rule of law and states of emergency does not take the interdependence between these two mechanisms of governance as its point of departure. Instead, over the course of a long history, these two modes of governance have been perceived as opposing concepts—despite attempts to reconcile them by controlling emergency powers through law. These attempts—often referred to as classical models of accommodation—include governing mechanisms such as "state of emergency," "state of siege,"[5] "state of alert [or alarm]," "state of readiness," "state of internal war," "suspension of guarantees," "martial law,"[6] "crisis powers," "special powers," "curfew," and so on. These exceptional governing mechanisms reflect a shared understanding, even by the most liberal thinkers such as John Locke,[7] that times of emergency necessitate the abandonment of rational law in favor of sovereign prerogative. Such a conception fosters the understanding that emergencies can take many forms, but the ability to prepare for them is limited. As such, emergency has become an umbrella term that refers to a variety of phenomena including but not limited to war, rebellion, epidemic, and economic meltdown. Thus, there is no precise definition of "emergency." The fundamental assumption of the models of accommodation is that once a threat disappears, normalcy can return without the residual effect of the emergency regime.

In this context, the scholarship on governing during times of emergency has focused on the question of whether the rule of law and emergency powers—seemingly contradictory modes of governance—can or should sit together. This question is at once normative and practical; the normative question is what are the conditions, if any, in which we should apply emergency powers, even if they violate the rule of law? The practical question is how can government ensure the security of the state and its people while respecting the rights of its citizens?

Indeed, legal-political theory,[8] particularly in the fields of constitutional theory and international law theory,[9] has spawned much debate about whether legal tools can tame emergency powers. On the one hand, we have *ratio* (rational law) as the highest right, and, on the other hand, we have *voluntas* (sovereign will) as the highest might. This dichotomy between the principles of the rule of law and the necessities of emergency powers has presented a great challenge to legal-political thinkers who have attempted to codify emergency powers into law books or place them under judicial review. The fundamental question is how to institutionalize emergency powers without overrunning the rule of law.

Several schools of thought have emerged to explain persistent states of emergency in democracy. First, there are the skeptics, following the German legal-political theorist Carl Schmitt,[10] who argued that emergency powers are fundamentally inconsistent with the rule of law. The term skeptics expresses the profound doubt that law can in any way control emergency crises. As the skeptics see it, emergency is elastic and ambiguous; it can appear in many different forms, and thus no legal form can foresee, let alone constrain, the measures needed to deal with an emergency crisis. Moreover, following Schmitt, they assume that emergency is what exists outside law.[11] In this respect, emergency powers are a necessity in times of an existential threat, and "necessity has no law" (Agamben 2005, 24). That is, necessity demands swift actions; it is not based on a legal norm, nor is there good-faith judgment about a necessity. Action that comes from necessity therefore cannot adhere to rule-of-law principles such as clarity, publicity, and generality, or protect against violations of human and civil rights. While for Schmitt this justifies suspending legality, for Giorgio Agamben and other thinkers who in some respects follow Schmitt (and whom I will to refer as radical skeptics), it is a source of continual abuse of power by liberal democracies.

A second school of thought maintains that legal tools can control emergency powers. Scholars in this camp suggest different legal models of accommodation to restrain emergency powers.[12] Members of this group are referred to as dualists (Zuckerman 2006) to indicate their conviction that times of normalcy and times of emergency should be governed by different legal measures (or extra-legal measures, in the case of the realists, as we shall soon see). The basic premise that guides this paradigm, and that was shared by political thinkers from Locke, Blackstone, and Jefferson to Machiavelli and Rousseau, is that emergency powers are at least partially legal; that is, based on "normative concepts" (Zuckerman 2006, 524). Yet this sizable group differs about the best legal means to use in a time of crisis.

Some members of the dualist group, following the tradition and work of Clinton Rossiter, base their analysis on the ancient model of the Roman dictatorship.[13] They advocate a neo-Roman model that asserts the legitimacy of emergency powers within a constitutional framework. They believe that either the material or the formal constitution, or both, should be significantly transformed to deal with potentially grave emergencies (Ararto 2006, 547). In this view, a sovereign is vested with extraordinary yet constitutional powers (Gross, 2013: 334–335). Members of this group include Bruce Ackermann, John Ferejohn, Pasquale Pasquino, Richard A. Posner,[14] and John Yoo.[15] The impact of this approach is extensive, because almost all constitutions contain provisions for emergency powers (Neocleous 2006, 194 and 206).

Other members of the dualist tradition advocate an alternative *legislative* model[16] in which emergency powers are delegated by ordinary legislation. The process of promulgating emergency powers is carried out by modifying ordinary laws or by legislating special emergency laws. Here too, emergency powers are considered exceptional, and once the crisis subsides, the system is to return to its ordinary legal and political processes. Advocates of the legislative model argue that its advantage over the constitutional model is that one need not anticipate the kind of emergency. This more flexible framework is an antidote to the chameleon-like nature of emergency. However, critics of the legislative model have warned that because the source of the legislation is ordinary, there is a greater risk that these emergency statutes will transform into normative laws.

The *realists*[17] are another subgroup of the dualists. Their name suggests that they share the skeptics' conviction that emergency exists outside law, but unlike the radical skeptics, the realists aim to restrain emergency powers by extra-legal measures. They are part of the dualist school of thought insofar as they approve the use of exceptional executive prerogatives in times of crisis—that is, governing measures that are different from ordinary legislation—but members of this group suggest that extra-legal alternatives should control emergency powers. Examples of this school are Oren Gross's extra-legal measures model (2003)[18] and Mark Tushnet's "extra-constitutional" measures. These models argue that executive action should be reviewed not by law, but by mobilized citizenry (2005b, 46).

In addition to the skeptics and the dualists, there are the *monists* (Ferejohn and Pasquino 2004), or as they are also called, advocates of the "business as usual" model (Gross and Aoláin 2006, 10).[19] While the monists agree that law and emergency are inherently at odds with each other, they argue that true democracy must govern by law and consistency, not by exception. The names of this school aim to capture the "strict" position (Posner and Vermeule 2005, 56) or the "inside" position (Lazar 2013, 138–159), in which even in times of crisis, the government should closely preserve and follow the rule of law and not go outside the legal realm (hence, stay "inside") by applying extra-legal measures. In other words, the monist position rejects the notion that emergencies justify circumventing law and diverging from the ordinary scheme of governance (Zuckerman 2006, 524). David Dyzenhaus, for example, has claimed that the rule of law prohibits the use of extra-legal measures, and that it is possible to respond to emergencies while respecting the rule of law (2005; 2006). One should not dismiss the monist approach as naïve; their conviction comes from the awareness of the "tendency of emergency policies to become entrenched over time and thus normalized and made routine."[20] This understanding is referred to as the ratchet theory (Posner and Vermeule 2005, 57–59), which states that emergency powers move forward, not backward. In other words, once used, they remain on the law books rather than being stricken from everyday governance.

Often the monist approach relies on the courts to control emergency powers, though often on the basis of an *ex post facto* review. Dyzenhaus (2006) is of the opinion that judges are obliged to adhere to the rule of law at all times, including times of emergency, and to control the actions of the government. Laurence Tribe and Patrick

Gudridge offer a more moderate version of this opinion, calling for "judicial responses within constitutional law" (2004, 1805).[21] Regarding *ex post facto* review, David Cole argues that despite the slow nature of the court, when considered over time, judicial review has successfully constrained the exercise of emergency power (2003, 2566).

Yet I argue that although this discourse is illuminating and important, it misses the reality of the matter, almost to the point of rendering itself irrelevant. Emergency powers and the rule of law are already profoundly commingled and have been for some time. This statement, based on empirical evidence, should be our point of departure. The Despouy Report, prepared for the United Nations, found that between January 1985 and May 1997, some hundred states or territories—that is, more than half the member states of the UN, states representing every continent except Antarctica—have at some point been under an SOE. The list includes Western liberal democracies such as France, the United Kingdom, Canada, and the United States. In the aftermath of September 11, the UN Security Council passed Security Council Resolution 1368 (2001), requiring all member states to enact laws to combat terrorism. This reality, I argue, calls for an alternative theoretical focus.

Alternative Theoretical Model

Unlike previous approaches, which base their analyses on the premise that law and emergency are at odds with each other, this book takes a different approach. My point of departure is the observation that the relationship between the two is more nuanced and complex than was previously thought; on many occasions law and emergency share an extremely intimate relationship, where the two modes of governance fuel each other.

While the realization regarding the commingling of law and emergency is in itself not new, it is generally taken to be merely an abstraction, albeit a significant one, which is to say, an obstacle to be overcome rather than a systemic phenomenon. As noted, a sizable number of scholars maintain that "emergency regimes tend to perpetuate themselves" (Gross and Aoláin 2006, 175), but this realization does not motivate them to shift their focus from how to make sure that emergency measures are only temporary and only during periods of exceptional danger or crisis—the two fundamental features of any model of accommodation. My alternative analytical model's basic premise, on the other hand, is that we should reject the notion that law and emergency are ontologically separate. Moreover, it requires the study of the relationship between the two, a study independent of a "genuine" crisis.

The book thus shifts the focus of legal-political theory from the question of whether and how emergency powers can conform to the rule of law to a new perspective, whose basic premise is that the rule of law and emergency powers make common, flexible governmental methods that empower political regimes. I argue that mutuality is the key, in which both modes of governance compensate for each other's weaknesses and together construct a stable political regime.

As such, this book addresses critical gaps in current theoretical studies of the relationship between the rule of law and emergency powers. As noted, most relevant scholarship on states of emergency—from radical skeptics and from ardent liberals—has focused on how law can control and restrain emergency powers, if at all. Both groups of thinkers, who otherwise do not agree on anything, take the same premise: an ontological separation between law and emergency. In this sense they all hold to the "emergency paradigm," which assumes that an ontological dichotomy exists between normalcy and emergency (Greene 2011, 1764–1765).

For liberals, law is autonomous, and thus emergency rule is an aberrational exception: They separate "normal" times and "normal" order of government from "exceptional" times of emergency and "exceptional" order of government. This assumption guides both the dualists and the monists. With regard to the dualists, the separation is clear; all models of accommodation are based on this split. The monists' point of departure is also based on this division; they simply choose the rule of law over the exception.

The radical skeptic's position in this regard is the mirror image of the monist's. Because radical skeptics assume that actions in a time of emergency are necessities, and since "necessity has no law," they regard governing by emergency powers as a perpetuate prerogative rule. Even more so, for radical skeptics, governing through sovereign prerogatives dominates and simply obviates normative law, to the point that "the exception is the rule" (Benjamin 1968, 257). At any rate, by taking the position that emergency is outside the rule of law, they separate law from emergency.²² Moreover, even the radical skeptics, albeit to a lesser degree, study emergency in the context of a crisis, at least initially.²³

Even realist scholars who recognize the interconnection of law and emergency, such as Oren Gross (2003; 2006), have focused on possible ways of controlling state power during an SOE. Such emphasis ultimately reinforces a false division of emergency and law. In Goss's book *Law in Times of Crisis* (written with Fionnuala Ní Aoláin), in which he clearly recognizes the commingling of law and emergency, the focus is on responses by democratic regimes to violent crises. In this respect, Gross is part of the mainstream scholarship on law and emergency that studies emergency only with the respect to crises.

I reject the notion that we need to study the relationship between law and emergency only in the context of a crisis, and I reject the premise that they are separate. I argue that in Israel, at the very least, the rule of law and an SOE have comingled continuously. In fact, the conjoining of law and emergency in the legal-political framework is reflected in the structure of many regimes around the world, including many liberal-democracies. Mark Neocleous argues even further that "the idea of 'normal times' is the biggest political myth" (2006: 204). For Neocleous, this myth is the product of the liberal paradigm, which assumes that there is "normalcy," where order is created by rules (ibid., 206–207). Against the false dichotomy of rule of law and emergency, he asserts that emergency powers are part of the normal mode of governing (ibid., 208). Historically, "Either the state of emergency is constantly re-enacted, or it remains in place by virtue of not being explicitly repealed, or it is eventually placed on the statute books as part of 'ordinary' legislation" (ibid., 204). Empirical evidence supporting Neocleous's assertion can be found in a collection of comparative studies on courts and terrorism, the conclusion of which asserts that "perhaps the most striking and potentially disturbing lesson repeated throughout this book is the tendency for [emergency] policies that are temporary to be transformed into permanent ones or for the extraordinary to become normal" (Volcansek and Stack 2011, 231). With time, their coexistence becomes a sustainable reality. Thus seemingly contradictory legal principles exist side by side (and in fact enhance one another), creating a regime that has incorporated both modes of governance.

The fact that scholarship has separated law from emergency has helped consolidate two unfounded conceptions, even by critical thinkers such as Agamben (2005): First, that there is a division between normal times and states of emergency; and second, that when such a division is engulfed by a state of permanent emergency—which has arguably developed since 9/11—it represents a new phenomenon (Neocleous 2006). In reality, these events, significant as they are, represent "more of the same" (Scheuerman 1999–2000, Neocleous, 2006). What helps to generate such separation, I argue, is the notion that we should study emergency in the context of crises. By considering the extensive use of emergency powers for economic regulation, for example, we quickly realize that many liberal democratic regimes in the past, such as Great Britain and the United States, as well as in Weimar Germany and France, have relied on emergency institutions and procedures for long periods of time well before the war on terror became a reality (Rossiter 1948; Scheuerman 1999–2000).

Working from this perspective, this book demonstrates the interdependent relationship between law and emergency, even in macroeconomic scenarios. Indeed, as William Scheuerman argues, the majority of studies on the use of emergency powers in economic matters are narrow in scope, and prominent voices within contemporary legal-political theory seem altogether uninterested in the problem of economic states of emergency (1999–2000, 187). Thus most of the work produced on states of emergency ignores the rich history of emergency powers used in political economy. But this history is crucial to understanding that they are far from exceptional methods of governance.

I join contemporary scholars such as Scheuerman, Neocleous, and Nomi Claire Lazar, who argue that the coexistence of the rule of law and emergency powers is a permanent political condition not only in authoritarian regimes, but also in liberal democracies. The state of Israel is perhaps one of the strongest examples of such mutuality.

Rather than concentrating on the question of how to allow government sufficient powers to meet crises while simultaneously preventing those powers from being abused, this book explores how a regime can include both modes of governance and how they support each other in shaping a long-term, stable rule. By "stable rule," I mean a regime that sustains itself over time despite its legitimacy being contested because of the political objectives it achieves with emergency powers. This book analyzes this relationship as a mutually reinforcing legal-political framework. I argue that only by acknowledging the true relationship between law and emergency, which is so prevalent in modern political systems of government, can we understand the challenge that emergency powers present.

Specifically, the book analyzes law and emergency as mutually dependent in Israel. Unlike previous scholarship, which is often preoccupied with *why* Israel relies on an SOE, this book asks how the regime has made two conceptually opposed doctrines coexist, and has fostered its convenient, if convoluted, government structure. It is a hands-on approach in studying this relationship as a co-constitutive correlation.

The Rule of Law, Law and Emergency Powers

I borrow from the emergency paradigm the monist's ratchet theory, that after emergency powers are enacted, they tend to persist as law and gradually become normal methods of government. I share the radical skeptic's understanding that law has something to do with this process; that is to say, it is not only that exceptional emergency powers derogate from the rule of law, but that legal mechanisms actually support emergency powers and their precarious effect.

To begin with, emergency powers are arguably the most effective tool for asserting sovereign will while maintaining a degree of legitimacy. During an SOE, law is ideally suspended *by* law to protect law. An SOE is not equivalent to a state-of-no-law; with its various legal-political institutions, the state continues to exist. As noted, many of the most prominent political thinkers, from Machiavelli and Rousseau to Locke and Jefferson, assumed that emergency powers are at least partially normative concepts. Moreover, while emergency powers, or better yet, emergency law, may have the authority to suspend a body of law and to violate all protected human and civil rights, they seldom do. With emergency law, rather than directly challenging the rule of law, power holders sneak up on the rule of law to meet desired ends. In the Israeli case, despite the volatility of emergency law, the regime has endured for decades with relative stability.

With that said, the rule of law is not a sham. While law often serves power, the rule of law does not equal power. Following a softer version of E. P. Thompson's conception of the rule of law (1975), I also contend that the principles of the rule of law matter, and that for law to mean anything, it must appear to be just, not simply to serve power.

In a postscript on the rule of law in his book *Whigs and Hunters: The Origins of the Black Act*, Thompson argues that despite the application of law as an instrument of class power, law, with its reference to universal standards and equality, is different from arbitrary power (1975, 262). He explains that "if the law is evidently partial and unjust, then it will mask nothing, legitimize nothing, contribute nothing to any class's hegemony" (ibid., 263). Thus, despite the fact that law is partly a sham (ibid., 266), for it to have credence, it must "pay" for the ideology of its principles, and thus impose some inhibitions on power. Thompson even argues that law is "an unqualified human good" (ibid., 266), for which he received ardent criticism. But even his fiercest adversary, Morton Horwitz, conceded in his review of Thompson's book that law "undoubtedly restrains power" (1976–1977).

For simplicity's sake, we can assert that the *rule of law* represents all the principles that adhere to universal standards and equality, while *law* represents legal tools that are comingled with political interests and are less pure.

To understand Thompson's conception of the rule of law we must return to Max Weber's assertion regarding the affinity between legality and legitimacy in modern times. Here lies the trick: to gain legitimacy, power must to some degree respect the principles of the rule of law and be restricted by law. Law remains effective only as long as we believe in its validity to constrain power. In this respect, Thompson explains that "rulers find a need to legitimize their power" (ibid., 263) and therefore adhere to law. In doing so, at times they must pay the "tax" that is attached to the rule of law.

What we have, therefore, is an ever-present tension between sovereign will (the highest might) and the rule of law (the highest right). As Franz Neumann articulates it, sovereignty and the rule law are irreconcilable, but they are two constitutive elements of the modern state (1986, 4). Neumann goes on to argue that "in a society which cannot dispense with power as principle, complete generality of law is impossible" (1964, 66). Hence, the rule of law cannot be fully adhered to as long as power has its way. This is why emergency powers, among other legal mechanisms, are so frequently used. Rather than directly challenging the rule of law, power uses tools associated with law, however roundabout they may seem, to maintain legitimacy. Put simply, power enlists law to legitimize its action. And more so, even illegitimate power (power based on non-democratic practices such as in the case of colonial or military rule) is at least partly built on law. As Eve Darian-Smith and Peter Fitzpatrick note, for law to rule, "Law must be ever responsive and indeterminate, capable of extending to the infinite variety that constantly confronts it" (2008, 3). Hence, in practice, political players use different legal apparatuses; chief among these are emergency powers, which are used to achieve their political will.

Analytical Framework

To best understand how Israeli authorities have extended emergency powers beyond their logical limit, this book illuminates the dynamics and interplay of law, politics, history, and economy. Specifically, my analysis brings together critical German political thought with colonial legal studies, and develops it into an advanced framework that reformulates the symbiotic relationship between law and emergency.

My point of departure is the work of Ernst Fraenkel, a German lawyer and political scientist, who in his book *The Dual State* (1941) articulated the existence of a co-constitutive dynamic between rational law and exceptional sovereign actions. Legal-political thought has been torn between two poles regarding the relationship between law and politics. It is a debate between a belief in the autonomy of law and the total politicization of law. In German legal-political scholarship, the former is represented by Hans Kelsen, while the latter is represented by Carl Schmitt.

Fraenkel's analytical framework lies between these poles, though it favors Schmitt's perspective. Analyzing the Nazi regime during the 1930s, he describes a symbiotic relationship between the *prerogative* state ("a governmental system which exercises unlimited arbitrariness and violence unchecked by any legal guarantees") and the *normative* state ("an administrative body endowed with elaborate powers for safeguarding the legal orders as expressed in statutes, decisions of the courts, and activities of the administrative agencies"). According to Fraenkel, the normative state is an essential aspect of the prerogative state; it is a "necessary complement to the Prerogative State," he writes (1941, 71). In fact, the prerogative state cannot function without the normative state. While legally the prerogative state has unlimited jurisdiction, in practice, however, its jurisdiction is limited. Only when joined with the normative state can the prerogative state sustain itself and gain some legitimacy by maintaining a connection to government by law. And thus, "the Normative State is allowed to function, where the Prerogative State does not require jurisdiction" (1941, 58). By maintaining such symbiosis, the prerogative state can present itself as a necessary exception rather than the actual rule of the land. In this context, law and emergency powers are hardly antagonistic to each other. Taken together, the regime is based on a sustainable and mutually reinforcing composition of the prerogative and the normative, which together make up the state's governance.

My goal here is to extend Fraenkel's analytical framework. I argue that the mutuality between law and emergency powers is present in various political contexts, including the state of Israel, rather than only in extreme dictatorships such as the Nazi regime. In fact, to a certain extent Fraenkel himself recognizes this when he applies his analysis to German capitalism.

The colonial state combined the prerogative with the normative state many years before the Nazi regime, mixing these modes of government to establish a hybrid regime that served its ambitious political objectives. In this respect, I apply a similar extension to the work of various scholars who study the application of law in the colony and legal imperialism. First and foremost, I posit that Nasser Hussain's assertion, in his work on *hyperlegality*,[24] that "the innovations and enduring legacies of a colonial governmentality offer a valuable resource for understanding the larger significance of specific [post-9/11] antiterrorism legislations" (2007, 514) goes even further. At least in the case of Israel, they shed light on sustainable governing apparatuses and legal structural complexity that date significantly before September 11.

In *The Origins of Totalitarianism* (1951), Hannah Arendt was perhaps the first to connect colonial or imperial rule to modern government.[25] In recent years, students of colonialism have advanced this understanding.[26] As they argue, rather than only operating in a might-makes-right mode, colonizers opted to achieve their discriminatory agenda through a kind of Weberian rational authority. Colonizers therefore carried out their will by legal mechanisms, however awkward, and thus maintained a veneer of legitimacy. In essence, colonial law had to serve a dual function: rationalization and discrimination. This duality demanded great flexibility in the use of law, and as a result, it was in the colony that Western law was most stretched to its limits.[27]

Hence, these scholars reveal several legal mechanisms that enabled colonizers to achieve discriminatory aims and still operate within the bounds of law.

Thus, despite the fact that colonial studies analyze extreme political settings, they illuminate fundamental aspects of law that are true for other regimes. Chief among these fundamental features is a nuanced understanding of the relationship between law and power. Students of colonial law drew a conclusion similar to Thompson's and Fraenkel's about the role of law. For these scholars too, law sustains a constant tension between constraining and serving power. Legal principles such as due process, validity, publicity, and so on all balance power, even if used in a repressive political environment.

More specifically, the study of law in the colony analyzes domains of jurisdictional complexity in political contexts in which emergency plays a dominant role. Such conditions exist in Israel too. The point of departure for this book is that Israel's emergency regime is an enduring fact. Contrary to some characterizations of Israel's emergency regime as an exception to the rule, it is just the opposite. The Israeli state has been under a legal SOE since its establishment, and has functioned without an official military government for only half a year.[28] As Amnon Raz-Krakotzkin (2007) argues, what is considered the exception in the history of the state of Israel is in fact the rule, and vice versa. This reality forces us to consider models in which an SOE is an enduring and dominant condition. And because colonial law and Israel's emergency enactment share acute similarities in terms of structural complexity and the administration of personal law for particular groups, colonial law studies offer an analytical framework in which to consider the Israeli condition.

Some scholars explicitly link the Israeli regime and colonialism (Rodinson 1973; Kimmerling 1983; Shafir 1989; Shoat 1992; Yiftachel 1996; Shamir 2000; and Massad 2006). I do not enter into this debate about whether Israel's mode of governance is colonial. There are legitimate parallels, but the book presents them as largely circumstantial. Instead, similar to Hussain, I am not offering a historical narrative that links the Israeli regime with colonialism. My objective in juxtaposing these two governing methodologies is more limited: to explain the dynamics and rationale of a regime that are based on seemingly opposing modes of government: the rule of law and emergency powers.

Ultimately my goal is to draw on colonial studies to demonstrate how law can extend the scope of power based on certain dynamics of law. I join Hussain in illuminating extensions of law. Hussian's hyper-legality model (2007) argues that current the antiterrorism legislation in the United Kingdom is not the withdrawal of law, but rather a hyperextension of law: the increasing use of classifications of persons in the law and the use of special tribunals and commissions. While I share Hussain's observation regarding the extension of law, I focus on a different characteristic: the *fluidity* of governance between several legal sources.

The Co-Constitution of Law and Emergency

The diagram below illustrates the relationship between law and emergency powers. Together they form an enduring government composition built on mutual reinforcement. I argue that as a mutual organ they compensate for an inherent "deficiency," or bottleneck, in liberal modern political regimes, namely, structural controls over sovereignty based on the principles of the rule of law. Put differently, the rule of law and emergency powers compensate for each other's weaknesses. The rule of law controls power, which seeks freedom from any restrictions. Emergency powers without law are simply naked power, thus creating a different costly regime given the sheer violence needed to sustain it, if it is at all possible.

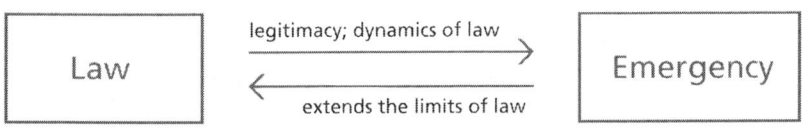

Figure 1. Diagram: The Co-Constitution of Law and Emergency

As the diagram illustrates, the first significant contribution of law to emergency powers is legitimacy. As noted, during an SOE the law is suspended *by* law. In this context, the measures taken under an emergency regime are under a legal framework, even if they violate protected civil rights, and are thus legitimate. In other words, when discriminatory or even oppressive actions are administrated by legal mechanisms—however awkward—the administration can maintain its character as a government by law.

Fraenkel (1941) subscribed to a similar notion in stating that the prerogative cannot function without the normative. I join Hussain in arguing that instead of viewing authorities' efforts as a cynical operation to disguise the arbitrary use of power, we should acknowledge the effort that power makes to channel its actions, however awkward, through administrative rationality. Analytically speaking, it is a much more productive approach (Hussain 2007, 523).

On the other hand, emergency powers complement law by extending legal measures beyond their limits. Emergency powers operate at the same time inside and outside the judicial order. They are inside the legal realm insofar as they suspend law *by* law. Emergency powers are activated by a formal legal procedure. But they operate outside the legal sphere inasmuch as they may trump all law and can execute what is traditionally considered illegal (violations of protected civil rights, for example). With the ability to play on both sides of the legal realm, emergency powers can achieve otherwise impossible-to-attain political ends while remaining within the boundaries of law.

Despite the fact that emergency powers may activate policies that are in a stark contradiction to rule-of-law principles, they preserve the ideal of the rule of law. In this respect, the dynamics between law and emergency is similar to the dynamics between racism and slavery. In the days of American slavery, racism perpetuated the belief that "all men are created equal" as established in the Declaration of Independence. The enslaved group was not considered fully human, so there is no threat to universal equality. Emergency powers operate in a similar fashion with respect to the rule of law. In a time of imminent threat, law can be broken, which is taken as an exception, while the rule of law—in its ideal, anyway—is ever-present, enduring, and universally applicable.

Understanding the dynamics of law, by which law also complements emergency powers, is my contribution to the co-constitutive theoretical model of the relationship between law and emergency. These dynamics extend the authority and power of emergency regulations even beyond this already all-powerful mechanism. The expansion of power is done from within—that is, without stepping outside the legal realm. Consider this, in numeric numbers one can expand by going to edges of infinity, but one can also find infinity in the numeric space between the numbers zero and one. Dynamics of law find space, which means more sovereign power, inside the legal realm. They can do so because of Israel's *fluid* legal-political structure.

Fluidity refers to the ability of a substance to flow freely between frames. This definition, I argue, is also appropriate for a legal-political context. In a fluid legal-political context, the system's boundaries are loosely defined. In this sense, a fluid legal system is based on multiple sources of law (as opposed to a single, uniform source) with a political system in which its branches and administrative institutions do not operate within a narrow scope. Such a fluid structure allows easy passage from one legal source to another, and the ability to patch two or more sources of law together, as well as for policy makers and other power groups to stretch their powers. Ultimately, stretched legality constitutes many ways to execute sovereign will while maintaining a connection to the law and the appearance of legitimacy.

The dynamics of law discussed in the book build on fluidity. With various emergency legal mechanisms available, governing officials can extend the authorities of discrete emergency regulations by mixing and matching them together or jumping from one legal mechanism to the next to serve desired ends. If one legal mechanism might be challenged or meet the limits of its authority, another is available. Thus, the fluidity and patchwork nature of Israel's legal structure has broader implications. Contrary to common understanding, convoluted legal structures are empowering. One might assume that a unified, original, and coherent system of emergency laws should consolidate the sovereignty of the state and simplify the application of these laws. But, as this book demonstrates, the opposite is true. Having an overlapping and ambiguous legal structure grants governing flexibility that extends sovereign power. All the while, the state maintains a degree of legitimacy by operating behind a veil of legality.

With emphasis on dynamics of law, my analysis extends beyond those that merely explore the political uses of emergency powers, whose assertions are often hard to prove. Indeed, it is difficult to identify whether a certain application of emergency powers is the direct outcome of the necessities of security or, merely a tool to implement political will. In trying to distinguish between these two objectives, one is bound to fall into the trap of subjectivity. In Israel, the availability of information only perpetuates this dilemma. Because state information is often classified, one does not know whether the government is maintaining secrecy for security reasons or is simply covering its tracks.

Moreover, deciding what constitutes a threat is too often subjective. For some, a certain condition is regarded as an emergency while for others it is not. It is particularly daunting to decipher in Israel, which has engaged in ongoing conflict with its Arab neighboring states and with the Palestinian people even prior to its inception. This conflict continues today with new factions such as Hamas in the Gaza strip and Hezbollah in Lebanon. Thus, matching between an objective threat and legal authority to execute emergency powers is challenging. Nonetheless, we can still delineate reasonable markers for recognizing uses of emergency measures in times without crisis.

The best indication that Israel's legal SOE has been applied despite the lack of immediate threat is the fact that on a few occasions the government has declared a *special* SOE. During the First Lebanon War in 1982 and the First Gulf War in 1991, a "special" SOE was declared, probably to distinguish it from the "regular" ongoing SOE. The emergency regulations[29] that followed the special declaration of emergency were distinct from the "regular" emergency regulations because they were not bound by the duration of the "regular" declaration.[30]

In this work, I review clear cases in which emergency powers were used to attain objectives beyond the defence of the state and its people. For example, in chapter 5 I examine the use of emergency powers to execute recurring governmental policies, such as economic fiscal or monetary programs.

Contribution to the Study of Israel's Regime

Existing scholarship has identified the impact of emergency powers in Israel's governance, but thus far none has recognized clearly that Israel's emergency apparatuses are a systemic element of its governance.

The premise of the majority of the studies on Israel's regime is that it contains internal contradictions. Thus, the objective of numerous studies has been to define the Israeli regime despite contradictions. The principal dialogue has been the "democracy debate"—namely, which type of democracy represents the Israeli regime, if it is a democracy at all.

Yonatan Shapiro, for example, defined the Israeli regime as a formal democracy (1977): a system that holds periodic general elections, that presupposes some degree of civil rights, such as freedom of speech and the right to associate, but still lacks a fundamental liberal component, which usually appears as a type of entrenched bill of human and civil rights. In this respect, Israel's national identity is based on a national-religious identity so the state is not separated from religion. Sami Smooha (1990), on the other hand, offered a different depiction of Israel's regime. He defined the Israeli regime as an "ethnic democracy," by which he means a regime that secures civil rights for all citizens as individuals, but simultaneously, maintains a structured dominance of the Jewish majority group.[31] Yet some scholars even went beyond the conception of a flawed democracy to argue that Israel is not a democracy at all. The most articulated account in this respect comes from Oren Yiftachel (2006). He defines Israel as an ethnocracy: a "regime characterized by an expansion of a dominant group in contested territory and its domination of power structures while maintaining a democratic façade."

Narrower scholarship has focused on the dominant role that Israel's emergency regime has played in the state's history and continues to do so. This body of work also recognizes Israel's internal contradictions. On the one hand, the long-standing SOE has had considerable bearing on Israel's governance, chipping away at its rule of law and democratic institutions. On the other hand, however, there has never been a period of lawlessness in the state of Israel. In fact, even in the Occupied Palestinian Territories (OPT), where democracy clearly does not rule,[32] the Israeli authorities have gone to great efforts to establish control and Jewish superiority via legal tools, however suspect.

In this respect, scholars highlight the charged concurrence of civil democratic principles and security-military values (Horowitz and Lissak 1988; Kimmerling 1993; Neuberger 1996; Ben-Eliezer 1998). Some go further and assert that Israel's security mandates extend beyond immediate threats and are directed at achieving political ends. For example, Ian Lustick's early study of Israel's regime asserts this notion (1978; 1980). He argues that the Jewish-Palestinian relationships inside the Green Line[33] should not be viewed through the prism of formal democracy, but through a system of control.[34] David Kretzmer (1990) has argued that an elastic concept of security has enabled the Israeli authorities, again inside the Green Line, to use emergency power not only to protect the state but also to discriminate against Palestinians. He writes, "There can be little doubt, however, that the concept of 'security,' as understood by the authorities in the Israeli context, encompasses a wider range of activities" (1990, 136). Hence, according to him, Israel's use of emergency powers is also for political reasons. Kretzmer introduces the "conflict management model" (1990, 137), in which administrative uses of emergency powers are not responses to security necessities but a means to achieve political ends. Similarly, Nadim Rouhana (1997) asserts that, in Israel, security has rationalized activities that extend well beyond the necessities of emergency and, in fact, reflect the Jewish majority's aspirations to supremacy.[35]

While this study does not reference this work directly, it complements the discourse with its understanding of the confusing elements of the Israeli regime.[36] The book does not evaluate which conceptualization of democracy best defines the Israeli regime, but it, nevertheless, contributes this body of work. It illustrates a governing mechanism that enables a system of control (Lustick 1978; 1980) and ultimately forges a gulf between Jews and Palestinians, but at the same time adheres to a government by law.

It does so by examining Israel's emergency jurisprudence and apparatus. I look inward to the legal order and its logic. I focus on Israel's emergency law as a multi-layered framework that establishes space within the legal system, which as a result, produces governmental flexibility. I illustrate how a regime's constant SOE may grant power that is based not only on the authority of the law but also on a convoluted legal structure. In addition, the book illuminates the depth to which emergency law is embedded in Israel's day-to-day governing routine.

Further, the book argues that Israel's continuing SOE has had a far greater impact on Israel's governing system and on society as a whole than has traditionally been understood. As the book demonstrates, the reach of Israel's emergency regime goes beyond defending the state and its people and even beyond political implications that stem from the ongoing conflict with the Palestinians. In Israel emergency powers have played a central role in shaping deep political processes, such as the allocation of resources and political representation, but their application has touched even seemingly unrelated realms, such as economic policies.

The book's geopolitical framework of analysis also sets it apart from previous studies on Israel's emergency jurisprudence. Earlier studies have focused on "Israel itself"—that is, the territory inside the Green Line—or on the OPT separately. Yet since Israel's emergency jurisprudence is not limited to either side of the Green Line, the scope of this study includes both "Israel itself" and the OPT. In this respect, I follow Baruch Kimmerling's "control system" concept (1989), which refers to *all* the territory under Israeli sovereignty. The timeline of this project begins at the inception of the state of Israel, since this is the moment we can relate to a sovereign Israeli legal-political system.

Ultimately, this study asserts that, contrary to the conception of Israel's SOE as the accidental outcome of trying times, it is in fact a governing tool. As I demonstrate, fostering a fluid emergency legal structure has yielded political benefits, whereas previous studies have labeled Israel's permanent emergency an exception. In doing so, these analyses back themselves into a theoretical corner.

Indeed, when analyzing the Israeli case through a liberal understanding of law, branding the SOE as an anomaly from "regular democracy" becomes the only option. Liberal positivism has no explanation for an enduring state of emergency other than to explain it away as an exception to democratic rule—even if this is inaccurate given the perpetual SOE in Israel. In other words, liberal positivism does not have the analytical tools to consider a more complex relationship between law and power. To view the SOE in Israel as anything other than exception breaches liberal theory's own conceptual boundaries.

For this reason, these studies ultimately have to turn to Israel's "exceptionalism," instead of rethinking the premise of their argument. They all recognize the enduring feature of Israel's emergency, but quickly bypass it. For example, Alan Dowty maintains that Israel's continuous emergency regime signifies a "routinization of crisis procedures" (1988, 34),[37] but he joins other scholars in asserting Israel's uniqueness. Both Baruch Bracha (1978) and Menahem Hofnung (1996; 2001) note that Israel's emergency regime has no parallel among Western liberal democracies. Bracha argues that in modern history, Israel is unique as a democratic state that is governed under a continuous SOE (1978, 297). Menahem Hofnung asserts that in Israel the emergency regime comes at a heavy cost, but concludes that Israel demonstrates that it is possible to maintain a democracy and a continuous emergency regime simultaneously (2001, 346). Thus, all scholars ultimately resort to Israel's "exceptionalism," rather than rethink the role of the SOE in Israel's regime, where Israel's emergency apparatuses are a systemic element of its governance.

The Chapter's Outline

In the next chapter, we take a quick detour to discuss Israel's legal-political system in general. This chapter does not discuss emergency powers but rather familiarizes readers with Israel's convoluted governing system. It thus, however, focuses on a main theme of the book: fluidity. This chapter reviews legal mechanisms other than emergency powers that grant governing flexibility, and ultimately, greater power, based on a fluid legal-political structure. Chapter 2 lays the groundwork for subsequent discussion by illustrating that a fluid legal structure is a constant in Israel, not an exception.

In chapter 3, I lay out all the emergency legal sources available to Israeli authorities. While Israel's emergency regime has long been recognized, the fact that Israel's legal system features several overlapping and incoherent emergency legal sources has received less attention. The chapter traces each legal source to its historical origin and follows its development. I concentrate on the complementary relationship between them. Chapter 4 continues the discussion and asks why Israel's emergency legal system is structured as it is. The chapter displays the complementary dynamics between Israel's multiple emergency legal sources. It argues that such dynamics are the reason for Israel's ambiguous emergency legal structure. I analyze historical events since the establishment of the state from inside and outside the Green Line. Analytically, the chapter draws on the work of colonial law scholars to explain jurisdictional complexity and the political motivation for maintaining structured ambiguity. I demonstrate how various complementary relations that are based on the fluid dynamics of law enable the state to extend its sovereign power and achieve political ends otherwise impossible. Chapter 5 considers the use of emergency powers for objectives beyond security and protection of the state and its people. The chapter explores how the Israeli authorities have used emergency regulations to execute economic policies. In this context, emergency powers were applied not to allocate resources in a time of war, or any other major crisis to help a population in need, but to regulate labor disputes and fiscal and monetary policies. Chapter 5 demonstrates the depth to which emergency law is embedded in Israel's day-to-day governing routine. In the conclusion, I address the critical question of how we are to conceive of this commingling of law and emergency, which, as I demonstrate with a short survey of secondary literature, is the governing condition in many countries outside of Israel.

As we explore the structure of Israeli governance, we come to understand that the initial SOE has prevailed by design, not by accident. Israeli authorities have used emergency measures in concert with a host of other laws to create an environment of legal expedience to achieve political ends. Israel's emergency jurisprudence is a foundation of a complex and intertwined set of laws that are used in ever-changing ways to achieve the desired end. By unveiling the layers and complexity of Israel's legal system, we can better understand the country's current legal and political environment, and the winding path to Israel's situation today.

2

ISRAEL'S LEGAL-POLITICAL SYSTEM

A Fluid Structure

This chapter provides an overview of Israel's legal-political system. Yet the overall objective is more ambitious. First, I wish to illustrate that fluidity is central to Israel's regime. Second, I wish to contribute to the debate on governability in Israel.

These two themes are connected: fluidity generates governability because it produces governing flexibility (that is, multiple paths for executing policy), and thus extends governing power. Israel's core legal-political structure, I illustrate, is loosely determined. As a result, its basic principles are not solidly defined. Thus Israeli politics constantly revolve around the prospect of defining and redefining the state's fundamental political identity and values[1] (for example, the relationship between religion and state, national identity, human rights, and even the size of government). On the one hand, such constant vacillations bear heavily on Israel's governability.[2] Yet, on the other hand, this fluidity allows for substantial governing flexibility. Ultimately, due to Israel's fluid legal-political structure, political players can rewrite the fundamental rules. And this capacity is a source of great sovereign power, at the very least in its potential. Often, in the debate over Israel's governability, the fact that Israeli politicians and administrators formally possess the power to execute almost any policy is overlooked.

Since my contention is that emergency powers in many nations are not separated from law, I see continuity between Israel's general legal-political fluidity and its emergency fluid jurisprudence. While emergency powers represent the most extreme apparatus in terms of the powers they grant, they are not different from the legal mechanisms I describe in this chapter in terms of their function; namely, they are a means to create "space" within the legal system and thus grant political flexibility and ultimately more power to policy makers.

Through the prism of fluidity, this chapter attempts to define Israel's legal political system. After an introduction, I describe Israel's multiple legal sources and the still-incomplete process of constitution making. I then move to discuss the fluid consequences of this process on Israel's legal hierarchy before and after the 1992 constitutional reform. I also review the role of the government, secondary legislation and the office of the Attorney General. Finally, I consider the way Israel's Supreme Court functions. I argue that it contributes to the overall fluidity of the system.

General Introduction

While Israel's political and legal systems have determined traditions and procedures, many are the outcome of temporary and ad hoc arrangements. In many instances, protracted temporary solutions have become permanent. These arrangements are often the result of compromises given political deadlocks. One way of thinking about Israel's political and legal system is to consider it incomplete, or a work in progress—that is, a young system yet to fully mature; another way is to consider Israel as governed by structured ambiguity.

Richard Posner has noted that all "constitutional law is fluid" (2006, 9), but in Israel, such an assertion is taken to the extreme. In this respect, defining Israel's political and legal systems is a challenging task. Israel is a parliamentary republic. But the State of Israel does not have a complete legislated constitution coupled with a complete bill of rights.[3] It does, of course, have a material constitution, which defines both the functions of and the relations between governmental branches, as well as civil rights. Israel's material constitution was shaped in part by formal legislation, juridical decisions, and the

Declaration of Independence (DOI) of 1948, which, although it is a nonbinding legal document,[4] has symbolic capital as a canonic declaration of intent. Still, Israel's constitutional framework has considerable gaps. Mainly, significant human rights do not enjoy formal entrenchment, the functions and relationship between its political branches are unresolved, and there is no constitutional law that formally defines the hierarchy between its laws and the process for making constitutional amendments.

British legal tradition is the main source of influence on Israel's political and legal structures. Such components as Israel's parliamentary supremacy, the supervisory power of the courts over administration and their authority to issue prerogative writs are tokens of British legal-political customs. Yet, Israel's legal-political framework is based on the British colonial model. Thus, relative to liberal-democratic states, the Israeli political structure is centralized, with limited separation of powers.

Indeed, Israel's political structure is relatively centralized. The Israeli Parliament, the Knesset, is only a single house of representatives and, formally, directly or indirectly all government branches and agencies depend on parliament's confidence. Thus, when the Knesset "speaks," other political and administrative divisions, including the court, listen. In addition, and even more significantly, the Knesset acts as a legislative branch and as a constituent assembly simultaneously. This peculiar conjunction is a source of great power, and indeed, the Israeli Knesset is defined as all-powerful.[5] Yet, as we shall see, the Knesset is controlled by the government coalition and therefore it is the government in Israel that holds actual power.

The fact that the Knesset acts simultaneously as a constituent body and as a legislative branch, creates significant fluidity in the operation of the Knesset and ultimately it is a source of great power. These concurrent roles are the practical result of the Transition Law, by which the 1948 elected constituent assembly was reconstituted as a legislative branch (the Knesset), as well as on the basis of the sovereign continuity between the first and the second Knessets and the Harrari Resolution. The Knesset's function as both a constituent body and a legislative branch was dubbed the doctrine of "two hats,"[6] a name that captures its ability to change back and forth between the two roles. And while the question regarding Israel's constitutional authority and the theory of two hats remains open from a theoretical, academic perspective (Salzberger 1996, 696), in practice this doctrine is settled. The alternative, which is politically impossible, would be to reelect or reappoint a constituent assembly (Rubinstein 2012, 109).

The outcome is that the Knesset functions as an eternal constituent assembly, which means it operates free from almost any limitations. Thus, as opposed to a more common situation in which legislation-making follows constitution-making, in Israel they overlap. This is a unique situation that makes the Knesset extremely powerful. It is true that in other democracies, such as the Scandinavian states as well as Holland and Belgium, the legislative body holds constituent powers and thus has the authority to amend constitutional laws (Madina 2007, 407). But the difference between these democracies and Israel is that this authority is rooted in a constitutional law, whereas in Israel, as we know, this fundamental constitutional law, namely Basic Law: Legislation, has never been enacted; it speaks to Israel's exceptionalism in terms of the fluidity of its constitutional law. As such, the Knesset operates in a fluid framework that allows it to change its own procedures at any time. Even with the constitutional additions of 1992, the Knesset has preserved its constitutive power to redirect its legislative procedures.

That said, the Knesset has only one house, which the government controls; this arrangement makes the government and not the Knesset, extremely powerful. The structure of the Israeli government is similar to the British model. As such, the government must have a majority in the Knesset, and most ministers are also members of the Knesset (MKs). Thus, formally speaking, the Israeli government, through its control of the Knesset and the lack of a fully legislated and binding constitution, has the power to enact any law, even when it would contradict liberal and democratic conventions.

Despite British influences, Israel's electoral system was constructed according to the continental tradition.[7] Thus, while in Britain elections are regional and absolute, in Israel they are direct and proportional. The British Mandate, of course, did not hold periodic elections. The State of Israel adopted its election procedure from its own pre-state structure, the *Yishuv*,[8] which was based on the continental tradition. On the one hand, this hybrid between British tradition with regard to most legal and political aspects and a continental electoral system has proved to be a source of instability. Yet, on the other hand, it is also a source of an important, unintentional separation of powers.

Several mechanisms serve as checks and balances over the Knesset and the government, but most are informal, consisting of public scrutiny and an ethic of responsibility on the part of members of government and MKs. By and large, Israel's checks and balances are an unexpected outcome of its direct and proportional electoral system. Furthermore, Israel's society is fragmented, particularly after the decline of the big party blocks, the Israeli Labor Party and Likud, in the 1980s. As a result of this combination, Israel's coalition is made up of several parties, including small ones. Hence the coalition is basically a small parliament, and has accidentally come to serve as a necessary internal check and balance, as the different factions within the coalition control one another.

Israel's Legal Sources

Israeli law did not emerge from a single unified legal source (Shachar 1995, 2). Rather, it is constructed from layers of legal traditions. The fact that Israeli law has merged various legal foundations is not unique. But what is notable is that Israel has sustained this complex legal structure for several decades. Israel's legislators were slow in creating a formal, coherent, and original legal framework that would replace its disjointed pluralistic legal structure. Moreover, to this day, certain sections of law—including emergency law, as we shall see—have maintained complex and multiple legal sources. Thus, Israel's continued legal structure points to a systematic fluid legal frame.[9]

Israel's legal sources stem from four different foundations: original Knesset statutes, British Mandatory enactments, remnants of Ottoman laws, and various religious laws that regulate the realm of personal-status law. Israeli law is a patchwork cobbled together from traditional and modern law and liberal and colonial legal practices.

British Mandatory law is the main source for Israeli law.[10] At the moment of its foundation, the State of Israel adopted a ready-made law in the form of the British Mandatory legal system. As discussed in the next chapter, as part of British Mandatory law, the State of Israel adopted a complete set of emergency regulations. All in all, the foundation of Israeli law is nondemocratic (Maoz 1988, 14), being based on two nondemocratic systems of law: the British Mandatory law and Ottoman law.

From the standpoint of law, there is continuity between the British Mandate and the State of Israel. As Ronen Shamir puts it, from a legal perspective, "Nothing significant happened in 1948" (2000, 7). The first act of the Provisional Council of the State was to issue a reception statute declaring that mandatory law in effect in Palestine would continue in force with limited adjustments. Section 11 of the Law and Administration Ordinance 5708-1948[11] asserts that "the law in force in *Eretz Yisrael* on May 14, 1948, will remain in force, insofar as it does not contradict this ordinance or other laws which will be passed by the Provisional Council of State."[12] The first minister of justice, Pinchas Rozan, in his address to the Provisional Council of State, stated that the LAO was "a transitory enactment which really contains only the barest minimum required at this moment so as to establish and provide a legal basis for our whole political system."[13] This temporary arrangement, however, became permanent. Until 1980, British law was applied where there was a gap or question about the proper law to apply.[14]

British Mandatory law profoundly enhanced the pluralist structure of Israeli law. By absorbing mandatory law, the State of Israel also integrated sections of Ottoman law into Israeli law. The mandatory government formally absorbed Ottoman law with section 46 of the Palestine Order in Council, 1922.[15] Accordingly, Ottoman laws that the British Mandate did not consider too remote from Western law or contradictory to the mandatory regime were kept intact. Then, as noted, section 11 of the LAO (1948), Israel's reception statute, added a layer on top of the mandatory reception statute, absorbing into Israel's domestic legislation the remnants of Ottoman law that were maintained during the mandate. The Ottoman legal system was a hybrid between traditional Islamic law and modern law; it merged East and West. In the nineteenth century, the Ottoman Empire reformed its legal system (referred to as the *Tanzimat*).[16]

Ottoman law primarily influenced Israeli law with regard to private law (contract law) and land regulations; however, between 1958 and 1984, under the leadership of the vice legal councilor, the influence of Ottoman law on private law was almost entirely superseded. Then, in 1984, the *Majalla*[17] was officially canceled. These new enactments nevertheless complicated the system because Israel's legislators were inspired by Jewish legal traditions and continental civil law (Maoz 1988, 14). These two legal traditions, a hybrid in themselves, were thus fused with British common law, adding another legal tradition to the hybrid.

In 1980, the Knesset enacted the "Foundations of Law,"[18] which established a new original foundation for Israeli law by declaring that "article 46 of the Palestine Order in Council, 1922–1947, is hereby repealed" (section 2[a]). The new Foundations of Law statute directs Israel's judges to Hebrew law as a source for legal interpretation in cases of legal gaps (lacunae). As such, it adds another normative legal source, which does not stem from Western legal traditions. But most legal scholars believe that the new Foundations of Law has little effect on Israeli law (Mautner 2008).

The Foundation of Law (1980), however, has no effect on laws integrated into Israeli law prior to its enactment (section 2[b]). One of the main sections of Israeli law still governed by Ottoman law is personal status law (matrimony, burial ceremonies, and so on). Indeed, to this day, the Ottoman millet system administrates personal status law in Israel. Accordingly, each ethnic religious faction operates autonomously under a different religious court. It is worth noting that what was progressive in the nineteenth century is not necessarily so from a twentieth or twenty-first century liberal perspective. In fact, the millet system was abolished in Turkey during the Young Turk Revolution of 1908 and was eventually replaced by a rather strict separation of state and religion. While there is religious tolerance in Israel, there is no separation of state and religion. The Ottoman millet system is an additional source of fluidity. It is stacked alongside Western normative legal sources. Incongruences between the traditions were sometimes patched together. For example, Western norms, such as banning polygamy, were enacted on top of the millet system.

An additional non-formal source is the Declaration of Independence, signed on May 15, 1948, by all the Jewish political factions at the time. The DOI, however, did not have formal legal standing, at least until 1994.[19] Nonetheless, it carries symbolic capital as a canonic "statement of intentions."[20] Already, in 1953, the former president of the Supreme Court of Israel, Justice Shimon Agranat, for example, used the declaration as a reference in his precedential decision *Kol HaAm*, in which he secured free speech and freedom of the press.[21]

The declaration asserts that the State of Israel will grant civil liberties in the form of freedom of religion, freedom of conscience, freedom of language, and freedom of education and culture. Further, it states Israel's commitment to the principle of civil equality. Accordingly, the State of Israel should grant political and social equality to all its citizens, regardless of their religion, race or gender. The declaration does not, however, list nationality or ethnicity as criteria for the principle of equality. Moreover, the DOI asserts that the State of Israel (*Eretz Yisrael*[22]) is a Jewish state. On the other hand, the word "democracy" does not appear in the declaration.

Constitutional Ambiguity:
The Harrari Resolution and Its Consequences

The process of constitution-making in Israel has only compounded the fluidity of Israel's complex legal sources. Israel's lawmakers and jurists have never brought coherence to the system. On the contrary, Israel's constitutional standing remains vague. At the moment of inception, however, the prospect of a constitution seemed promising. Both the United Nations General Assembly Resolution 181 (November 29, 1947) and Israel's DOI proclaim that the State of Israel shall have a constitution. In fact, it is stated in the DOI that, no later than October 1, 1948, the new State of Israel shall have a constitution which will be based on its principles. This intention, however, was never realized.

Indeed, early on the process of constitution making went awry. With the fading of the 1948 war, on January 25, 1949, a constituent assembly was elected in Israel's first general elections. However, the first act of the constituent assembly—the Transition Law, 5709-1949[23]—was to reconstitute itself as the First Knesset (a legislative branch). Since then, the issue of whether the Knesset is a constituent body, a legislative branch, or both, has been open to different interpretations.[24] But, ultimately, from a practical perspective, in Israel, the constituent body and the legislative branch are one and the same.

The ruling Mapai party, headed by Ben-Gurion, opposed a constitution in fear that it would limit its power. It is probably for this reason that Menachem Begin, head of the opposition party Herut, who in 1977 became prime minister, stated, in approving constitutional drafting, that "if the Constituent Assembly legislates a constitution, then the government will not be free to do as it likes."[25]

Thus the process of constitutional drafting as a whole was rejected. Following the Transition Law, by which the constituent assembly became a legislative assembly, the Knesset also adopted a compromise, the Harrari Resolution,[26] named after the Knesset Member (MK) who sponsored it. The Harrari Resolution states,

> The First Knesset instructs the Constitutional, Legislation and Judicial Committee to prepare a draft State Constitution. The constitution will be built *chapter by chapter*, in such a way that each will constitute a separate *Basic Law*. The chapters shall be presented to the Knesset when the committee completes its work, and all the chapters shall be combined into the Constitution of the State.[27]

Hence, instead of launching a rigorous process of constitution making, the process was delayed and fragmented. A Knesset committee—the Constitutional, Legislation, and Judicial Committee—was commissioned, and it was decided that the constitution should be enacted in chapters called basic laws, with the idea that, once enacted, the basic laws would be integrated into a complete constitution. However, in the Harrari Resolution there is no explanation of the process by which the basic laws would be integrated into a constitution or whether the Supreme Court will have judicial review (Landau 1996, 701). Further, the resolution was vague about when or whether the basic laws would have superiority over regular laws.

In effect the Harrari Resolution was a decision not to have a constitution.[28] The execution of the resolution was very slow. Neither the first nor the second Knessets enacted any Basic Laws. Thus, the first basic law was finally enacted eight years after the resolution was passed. On the other hand, however, shortly after the resolution was accepted, the Knesset enacted statutes of a constitutional nature: the Law of Return (1950)[29] and Women Equality (1951), both of which were passed without being declared basic laws. The prospect of enacting constitutional laws outside the Harrari Resolution suggests that, in fact, the Harrari Resolution was a vote against a constitution.

To this day, the key Basic Law: Legislation still has not been enacted, despite several law proposals, the first in 1975 and the most recent in 2012. Without this missing central component, Israel's legal hierarchy remains undefined by law, and the ambiguous relationship between the Knesset as a constituent body and as a legislative branch is maintained. Moreover, the procedure for amending the constitution is left vague.

In addition, the basic laws' form and content are also indecisive. While some constitutional enactment procedures were followed as they appear in the Harrari Resolution, others were ignored. In this respect, in terms of their form, all basic laws are titled "Basic Law," and the years in which they were enacted are not specified. On the other hand, other formal terms of their enactment are ignored. Only Basic Law: The Knesset and Basic Law: The Government were enacted according to the Harrari Resolution, by which they were prepared and presented by the Knesset's constitutional committee. The rest of the basic laws were prepared by private MKs and delivered as private laws.

Considering the content of the basic laws we find that they also suffer from irregularities and ambiguities. Traditionally the content of constitutional laws defines the structure, operation, and relations between different governmental institutions, including procedures for amending the constitution and a set of civil rights. However, a number of basic laws do not address these issues. Instead, they regulate matters commonly dealt with by regular laws (for example, Basic Law: Israel Lands [1960] and Basic Law: Jerusalem, Capital of Israel [1980]). In addition, unlike traditional constitutional laws, which are short and assert only the spirit of the law or general principles, some basic laws are highly detailed and do not leave much room for interpretation. On the other hand, some regular laws in Israel, in terms of their content, deal with constitutional norms. Aside from the laws mentioned above (the Law of Return and Women Equality) we can also list the Transition Law and the Law against Racism as examples.

Overall, before 1992, nine basic laws were enacted: Basic Law: The Knesset (1958), Basic Law: Israel Lands (1960), Basic Law: The President (1964), Basic Law: The Government (1969), Basic Law: State Economy (1975), Basic Law: The Army (1976), Basic Law: Jerusalem, Capital of Israel (1980), Basic Law: The Judiciary (1984) and Basic Law: The State Comptroller (1988). As we can see, not all of these laws deal with the structure and operation of governmental and administrative institutions, and none of them define any civil rights. Moreover, apart from section 46 of Basic Law: The Knesset, none of the basic laws restrict the Knesset in future legislation. As I shall soon discuss, this was changed to a degree in 1992, when two additional basic laws were enacted, Basic Law: Human Dignity and Freedom and Basic Law: Freedom of Occupation. Including the last two enactments of 1992, there are a total of eleven basic laws to date.

Fluid Legal Hierarchy Before and After 1992

Israel's constitutional fluidity has left the questions of when and whether basic laws have normative superiority over regular laws open. As noted, one interpretation of the Harrari compromise maintains that the basic laws, by title, are superior to regular laws. However, according to an opposing approach, only when they are integrated into a complete constitution will they gain normative superiority—meanwhile, their status equals that of regular laws. This ambiguity ended up at the door of the Supreme Court.

In many respects it was left for the Supreme Court to decide whether basic laws override regular law?[30] In fact, prior to this constitutional question, the court had to rule whether it had the authority to review and invalidate the Knesset's enactment.[31] Ultimately, before 1992, the court ruled that basic laws are not superior to other laws, even specific, entrenched sections of the law (at the time, section 46 of Basic Law: The Knesset was being debated). At the same time, the court decided that the Knesset could set limits on its future legislation (HC 107/73). Yet, all things being fluid, with few exceptions, the court has proceeded as if explicit entrenched clauses have superiority over regular laws.[32] Still, on other occasions, the court has argued that because basic laws are often general and because regular laws are normally more detailed, the latter are therefore more effective.[33] Overall, without a clear legal normative hierarchy, we are left with the following rules: *lex posteriori derogat legi priori* (a later law overrides a previous law) and *lex specialis derogat legi generali* (a detailed statute overrides a general bill). I will return to discuss the Supreme Court in a separate section.

The Supreme Court's decision that basic laws do not have superiority over regular laws produces greater fluidity in the system as a whole. A fluid relationship between basic laws and regular laws is the outcome of the ambiguous relationship between the two roles the Knesset plays. Thus, what follows is that basic laws, which are the product of the Knesset sitting as a constituent body, can and often do pass by a regular majority. As a result, until recently regular laws could be used to amend most basic laws—that is, by the Knesset sitting as a legislative branch.

The outcome of such a fluid structure can be rather severe from a due process perspective. Since the Knesset, sitting as a constituent body, can enact basic laws by a regular majority, it has the power to restrict future Knessets by asserting that only a special majority can amend these enactments. Thus, the Knesset can entrench a bill by a regular majority and therefore direct future Knessets because these bills can only be altered with a special majority. In other words, with only a regular majority, the Knesset has the power to restrain future Knessets with a special majority.[34] In some respects, this was the case with the 1992 constitutional reform.

The two additional basic laws enacted in 1992, which some defined as a constitutional revolution, were passed by a regular majority. In fact, less than half of the Knesset members participated in the final voting on the basic laws. Only twenty-three MKs out of one hundred and twenty participated in the last two votes (which came one right after the other) on Basic Law: Freedom of Occupation. All of them approved the bill (DK 125 1992, 3393). Basic Law: Human Dignity and Freedom was passed thirty-two to twenty-one (DK 125 1992, 3793), which reflects that this bill was and remains very controversial.[35]

Indeed, the manner in which the 1992 basic laws were enacted weighs heavily on their legitimacy, particularly as tokens of a constitutional revolution. Thus, even before considering their level of entrenchment (and thus their superiority over regular laws, which, overall, is unimpressive) and their power to discipline future Knesset enactments, the constitutional standing of these new basic laws is not sound. Religious and right-wing advocates argue that these basic laws were enacted in an underhanded process by a liberal ad hoc coalition that "kidnapped" the Knesset. Gideon Sapir (2010, 59–85) summarized the critique against these statues arguing, inter alia, that MKs were given partial or even wrong information about the nature of the laws and that their enactment lacked almost any public debate.[36] The then MK, Amnon Rubinstein, one of the leading figures behind the bill and a longtime professor of constitutional law, rejects this critique, arguing that the protocols of the Knesset's committees and the changes made to the original proposal of Basic Law: Basic Human Rights and Freedom—changes, as we shall see, that watered down the provisions—reflect that the MKs understood what was at stake (2012).

All in all, even this constitutional moment was ultimately the outcome of a fluid legal patchwork in the tradition of the Harrari Resolution, rather than a profound constitutional reform. Ultimately, these basic laws came as a compromise, kicking the can down the road, so to speak. Despite the fact that for the first time in Israel's history the Knesset proposed giving constitutional status to human rights, these constitutional amendments were the result of a major compromise that, overall, left the status of human rights in Israel in a precarious state. Little was left from the original bill that was introduced in 1989, Basic Law: Basic Human Rights, which included judicial review. Eventually it was split into two laws: Basic Law: Freedom of Occupation (henceforth "Freedom of Occupation") and Basic Law: Human Dignity and Freedom (henceforth, "Human Dignity"). In this respect, only rights that more or less were in a consensus among Jewish Israelis were left in and other fundamental rights, such as equality, freedom of movement, freedom of religion, freedom from religion, freedom of speech, freedom of association, freedom of demonstration and artistic freedom were intentionally removed in the process of legislation.[37] Moreover, Basic Law: Legislation was not part of this constitutional moment; therefore, the basic principles concerning legal hierarchy and the process by which constitutional changes are introduced are unaccounted for. If they exist, it is only through court rulings, not by constitutional legislation.

Thus, the enactments of the 1992 basic laws are further indications of the fluidity of the system. Overall, the signing of these bills into basic laws did not bring coherence to the system and was yet another example of the patchwork legal system. The limitations that these basic laws have introduced on future enactments were coupled with limitations on the limitations: namely, limitations that provide paths to overpass the protected human rights proclaimed by these statutes.

Of these two basic laws, only Freedom of Occupation, which initially seemed rather harmless to the religious factions, was formally entrenched from the outset. This is exactly an example in which the Knesset, by a regular vote, restrained future Knessets by asserting that any change would have to gain a special majority. At any rate, soon after the Freedom of Occupation enactment, when the "sinister" outcome of this statute manifested as a result of a debate over the right to import non-kosher meat,[38] the law was changed and retracted. An overcoming clause[39] was added as part of a 1994 amendment to the law; this clause sits side by side the entrenched clause.[40] According to the entrenched clause, changes to this basic law can only be made through another basic law, meaning that in order to enact a change there must be an explicit vote with a majority of Knesset members voting in favor. The overcoming clause, however, asserted a path by which a regular law can override this basic law. Thus a regular law that contradicts protected rights granted by Basic Law: Freedom of Occupation is valid, as long as it is supported by a majority of the MKs and formally declares the violation of the basic law. This regular statute is restricted for four years, but can be renewed.

The political battle over Basic Law: Human Dignity was much harsher and therefore sections of the law were immediately gutted. First, the law was not entrenched; from the outset a regular law could be enacted to alter it. Second, a special order was added to the bill (*Smirat Hadinim*) with the objective of protecting the old "victories" of the orthodox religious parties; this means that old laws, even if they violate human rights asserted by the new basic law, gain immunity and thus continue in force. In 1994, as part of the amendment to the two 1992 basic laws, an additional double-edged article was introduced: a limitation clause. This clause protects the basic laws from the content (objectives) of future enactments. It restricts the Knesset in its role as a legislative branch that enacts regular laws by asserting that there should be no restrictions to these rights unless achieved through the enactment of a law, for a valid objective and for the good of the general public. This clause, as we shall see, is an interpretive battleground; it is debatable whether it protects the basic law and the proclaimed rights or opens a path to violations of law.[41]

These rather confusing ad hoc enactments were considered by some as nothing more than a "constitutional revolution."[42] The advocates of the constitutional revolution, chief among them the then Chief Justice Aharon Barak, highlighted the fact that for the first time in Israel's history, the Knesset had put forward a constitutional status of human rights in Israel, and more significantly, the Knesset had restricted its own power.[43] Previously, as noted, the court had already recognized certain civil rights in a judicial bill of rights; yet some civil rights, not necessarily those acknowledged before, were formally recognized for the first time by the 1992 statutory law. Moreover, these laws marked a significant milestone inasmuch as the Israeli Supreme Court extended its review to include not only secondary legislation by the government as before, but the Knesset's primary legislation as well.

On the other hand, prominent legal figures such as former Chief Justice Moshe Landau resisted the notion of a constitutional revolution. They argued instead that the enactment of the last two basic laws "was hardly an Ackermanian 'Constitutional moment'" (Gross 1998, 88–89).

The outcome is a limbo of interpretations, the chief question being whether these enactments granted the Supreme Court the authority to interpret the Knesset's legislation. This, however, did not prevent the Supreme Court, headed by Chief Justice Barak, from taking the lead in asserting the constitutional revolution with judicial activism. Shortly after the 1992 enactments, Barak published an article introducing the possibility that human dignity is superior despite the missing entrenchment (Barak 1992). A few years after the 1994 amendment that added the limitation clause, the court validated Chief Justice Barak's suggestion (CA 6821/93). The majority decision asserted that although these two new basic laws do not explicitly facilitate judicial review, by limiting the Knesset they invite the Supreme Court to validate future enactments. The court validated the limitation clause ruling that, according to this clause, any law can be canceled if it violates the principles, regardless of the majority by which it was enacted. However, in a later case, the court affirmed that the limitation clause is not valid with regard to changes enacted by basic laws.[44]

The fact that much of the constitutional revolution is based on case law instead of on legislation amounted to yet another layer of instability in Israel's legal-political structure. Gideon Sapir termed it a "continuing revolution" (2010, 8) because the actual cornerstones of the constitutional reform were based on court decisions that came after the legislation. As a result, the foundation of these constitutional achievements is insecure. Some might argue that this process is characteristic of the common law system, but the conditions in Israel (the lack of a complete formal constitution) render the prospect of the court writing a constitution unique and problematic.

At any rate, the outcome of the 1992 basic laws enactments and subsequent Supreme Court decisions left Israel's legal system flexible and overall fluid. What is left is an ongoing dialog in which the Knesset has the ultimate word. On the one hand, the Supreme Court did receive a substantial tool to review and revoke Knesset legislation. On the other hand, however, it kept the Knesset's power to immediately counteract and withdraw the court's decisions.[45] I shall elaborate on this dialog, particularly, the Knesset's reaction to the court's activism following the 1992 enactments in a subsequent discussion about the Israeli Supreme Court. All in all, so far, by the time of this book's writing, in a period that stretches over two decades, the Israeli Supreme Court has revoked thirteen laws altogether. The Knesset, for its part, did not change the 1992 basic laws as a response to the Israeli Supreme Court's activism, and thus far, despite growing calls, particularly from the right, to limit the court's power, has been rather reserved. I shall return to this issue later in the chapter.

Ultimately, the question regarding the level of entrenchment and the normative superiority of the basic laws remains open.[46] The essential entrenchment that was initially attached to Basic Law: Human Dignity (CA 6821/93), as opposed to the formal entrenchment that protected Basic Law: Freedom of Occupation, was extended to all of the basic laws (HC 212/03). Thus, any changes to the basic laws must be made by new basic laws. As such, the legislation process examines new bills' compatibility with the basic laws following the understanding that the latter are superior to the former.

This has led to a rather grotesque outcome. Basic Law: State Economy (1975) asserts that the state budget will be allocated for only one year. In order to pass a budget for two years the Knesset enacted Basic Law: State Budget 2009 until 2010 (Special Provision) (Temporary Order). Thus we are left with the absurd situation of having to pass a constitutional law that is at the same time a special provision and temporary.

The overall result is a fluid arrangement of the constitutional legal hierarchy and an insecure status for human rights.[47] As noted, Israel is still missing the most basic law among all basic laws: Basic Law: Legislation. Without which the Knesset continues to sit as both a constituent assembly and a legislative body with the power to reconstitute any protected right or protocol. Moreover, the "dialog" between the court and Knesset continues, and ultimately the Knesset has the upper hand. As a result, no human right is fundamentally secure and many are not even legislated. On the other hand, the law protects previous violations of human rights.

The Government and Secondary Legislation

Israel's fluid constitutional framework has a direct effect on the power and operation of its executive branch. Moreover, the Israeli government enjoys administrative flexibility that goes even further then its capacity to control the Knesset,[48] which in itself, as we saw, operates in according to an ambiguous constitutional structure. The Israeli government has the power to enact primary arrangements without being reviewed by the Knesset (Maoz 1988, 30). Indeed, Israel's government is able and enables itself to operate outside the Knesset's supervision. One of the ways the Israeli government operates outside the Knesset's control is by using emergency powers—the focus of this book. As we shall see in subsequent chapters, for example, Israel's government has used emergency powers even for administrating routine economic policies, thus bypassing the Knesset.

But Israel's government has other means, other than emergency powers, to bypass the Knesset's sovereignty and extend its power. On top of the general constitutional fluidity that generates governing flexibility, administrative legislation (or secondary legislation) executed by government members plays a central role in extending sovereign power. This mechanism fits with the central theme of this book: the ability of power to find the means, preferably legal ones, to execute its will.

Following the mandatory tradition, Israel's ministers have the power to issue orders as secondary legislation. In many respects secondary legislation is more significant than primary legislation and should be taken seriously in the debate over Israel's governability. First, the majority of legislation is passed with secondary legislation. Second, secondary legislation's impact is more substantial than primary insofar as it is more detailed and actually executes policy.

Since the Knesset does not have control over secondary legislation, the Israeli government operates in a fluid environment. Michal Elef-Shilo (2012) demonstrates that compared to liberal democracies such as Australia, the US, and the UK, the Israeli government, in terms of the way it executes secondary legislation, operates with little supervision or control. Ideally, secondary legislation only implements policies that were enacted as primary legislation. One of the basic principles of the democratic rule of law is that core regulations should be enacted as primary legislation, since this process safeguards the principles of participation, publicity, and majority rule. Under regular conditions, secondary legislation cannot contradict primary legislation, but there are exceptions to this rule. Primary legislation is usually general, and therefore executing its orders requires additional implementation orders, which is the purview of secondary legislation. Secondary legislation that simply implements the orders given by primary legislation is described as *juxta legem* (according to law).[49] When operation instructions are not specified by the primary legislation, the government can set implementation orders, thereby extending the law, as long as these orders do not contradict the law. This kind of secondary legislation is termed *praeter legem* (outside the law).[50] On certain occasions—as in the case of emergency regulations, which are used in some countries more than others—the government can even issue secondary legislation that contradicts the law: *contra legem*.[51] Yet in Israel, even the first two normative kinds of secondary legislation (according to law and outside the law) function without granting meaningful control to the legislative branch, thus, in some respects, rendering its operation similar to the third kind, contrary to the law.

In bypassing the Knesset, even secondary legislation that does not necessarily contradict existing law produces a similar effect as emergency powers, inasmuch as both challenge the sovereignty of the legislative branch. Unlike government acts that usurp their authority from the legislative branch, in many ways the performance of the Israeli government challenges the sovereignty of the legislative branch and violates the separation of power.

The Israeli government often operates without transparency and outside the Knesset's review. The Knesset does not have a complete procedure to review the government's enactments. This lacuna allows Israel's government to function without any external review and moreover to work outside the public eye (Elef-Shilo 2012, 62).[52] There is a general lack of transparency in the operation of the government. For example, both the protocols of the ministers' committees as well as the minister's voting records are kept hidden from the public eye. Moreover, the government has a procedure that bypasses almost all forms of review; this procedure basically allows the ministers to operate at their own discretion similar to emergency powers. According to "Procedure 19B," a minister sends a decision in an envelope (today a virtual box) and if no other government member raises objections—it should be noted that it requires other very busy ministers to actively check the box—one week from its distribution it is approved.[53] All in all, secondary legislation in Israel is yet an additional layer that extends power due to lack of defined legal borders.

Additional Fluidity: The Attorney General

Despite significant gaps in the 1992 constitutional reform, it has resulted in an increase in the roll of legal consultants working for the government and the Knesset. It has become more prudent for legal consultants to advise if new legislation will withstand judicial review. Chief among these institutes is the Office of the Attorney General. Yet even this bureaucratic agency that performs a crucial role in Israeli public life operates in a fluid context.

The attorney general's sources of authority and functions are based on ambiguous, mixed arrangements. In this respect, there is no legislation that outlines such things as the nature of the office, its general standing, its authorities, the process by which an attorney general is elected or the process by which an attorney general can be discharged. Thus, even this central legal office is the outcome of a patchwork system rather than a formal act of legislation.

Indeed, the Office of the Attorney General is the outcome of a hybrid mix between mandatory legacy, court rulings, several unbinding decisions reached by Knesset committees, and even unilateral actions taken by various attorney generals over the years. As a side note, liberal powers in Israel are afraid that that formal codifying of the office's authorities will mean stripping it of some of its powers, thus leaving the attorney general less affective in setting controls over the government. Inasmuch as the State of Israel suffers from a general lack of controls over its administrative agencies, they are right. But this does not take away from the underhanded methods this office employed to usurp its authorities.

As with any case of fluidity, the flexible foundation of the office of the attorney general is a source of power. Other than professional capital—attorney generals are expert jurists, many of them later become Supreme Court justices—the power of this office is based on a combination between the authorities it usurped over the years. The government can replace the attorney general, but cannot revoke his authorities.

One of the powers of the office of the attorney general has to do with the attorney general's ability to nullify a statute in practice by asserting that its orders will not be enforced. For example, in 1972 the attorney general did not enforce the statute against male homosexual intercourse (vol. 5 50.049). Other attorneys general did not enforce the law against meeting with PLO members when it was forbidden. Yet this is highly fluid insofar as a conservative, nationalist or reactionary attorney general can use this power for different agendas.

Ultimately, the basic fluidity of the Office of the Attorney General is structured upon its dual basic authorities. In accordance with Israel's convoluted arrangements, the attorney general serves, on the one hand, as the legal adviser to the government and, on the other hand, as the head of the prosecution. Thus, the Attorney General has to constantly overcome this inherent contradiction in which, formally speaking, the same person is responsible to indict and defend government members at the same time.

The Supreme Court: Enhancing Fluidity

The Israeli Supreme Court has contributed significantly to Israel's fluid legal structure. Generally, I argue that the Supreme Court does not only operate in an incoherent framework, but also maintains, and even reinforces, the complexity and ambiguity of Israel's legal-political structure as a whole.

The court, as is the case with other institutions in Israel, operates in under-defined circumstances in terms of its authority, and often the court itself decides its own jurisdictions. As discussed, the court functions without a full formal constitution or a complete bill of rights. Moreover, the Supreme Court is not explicitly commissioned to sit as a constitutional court. However, the court has played a central and active role as a policymaker within the Israeli political system. In general, judicial precedent (judge-made law as opposed to statutory law) plays a major role in the Israeli legal tradition. Israel's administrative law is based on judicial decisions rather than legislation. This tradition has been a major force in making Israel more liberal (by introducing a judicial bill of rights, for example) and probably the reason that many critics turn a blind eye to the ambiguity the court adds to an already fluid structure. In the future, however, other political factions might promote different agendas by using the court.

Of course, extending the judicial mandate is a common phenomenon. The Israeli Supreme Court, in this respect, is far from being the only court that actively applies judicial precedent. Yet it is unique because the Israeli court operates in an obscure constitutional context. In other words, it is the lack of a fully drafted, formal constitution that makes the Supreme Court unique among other courts around the world, which could be even more active.[54] Granted, of course, that courts can legislate from the bench despite having a fully drafted, formal constitution. But unlike other courts, the lack of a grounding constitutional framework allows the Supreme Court to operate with fewer restrictions. All in all, I argue, the court is not only a "victim" of Israel's fluid constitutional foundation, but also a "perpetrator" of that reality.

The Israeli Supreme Court stands out due to its unique function as a High Court of Justice (HCJ). Beyond the typical role as the highest court of appeals, the Israeli Supreme Court, based on mandatory tradition, serves as a court of first instance in cases pertaining to administrative law. Historically, as opposed to criminal and private law, which were left in the hands of the lower courts and often run by the local residents (Palestinians and Jews), it was important for the mandatory regime to preside over all matters concerning administrative law. Thus, because the HCJ served as a court of first instance, the British Mandate managed to preserve its control over all administrative issues. In order to maintain legal continuity, the HCJ continued to function in this role even after the establishment of the State of Israel (with a short gap; the HCJ reopened on September 14, 1948).[55] Hence, following mandatory tradition, the HCJ reviews the policies and activities of Israel's political and administrative institutions based on direct appeals by plaintiffs to the HCJ. The HCJ may grant plaintiffs relief in the form of prerogative writs against government actions, "in the interests of justice." The HCJ's decisions cannot be appealed. In extraordinary circumstances, however, the sides may be granted additional hearings.

An additional source of Israel's HCJ exceptionalism has to do with its judicial authority over the Occupied Palestinian Territories (OPT). This is yet another case of fluidity. In a way almost unprecedented in international law,[56] and also without formal authorization by Israeli statutes, the HCJ reviews appeals that are put forward by Palestinian residents of the occupied territories. In other words, Palestinians from the OPT were granted access to the Israeli Supreme Court. It is still unclear, to date, if the court has judicial authority when reviewing cases from the OPT. What is clear is that the court's jurisdiction in the OPT is extraterritorial (Sheleff 1993, 763). The court's understanding of sovereignty pertains not to territorial sovereignty in this regard, but to juridical sovereignty. The HCJ asserts its jurisdiction from its authority over all of Israel's administrative agencies, including the army. In other words, according to the court, its jurisdiction does not stem from Israel's territorial sovereignty over the OPT—it is a recognized fact that Israel never officially annexed them—but from the court's authority to review the activities of all Israeli administrative bodies.[57]

The numerous cases from the OPT have certainly challenged the HCJ. I shall not elaborate on this topic, which deserves and has indeed received[58] a full discussion on its own. Generally speaking, these cases have added tension to the relationship between the court and Israel's political and administrative branches.

In the first three decades of the state, the cultural-political atmosphere coupled with the lack of a constitution, hindered the power of Israel's juridical branch.[59] Yet, even in the first years of the State of Israel, when the court was relatively weak as opposed to the powerful central government, the court established, step by step, a Judicial Bill of Rights. Indeed, the HCJ has often been called the "Guardian of Civil Liberties" (Maoz 1988, 50). The Israeli HCJ has actually received international recognition as a court that is able to protect civil rights without a formal constitution or bill of rights (Sheleff 1993, 758). Still, judicial human rights are "soft" principles. They cannot override primary legislation, and as a rule, case law based on an interpretation of the court cannot serve as an independent source of law (Shachar 1995, 7).

All in all, the continued back and forth (the "dialogue") between the legislative, executive, and juridical branches has produced fluidity and instability. The dialog between the Knesset and the HCJ intensified after the 1980s and even more so after the 1992 constitutional reform. And the lack of a binding legislation, particularly in cases when the political system is fragmented,[60] can also lead to a more powerful court. In this respect, since the 1980s, the changing conditions in which the HCJ has operated have had the opposite effect;

they have made the court more dominating At some point in the late 1970s and early 1980s, with personnel changes, the court adopted an activist approach to applying more vigilant judicial review.[61] Around that period, the court loosened standing rights. As a result, plaintiffs no longer had to be directly involved in the case in order to appeal to the HCJ. Since then, different civil society associations have been able to appeal against unlawful acts by an administrative authority. Moreover, as noted, the basic laws of 1992 also ignited the court's activism. The significance of the 1992 basic laws, as we know, was the creation of a legal normative hierarchy, which allowed more legal scrutiny. The court, as a result, acquired better tools for interpretation and could validate or invalidate laws accordingly. And as noted, the court also extended these review tools on its own authority.[62]

Without going into great detail, with a lack of defined constitutional borders, there are no substantial limits on an activist[63] HCJ. And when the court by its own discretion, regardless of whether justices are right or wrong, decides on matters without any substantive legal reference, it furthers the legal complexity, particularly if it triggers the Knesset to strike back. Overall, my basic argument with respect to legal activism is as follows: from the perspective of the production of fluidity, it does not matter if the source is a politician or a justice. Despite the current reserved and often positive outcome, from a liberal perspective, the court is extending the limits of the law. Fluidity, we should remember, ultimately does not limit power; on the contrary, it enhances power insofar as it adds flexibilities.

As expected, the court's activism has met with a reaction from the Knesset. The negative reaction came from across the political spectrum, but it has been the voices from the Israeli right that were most ardent in their desire to limit the power of the court. For example, Israel's current rightwing, yet liberal, President Reuven Rivlin, in his tenure as the Speaker of the Knesset, spoke harshly against the court's activism, which he regarded as a threat to the Knesset's sovereignty (Sapir 2010, 131). A major milestone that heightened the Israeli right fury against the court was the court's ruling on Gaza Withdrawal plan in 2005 (HC 1661/05). In a decision of ten to one, the court upheld the government's plan that was approved by the Knesset to remove Jewish settlers from Gaza. In recent years, particularly during the seventeenth, eighteenth, and nineteenth Knessets (from April 2006) under rightwing coalitions, the Israeli Supreme Court has been under attack from the government and the Knesset.[64] These institutions have worked to weaken the court by attempting such tactics as trying to reform the process for electing justices, changing the number of justices, establishing a new constitutional court, etc. Chief among this reaction was the attempt, headed by the former minister of justice Professor Daniel Friedmann, to reform the procedure for electing justices.[65] This program eventually did not materialize, but the Knesset did succeed in interfering with court's seniority customs, thereby pushing a more conservative justice, Judge Asher Grunis, into the position of chief justice. Moreover, during the nineteenth Knesset, for example, new bills were pushed forward with the intent to weaken the HCJ by granting the Knesset the power to determine the court's personnel and to loosen the conditions by which the Knesset can overcome the court's rulings.[66] Overall, it is too soon, however, to determine the outcome of this process.

Conclusion

Israel's political and legal systems operate in a fluid structure. Its political branches and administrative agencies function in an open and flexible jurisdictional structure whereby the roles or authorities of its different institutions are often up for grabs. These circumstances give rise to an empowering ambiguity. As noted, it allows governing flexibility inasmuch as different agencies can usurp additional authorities, giving them multiple options to execute their will. Ultimately, this structured fluidity translates into power.

Thus, I argue, from the perspective of formal power to execute political will, Israel does not have a governability crisis, but just the opposite. In terms of legal authority, Israel's policymakers have plentiful power, to the point, in fact, that they can operate almost free from any formal barriers. In other words, the sources of Israel's governability problem are not in any way related to a lack of formal legal muscle. On the contrary, I would argue that Israel desperately requires deep reform that will place constitutional limits on its political branches and administrative agencies. This reform is even more urgent if we also consider its readily available emergency powers.

In fact, the constituted legal ambiguity I describe in this chapter, and the political possibilities it extends to Israel's ruling elite, raises questions about the regime's strong allegiance to emergency powers. In other words, if Israel's general fluid structure allows such governing flexibility and thus power, does it not make emergency powers rather redundant? The first and immediate answer is that power does not wish to give up any sources of authority. But I think it also speaks to the values of the rule of law and the unique political quality of emergency powers. Even in such a fluid legal structure, the basic principles of the rule of law set limits on power. Particularly, I would argue, it produces an ethic of responsibility. Politicians cannot abuse the rule of law to the point that they simply render it totally insignificant. But with emergency powers politicians can stretch the law and their political possibilities much more. As noted in the introduction, unlike any other legal mechanism that is based on fluidity, emergency powers operates at the same time inside and outside of the judicial order and thus they are capable of extending power beyond any other legal mean. We now turn to explore Israel's fluid emergency jurisprudence.

3

FLUID EMERGENCY LEGAL SOURCES

Since its establishment in 1948, Israel has been under a legal state of emergency. Less known, but equally important, is the fact that Israel's legal system features several overlapping and incoherent emergency legal mechanisms that exist side by side. As a legal patchwork of sorts, Israel's complex system of emergency enactment has cobbled together various emergency legal mechanisms that sometimes overlap and sometimes complement one another. Two of the three main emergency legal mechanisms are quite comprehensive—some would argue excessive—and need no additional emergency apparatus. But during the years of its establishment, Israel's legislative body has never unified these various legal emergency procedures, nor has the judicial branch challenged this legal complexity.

The fact that Israel's authorities have failed to bring coherence to the system begs the question of whether maintaining such a complex legal structure serves its political purposes. But before I can address this question in the following chapter, it is necessary to outline Israel's convoluted emergency legal structure. Indeed, Israel's emergency powers are based on an extremely complicated array of legal sources, which makes it imperative to sort them out. In this chapter I trace each emergency legal source back to its historical origin. I consider all the laws available to Israel's authorities. Thus, it encompasses shared emergency laws that apply in "Israel itself" as well as in the OPT, military orders in the OPT, and legal mechanisms that bridge between "Israel itself" and the OPT.

A Fluid Jurisprudence

Scholars have identified the convoluted nature of Israel's legal system (Bracha 1978; Cohn 1998; Dowty 1988; Goldstein 1978; Hofnung 1996 & 2001; Klinghoffer 1962; Rubinstein 1996; Saltman 1982, Shetreet 1984 and Saban, 2002). But few have connected its complex structure to the Israeli regime's intentions. As previous studies have outlined, Israel's law books house three distinctive legal bases for enacting emergency powers: mandatory emergency defense regulations; administrative emergency orders; and primary emergency laws, which I refer to also as primary laws. Because my frame of reference is Israel's control system (Kimmerling 1989), I also consider a fourth category, belligerent occupation, whose foundation stems from international law. This fourth category is key to understanding Israel's governing powers in the OPT.

What all these divisions clearly reflect is that the State of Israel does not have a unified legal methodology for emergency enactment (Hofnung 2001, 52). Never has a general legal mechanism been issued to organize all the different emergency legal procedures. Only a few clauses in the Israeli law book define a legal hierarchy in which contradictory procedures take precedence over others.[1] Moreover, as Margit Cohn shows, neither the government, nor the Knesset, nor the court formally disapproved of the structure of this system (1998, 637). All in all, Israel's authorities have made little effort to solve these internal contradictions. Augmenting this problem is Israel's lack of a constitutional arrangement that asserts normative hierarchy in its body of law.

Table 1 outlines and summarizes the relationship between these legal mechanisms; their sources; their status as primary or secondary laws; their dependence on a declared SOE; the type of authorities they grant (explicit or legislative); and those who are authorized to use or issue emergency regulations.

The first two and main legal sources are the mandatory emergency defence regulations and the administrative emergency orders. Whereas mandatory emergency regulations are independent from an official declaration of an SOE, administrative emergency orders are conditioned by it. Moreover, because of a court decision, while mandatory emergency regulations are explicit in the authority they grant, administrative emergency orders carry a legislative power by

Table 1. Emergency Legal Mechanisms.

	Source		Status		Dependency on a State of Emergency		Authorities		Authorized Authority	
	Foreign	Original	Primary	Secondary	No	Yes	Explicit	Legislative	Military Commander	Minister
Mandatory Emergency Defence Regulations	✓		✓		✓		✓*		✓	
Administrative Emergency Orders		✓		✓**		✓		✓		✓
Formal Emergency Laws — Renewal		✓	✓			✓	NA	NA	NA	NA
Formal Emergency Laws — Dependent		✓	✓			✓	✓	✓	NA	NA
Formal Emergency Laws — Independent		✓	✓		✓		NA	NA	NA	NA
Belligerent Occupation	✓		✓		✓		✓	✓	✓	

* Originally the mandatory emergency regulations also had legislative powers, but after a court's ruling, new emergency regulations must be enacted through administrative emergency orders (AEOs).

** But AEOs can override primary laws.

which ministers can issue regulations as they deem necessary. Further, mandatory emergency regulations and administrative emergency orders authorize different agencies. The mandatory emergency regulations stem from a British colonial enactment and follow that tradition in authorizing military commanders. By contrast, administrative emergency orders, which are original Israeli enactments, authorize a minister, who can then delegate power to an administrative agency. On the other hand, mandatory emergency regulations and administrative emergency orders overlap. Mandatory emergency regulations and administrative emergency orders can stand on their own; each grants comprehensive emergency powers and, thus, each makes the existence of the alternative emergency legal mechanism redundant.

The array of legal mechanisms underlying Israel's emergency powers is even more complex than this description suggests. Formal emergency laws, for example, are in fact made up of several clusters of laws:

1. Renewed administrative emergency orders (or renewal laws), which demonstrate the fluidity between legal mechanisms insofar as secondary orders are transformed into primary laws;
2. Laws dependent on a declared SOE (dependent laws); and
3. Laws that do not depend on a declared SOE (independent laws).

Moreover, primary laws feature the same complementary relationship as mandatory emergency regulations and administrative emergency orders. While some primary laws are explicit in the authority they give to an administrative agency, others simply grant legislative power to use at the discretion of the authorized authority.

Table 1 thus illustrates the immense complexity and ambiguity of the relationship between these various emergency legal mechanisms. Unlike a well-constructed system that is organized in different chapters and where each defines a separate section of law, the legal sources of Israel's complex emergency enactment define and redefine similar legal sections. Whereas a well-constructed system sets "one building block on the side of another," a complex system patches one on top of another (Cohn 1998, 633).

The Mandatory Emergency (Defence) Regulations

The Expansive Power of Mandatory Regulations

Mandatory emergency regulations have an inauspicious foundation. They stem from British enactments between 1937 and 1945, during Britain's mandatory rule over Palestine. Born in the context of a colonial regime whose aim was to suppress Palestinian and Jewish insurgency and to consolidate British control during World War II, these laws are sweeping in scope and delegate emergency powers for nearly any foreseeable emergency need. Still, while these laws are more than all-encompassing enough to stand on their own, Israel has instead coupled them with additional emergency mechanisms, creating overlap and redundancy in its emergency legal regime.

Indeed, mandatory emergency regulations originated in three sets of emergency enactments. The first set, the Palestine (Defence) Order in Council of 1937, came as a response to the 1936–1939 Arab revolt in Palestine. These regulations were promulgated by virtue of article 6 of the Palestine (Defence) Order in Council, 1937.[2] The privy council in London adopted emergency regulations that were previously formulated during other insurgencies in its colonies—mostly the Boer War in South Africa. Accordingly, the High Commissioner, who acts as the executive as well as the legislative authority, was authorized to enact any defence regulation "as appears to him in his unfettered discretion to be necessary or expedient for securing public safety, the defence of Palestine, the maintenance of public order and the suppression of mutiny, rebellion, or riot and for maintaining supplies and services essential to the life of the community." The defense regulations apply notwithstanding any law; they may amend any law with or without modification. The second set, the Emergency Powers (Defence of the Colonies) Order in Council of 1939,[3] was enacted in the context of World War II. As such, these were general orders as opposed to the regulations of 1937 and those that would come in 1945, which were specific to Palestine. In other words, the emergency regulations of 1939 were enacted in order to protect against external threats, whereas those of 1937 as well as 1945 were enacted in order to protect against internal threats. Yet, during the war, additional orders particular to

Palestine were enacted.[4] Some of the 1939 regulations were made void by the end of the war in 1945. In September of 1945, Lord Gort promulgated under the authority of article 6 of the Palestine Defence Order in Council, 1937 a collected set of 147 regulations, was spread on forty-one pages and established a virtual regime of martial law (Dowty 1988, 35). These emergency regulations came in response to Jewish insurgency.

At the time, the Jewish leaders of the *Yishuv*[5] were strongly criticizing the Emergency (Defence) Regulations of 1945. Indeed, some of the future political leaders of Israel were especially targeted by them. The Jewish Bar Association of Palestine publically denounced them, stating that the "granting of such wide powers to the authorities without judicial control is a serious breach of the fundamentals of any orderly regime and undermines the very existence of the regime itself."[6] However, in May 1948, Israel incorporated mandatory emergency regulations, along with the mandatory law in general, into its domestic legislation (section 11 of the LAO). It is worth noting that the same statute also gave birth to the administrative emergency orders: Israel's original emergency powers.

Israel officials at the time justified incorporating mandatory emergency regulations into their system of governance because of the hasty establishment of the state during a time of war. The general attorney argued that, while mandatory emergency regulations were indeed despicable, given their history, there was simply no time to replace them with a new, original law. While Britain has removed or replaced mandatory emergency regulations, Israel has kept them in place—long after the end of the war, which was the source of their temporary "patchwork" justification—and they continue to apply today. Out of a total of 162 sections, some with sub-articles, the Knesset formally canceled or replaced only a handful of sections.[7]

It thus seems that incorporation of the mandatory law, upon its emergency enactment, may well have begun as a pragmatic solution, but later turned into a programmatic tool. Menahem Hofnung (2001, 83) and Michael Saltman (1982, 393) suggest that the merit of the mandatory emergency regulations lies in the fact that they are not an original Israeli law. As such, despite the fact that formally they are part of the Israeli law, they are perceived as "foreign" to the Israeli democracy.

Mandatory emergency regulations have the status of primary laws, they apply notwithstanding any law, and they may amend any law with and without modification. They also remain in force with no time limit; and they are valid regardless of whether a SOE has been formally declared. Mandatory emergency regulations can be divided into three kinds of emergency regulations:

1. Execution authorities, such as arrests, inspections, and the opening or closure of roads and businesses.
2. Prevention authorities, such as limiting or preventing movement or speech.
3. Punishment authorities, such as the demolition of houses.

These various categories of enforcement cover a broad swath of emergency powers and provide authorities with a wide range of possibilities for action. In sum, mandatory emergency regulations are both comprehensive and excessive. Indeed, their authority applies to many areas of daily life, from business operations to road closings to detentions and other punitive measures.

The mandatory emergency regulations that eventually remained in force and then integrated into Israel's domestic law can also be divided between regulations pertaining to security and those who regulate services and organize the economy in a time of emergency. The security-based orders enacted in 1945 were issued without an expiration date and continued to be valid indefinitely as part of the Israeli law. An important bulk of the mandatory emergency regulations pertaining to economic regulations, however, had to be renewed since their validity was temporal. Some of the "economic" regulations were renewed indefinitely by the power of the King-in-Council in 1946 and by the Supply of Products and Services (Transitional Provision) Decree of 1946.[8] Yet, the rest of the economic regulations were only renewed for 5 years in 1947 by the mandatory regime, shortly before the establishment of the State of Israel.[9] In fact, this renewal was used as a justification for keeping them "for the time being" by the Israeli government (Hofnung 2001, 67). Yet just before their expiration date these regulation were prolong the State of Israel, in a series of renewal laws,[10] for a few months each time, sometimes with some corrections, until[11] they were replaced by an original Israeli law, the Control of Products and Services Law, 1957,[12] and the Currency Supervision Law, 1978.[13]

Originally, and according to the British colonial legal tradition, mandatory emergency regulations delegated powers to a military officer. With the adjustments, in the integration of the mandatory emergency regulations into the Israeli law, the powers were conferred to a "Military Commander," who is an officer appointed by the chief of staff with the approval of the defense minister.[14]

Because mandatory emergency regulations grant such vast authority, it is impossible to restrict their power by arguing that a particular action goes beyond the law's actual authority. This vast authority poses problems, of course, where mandatory emergency regulations' use can easily become capricious and arbitrary.

Maintaining Fluidity

Given their history as British colonial orders, mandatory emergency regulations met substantial challenges. Early on, the Israeli Supreme Court, sitting as a High Court of Justice (HCJ), decided on the legal status and validity of mandatory emergency regulations.[15] The HCJ continued to sustain this position in which mandatory emergency regulations are a valid part of Israeli law.[16] As early as 1948 in the *Altalena*[17] case, the HCJ rejected the argument that mandatory emergency regulations were foreign colonial laws and that they thus contradicted Israeli law (Cook v. the Minister of Defence, 1948). Soon after, in the canonic case Levon v. Gubernik (1948), the HCJ reaffirmed its decision. In Levon v. Gubernik, the court ruled that only regulations that have been explicitly revoked are no longer part of Israeli law. The court concluded that the suffix of section 11 of the LAO, 1948, refers only to technical changes.

> The legislator would not have hidden in the words 'within the modification from establishing the state and its administrations' such an important decision regarding the nullification of the emergency regulations. The legislator did explicitly nullify in section 13 [of the LAO, 1948] two laws from the White Book from 1939;[18] that is, sections 13 to 15 of the Immigration Ordinance of 1941, sections 102 to 107 of the Emergency (Defence) Regulations, 1945, and the Land Transfer Regulation of 1940. If the legislator was of the opinion that all or some of the emergency regulation from 1939 or from 1945 should be nullified, similarly as he did with regard to section

13, the path to do so was explicitly open. Nevertheless, it did not do so. (Levon v. Gubernik, 69)

The HCJ continued to sustain the position that mandatory emergency regulations are part of the Israeli law in subsequent cases: "Emergency Powers (Defence) Act, 1939, and Emergency (Defence) Regulations, 1945, . . . are part of the *law* that rules the State of Israel" (22/49, 706. Emphasis added).

Later, the court even expanded the validity of the mandatory emergency regulations by confirming their application on the OPT.[19]

Over time, the HCJ has introduced some procedural limitations on mandatory emergency regulations.[20] However, more significantly, the HCJ also ruled that the authorized authority's discretion with regard to mandatory emergency regulations is not subject to judicial review.[21] With the HCJ rulings, since the 1960s only high-level officers (generals, who head one of the three commands and the commander of the navy), as opposed to merely any "military commander," could execute mandatory emergency regulation 111 (Detention), and only for a duration of three months (or one to three months in East Jerusalem). Moreover, only the chief of staff could detain someone for more than three months, but only up to six months, and provided that the advisory committee headed by a Supreme Court justice approved. The attorney general asserted that the detention should be preventive rather than punitive. Later, the Emergency Powers (Detention) Law of 1979, which replaced mandatory emergency regulation 111, added a requirement for judicial approval within forty-eight hours of the detention order and periodic judicial supervisions.

Prior to 1967, various attempts to remove mandatory emergency regulations from the Israeli law books failed. The first attempt was in December of 1950 just before some of the mandatory emergency regulations, were about to expire. The government, represented by the then-minister of justice Yitzhak Rozen, laid out a suggestion, which never materialized, for a comprehensive original emergency enactment[22] to replace and unify all the different emergency enactment procedures. The intention of the law was to grant authority to a military commander to detain, deport, limit movement, evacuate, and censor (but not to demolish houses). However, unlike mandatory emergency regulations, they would not adhere to primary legislation. The law was brought to the Knesset for a first vote and passed thirty-four to twenty-six.[23] The bill then went to the Knesset committee, but the opposition from the three biggest parties, notwithstanding the ruling party Mapai, forced the government to bury it in the committee and finally to drop it altogether.

Indeed, during the first seat of the Knesset, there was a tendency to replace the temporary arrangement with a formal one, but the government faced opposition from left and right in its attempts to secure emergency powers in primary legislation. In the final analysis, all the major parties preferred a temporary solution rather than as a permanent one. The two cardinal events that killed such attempts were: the Harari compromise that ended the process of constitution-making as one unit, and the renewal law, the Order for the Extension of the Validity of Defense Regulations (Temporary Provision),[24] which was passed despite opposition from right and left, and by which the mandatory emergency regulations were renewed.

In 1951, fifty-three members of an ultra-orthodox, anti-Zionist, Jewish underground (suspected of arson and of stockpiling weapons and explosives to be used against the state) were detained by the power of mandatory emergency regulation 111. These detainees became known as the "Jellamy detainees."[25] This event ignited a heated debate and a call to remove the mandatory emergency regulations altogether. However, the government forcefully resisted revoking the mandatory emergency regulations unless they would be replaced by law.[26] Menachem Begin, then the opposition leader, who himself was targeted by mandatory emergency regulations during the British Mandate as the leader of the *Irgun* underground, gave an emotional speech:

> The law you have used is Nazi, tyrannical and immoral; an immoral law is also an invalid law. Therefore, the detention is illegal and your order is arbitrary. You had no right to do this; when there is a Knesset in existence, courts in existence. . . . If these laws, the laws of terror of an oppressive regime [the British Mandate] will remain in force in Israel, the day will come when no single group will remain unharmed by them, and it matters not which group.[27]

The Knesset debate ended with this declarative statement:

> The Knesset declares that the [Emergency] Defence Regulations, 1945, which are valid in the state since the British Mandate, are in contradiction to the basic principle of the state; the Knesset therefore submits that the Committee of Law and Justice be obliged to prepare and present before the Knesset a bill for the removal of these regulations.[28]

After two weeks, the committee introduced a statute, a Bill for the Canceling of British Emergency Enactment (Security Matters), 1951,[29] but the coalition managed to postpone the debate for two further weeks and it has never been picked up since.

During the 1960s, there were other proposals to revoke the mandatory emergency regulations (as well as the military government). Yet, as before, they failed for the same reasons. On the one hand, the government refused to cancel the mandatory emergency regulations without an alternative in the form of an original enactment. On the other hand, the opposition from left and right did not wish to grant such powers to the government and preferred, as the lesser evil, to keep them as temporary foreign procedures. In 1962, Pinhas Rosen, once Israel's first minister of justice, introduced a private bill that suggested bringing the mandatory emergency regulations under section 9 of the LAO, or subjecting them to a declaration of an SOE. In 1966, another minister of justice, Yaakov Shimshon,[30] initiated another reform, which came to a halt due to the Six Day War in June 1967.

Since the war in 1967, however, no serious effort has been undertaken. The fact that there was no attempt to revoke mandatory emergency regulations after 1967 is not mere coincidence, I argue. Despite Jordanian opposition, Israeli officials insisted that mandatory emergency regulations were in force in the OPT because the region was also historically part of the British mandate and has had no other recognized sovereign since that time.

This line of reasoning served Israel's purposes. It gave Israeli's occupation authorities a comprehensive, ready-made set of emergency powers in the form of "local" laws. Israel coupled together the OPT with "Israel proper" as the old territory of the British mandate in which mandatory emergency regulations apply. Hence, revoking them in one region but not the other could have posed a problem that Israel wanted to avoid.

Indeed, removing these colonial mandates only from Israel proper might have raised more questions about unequal treatment of the occupied territories. When it came to power in 1977, the Likud party—which, in its previous incarnation as Herut, consistently voted to revoke mandatory emergency regulations—did not attempt to remove mandatory emergency regulations from Israeli law. The Likud party made one concession, and enacted only the Emergency Powers (Detention) Law of 1979, which replaced two mandatory emergency regulations that addressed detention and deportation (mandatory emergency regulations 111 and 112).[31] Nevertheless, the bulk of mandatory emergency regulations not only remained in place but also were applied more extensively, including mandatory emergency regulations 111 and 112, in the OPT.[32]

Administrative Emergency Powers

In the Israeli legal system, administrative emergency orders create further convolution and redundancy. Unlike mandatory emergency regulations, which were inherited from British colonial rule, these emergency legal mechanisms stem from original Israeli law. They carry legislative power, enabling ministers to issue emergency decrees as they deem necessary. Insofar as administrative emergency orders have a status of secondary legislation, they are distinct from the other emergency legal sources. Yet their status as secondary legislation does not dilute their power because they can trump primary law. Unless a primary law or a section of it has been specifically and expressly entrenched, these secondary laws can override primary law.[33]

Like mandatory emergency regulations, the administrative emergency legislation is excessive in the power it grants, yet for different reasons. Administrative emergency orders' expansiveness lie in the extensive legislative power these orders delegate to the ministers. Once commissioned by the government, ministers can issue emergency orders at their own discretion. In May 1948, in the days that followed the declaration of the SOE, the government commissioned ministers in key positions, such as the minister of defense and the minister of finance, to enact emergency regulations. Since then, most ministers—other than the foreign minister and the minister of religion—have been granted this power.[34] None of these general powers have been revoked.³⁵ Because administrative emergency orders can serve virtually any emergency need, having alternative emergency legal mechanisms alongside them is redundant.

Restrictions on Administrative Emergency Orders

Section 9 of LAO (Emergency Regulations) states the following:

(a) If the Provisional Council³⁶ of State deems it expedient so to do, it may declare that a state of emergency exists in the State, and upon such declaration being published in the *Official Gazette*, the Provisional Government may authorize the Prime Minister or any other Minister to make such Emergency Regulations as may seem to him expedient in the interest of the defense of the State, public security and the maintenance of supplies and essential services.
(b) An emergency regulation may alter any law, suspend its effect or modify it, and may also impose or increase taxes or other obligatory payments.
(c) An emergency regulation shall expire three months after it is made, unless it is extended or revoked at an earlier date, by an Ordinance³⁷ of the Provisional Council of State, or revoked by the regulation-making authority.
(d) Whenever the Provisional Council of State thinks fit, it shall declare that the state of emergency has ceased to exist, and upon such declaration being published in the *Official Gazette*, the emergency regulations shall expire on the dates of prescribed is such declaration."³⁸ (Emphasis in original.)

Upon review, the restrictions on administrative emergency orders are rather slim, with only three limitations all told. The first states that an administrative emergency order can be issued only during an SOE. This condition is a theoretical limitation, of course, because the State of Israel has been under a continuous SOE since its establishment. Thus, in terms of enforcement and practical application, this limitation is hollow, and in practice has no effect.

The second restriction outlines the objectives of administrative emergency orders and stipulates that they must be in accordance with "the defense of the State, public security and the maintenance of supplies and essential services." Hans Klinghoffer (1962, 87, 93) argues that, like the first constraint on administrative emergency orders, this limitation is also only theoretical because the objectives are so broad. Therefore, almost any administrative emergency order can be positioned as being linked to these objectives. As with mandatory emergency regulations, it is difficult to argue that enacted administrative emergency orders exceed their granted authority. In addition, administrative emergency orders have been drafted to grant general authority, as opposed to particular powers, and it remains unclear whether ministers can issue administrative emergency orders that relate only to their jurisdictions. In the past, ministers have issued administrative emergency orders that extended beyond their ministerial responsibilities.

The third restriction limits administrative emergency orders' validity to a three-month duration. This restriction is crucial to the democratic character of the state (Klinghoffer 1962, 89). Otherwise, the emergency regulations could simply trample over the normative governmental rule. Yet in Israel, even this restriction has loopholes that neutralize its sting: by copying administrative emergency orders and reissuing them as new orders, the government can renew old orders endlessly without the Knesset's direct approval—so long as the Knesset has not ended the SOE. This procedure is generally regarded as stepping outside the renewal protocol, but in the past the Israeli government has used it.

The crudest use of such "renewal" took place in 1957. During the Suez War, the government published a corpus of 222 administrative emergency orders, which were due to expire three months later. Just two days before their expiration date, the minister of defense issued new administrative emergency orders that basically copied the previous set of administrative emergency orders with only minor changes. To date, some administrative emergency orders that were enacted during the 1948 war have been reissued as "new" administrative emergency orders, others have become renewal laws, and still others have been replaced by original primary law.[39] These various instances of administrative emergency orders' renewal indicate the fluidity of this emergency legal mechanism. If an authority wishes, an administrative emergency order never need die; instead, it can be reissued as a new order. All in all, the control mechanisms over administrative emergency orders are weak. For the most part, it is the Knesset that should set limits on the government's use of administrative emergency orders, but because in Israel the government's coalition controls the Knesset, it has the power to ratify its actions.

Besides reissuing the administrative emergency order as a way to renew them or bringing them in front of the Knesset for a formal renewal, there is an administrative renewal procedure.[40] An administrative emergency order can also be renewed as a secondary administrative regulation by the minister who issued it. According to this procedure, the minister has to submit his request to the government's cabinet for approval. If approved, the proposal goes to the Knesset, where it has to be approved, but only by one vote instead of three votes as any other law, including formal renewal laws. This procedure was formally codified in section 50 of the Government Rules of Order, 1977.

Over the years, more procedural restrictions were introduced. These additional limitations were drafted in the Government's Working Rules and in the Attorney General's Guidelines.[41] The Government's Working Rules assert that a minister who seeks to use his or her power according to section 9 should obtain an authorization from the government. The minister should bring his or her proposal before the government for discussion and, if needed—because of especially urgent necessity—the approval vote can be given over the telephone.[42] The Government's Working Rules protocol also provides the procedure for renewing the regulation by the Knesset as renewal laws. The proposal is then discussed in a governmental forum and, if agreed, it passes to the Knesset as a draft statute.[43] These procedures provide minimum review to prevent arbitrariness, but only as an internal review by the same body that also issues the emergency regulations. Other than that, there is no other substantive review. With respect to the HCJ, the court generally followed a formalist approach. As such, as long as the minister did not violate due process or the objective as described by section 9 of the LAO or the Basic Law: The Government, the court did not intervene. Indeed, the court until 1990 did not disqualify any administrative emergency order on reasonableness grounds. Only on July 1990 was an administrative emergency order canceled on the grounds that a swift primary formal legislation was in process.[44]

In 1992, the Knesset amended the Basic Law: The Government. This amendment replaced section 9 of the LAO of 1948 as the legal source for administrative emergency orders in a time of a SOE. The new law came into force in 1996. The law was then amended again in 2001,[45] and came into force in 2003. According to section 38(a) of Basic Law: The Government, the Knesset has the authority to declare a SOE by its own recognition or by approving the government's request. section 38(b) of the same law asserts that the Knesset can declare an SOE only for a period of one year. As such, it appeared that this amendment turned the restriction, by which the administrative emergency orders are valid only under an SOE, from a theoretical limitation to an actual one. However this new procedure, in practice, did not have any effect, because the legal SOE in Israel has continued to be in force ever since. The SOE has been renewed almost automatically. Section 38(c) states that the government can also declare a SOE if the Knesset is unable to meet. This declaration will remain in force for seven days unless the Knesset approves it during this time. If the Knesset does not meet during these seven days, the government can renew its decision for an additional week. Section 38(e) asserts that the Knesset may at all times revoke the declaration.

Section 39(a) of Basic Law: The Government states:

> During a state of emergency the Government may issue emergency regulations for the defense of the State, public security and the maintenance of supplies and essential services. The emergency regulations will be submitted to the Foreign Affairs and Security Committee at the earliest possible date after their enactment.

This article essentially copies section 9(a) of the LAO, with one addition and one modification. The addition ascribes to the Knesset more oversight, since the administrative emergency order has to be submitted to the Knesset's Foreign Affairs and Security Committee. Yet, this arrangement is rather weak and vague insofar as the timeframe is not explicitly marked and also by the fact that the Knesset committee is not authorized to revoke the administrative emergency order. In the new arrangement, the power is vested in the government as a whole. Indeed, section 39(b) replaces the previous ministerial independent power and instead commissions all powers to the prime minister as a representative of the government as a whole. If the government is unable to meet, the prime minister can then delegate powers to himself or any other minister. This is a partial recognition of different stages of emergency. Section 39(c) copied section 9(b) of the LAO, 1948 with the addition "unless there be another provision by law." This is recognition in the existence of entrenched laws or sections of laws. Another restriction that was added with respect to section 9 of the LAO is judicial review. Section 39(d) asserts that the regulations cannot prevent judicial review and should not approve any act that violates human dignity. This provision does not apply to existing emergency enactments. In this respect, new administrative emergency orders cannot prevent appealing to a court, cannot allow retroactive punishment, and cannot violate human dignity. Moreover, as opposed to the previous legal mechanism, Section 9 of the LAO, administrative emergency orders are valid only for three months; then the Knesset must renew it with a law (section 39[f]). In addition, the Knesset can cancel an emergency regulation with a majority of the Knesset members (ibid.). Finally, if the SOE ceases to exist, the administrative emergency order will not be sustained longer than sixty days after the termination of the SOE (section 39[h]). Section 41 protects Basic Law: The Government by stating that the administrative emergency orders, promulgated by the power of this law, cannot alter, suspended, or condition it. Margit Cohn has argued that the new restrictions were in some respect counterproductive, since, due to the new limitations, the government has become more tempted to enact emergency regulations outside this procedure using the existing alternative legal mechanisms (1998).

By and large, the HCJ maintained a formalistic judicial approach with respect to both administrative emergency orders and mandatory emergency regulations. In cases pertaining to administrative emergency actions that stem from administrative emergency orders, the HCJ did not intervene as long as the minister did not violate due process or the objective, as instructed by section 9 of the LAO (and later Basic Law: The Government). As noted, until 1990, the court did not disqualify any administrative emergency order. Then, in Poraz v. Government of Israel (HC 2994/90), the HCJ, already in its more activist era, overruled a case on the grounds that a swift primary formal legislation was in process.

The Coexistence of Mandatory Emergency Regulations and Administrative Emergency Orders

As early as 1948, the ambiguity between mandatory emergency regulations and administrative emergency orders came under fire. In Ziv v. Gubernik (1948), the HCJ had to decide whether the overlapping powers of administrative emergency orders and mandatory emergency regulations contradicted each other. The court ruled that section 9 of the LAO (administrative emergency orders' original legal source) does not, in fact, override or contradict mandatory emergency regulations. In its holding, the court further validated the patchwork relationship between mandatory emergency regulations and administrative emergency orders, by asserting that any *new* emergency regulations be enacted through administrative emergency orders, not through mandatory emergency regulations. Following the decision, sections of mandatory emergency regulations that granted the authority to enact new regulations were invalidated, but all pre-1948 regulations—unless explicitly revoked—remained valid.

With sanction from the court, and because the 1992 amendment (in Basic Law: The Government) had virtually no effect on the affiliation between administrative emergency orders and mandatory emergency regulations (where the 1992 amendment was itself a Band-Aid), this patchwork relationship is a powerful tool for Israel's authorities and grants great political flexibility. First, mandatory emergency regulations complement administrative emergency orders; mandatory emergency regulations are a complete set of emergency regulations that remain in force with no time limit, and also apply in the OPT. On the other hand, as I discuss in the next chapter, administrative emergency orders' legislative power complements that of mandatory emergency regulations by extending their validity.

Primary Emergency Laws

Primary Laws: Lost Opportunities for Cohesion

Israel's primary emergency laws illustrate the state's lost opportunity to unify its convoluted legal system. Israel's law books contain yet another class of emergency laws that were formally enacted by the Knesset; thus I term them, as noted before, "primary emergency laws." However, other than being formal and pertaining to some emergency condition, nothing classifies them as a single category of laws. The Israeli legislator could have used primary laws to unify Israel's emergency law by signing into law a body of statutes that would replace and unify all the existing dispersed emergency legal mechanisms. Instead, over the years, random primary laws were enacted as a continued legal patchwork.

Fewer in numbers, primary laws perpetuate Israel's legal complexity by replicating the complementary relationship between mandatory emergency regulations and administrative emergency orders (explicit/legislative and dependent on/independent of an SOE), and by redefining similar authorities already outlined by mandatory emergency regulations without replacing them. Primary laws also augment the fluidity of Israel's emergency legal structure, because the majority of primary laws are in fact renewed administrative emergency orders.

Not only is it difficult to recognize primary laws, but sorting them into categories presents a problem as well. Indeed, over the years scholars have suggested different divisions, some of which contain further subcategories. Alan Dowty's first category (1988) contains laws which are dependent on the existence of an SOE (henceforth, "dependent laws") as instructed by section 9 of the LAO and later by section 39(a) of Basic Law: The Government. Shimon Shetreet (1984) offers a further subdivision of this category. The first subsection is explicit dependent laws, which provide detailed arrangements for the execution of the law. The second subcategory is legislative dependent laws. These laws provide secondary legislative power to the authorized authority to promulgate regulations in certain matter under condition set forth in the enabling legislation. Dowty's second category is original laws, whose function is related to emergency or security matters. I shall term these "independent laws." Menahem Hofnung (1996, 2001) provides a third category of primary laws, termed "renewal laws." In his division, as we shall see, he adopts Huns Kimghufer's subdivision (1962). My division will include renewal laws, dependent laws (on a SOE) and independent laws upon all their subcategories.

Renewal Laws

Renewal laws represent one of the systems' most flexible elements and illustrate the fluidity of the system as a whole. Originating from administrative emergency orders, renewal laws form the majority of primary laws. According to the convention, administrative emergency orders can remain in force after they expire (three months from the day of their enactment) only if the Knesset renews them. Once renewed, these emergency arrangements take on primary, rather than secondary, legislation status. Thus, a regulation born as a temporary, emergency exceptional act becomes a primary bill. As a consequence, the hierarchy between primary and secondary legislation changes and allows the latter to take on greater power. Indeed, if Israel's authority so wishes (note that the government controls the Knesset in Israel), it can convert temporary laws into formal emergency powers. As a result, to a significant extent, emergency powers do not fade away, but instead simply change status, and in doing so, become more powerful.

The superiority of renewal laws over regular laws was affirmed by the HCJ. The HCJ affirmed that renewal laws have the status of primary laws and thus supported the fluidity of the legal structure. In a case from 1953, the court stated,

> It is clear that once the Knesset renews, by law, the duration of emergency regulations, which were enacted by a certain Minister, it asserts that these regulations are expedient and moreover, that, for the duration of their renewal, they receive the validity of a primary law. It [also] means that at least from the moment the emergency regulations were renewed they obtain a legal validity regardless of their origin and even if it is feeble (HC 243/52; henceforth the "Bilar precedent")

The Bilar precedent came under harsh criticism. Benjamin Acktzin (1953–1954) asked, in his potent critique, "Since when does an executive order become a law?" To him, administrative emergency orders are executive orders and cannot be made into primary law. Hans Klinghoffer was less critical of the court; as he saw it, the administrative emergency order can be only a second-rate law with lower status (1962, 109). Klinghoffer also argued that renewal laws should not escape judicial review.

At any rate, by affirming that renewal laws are primary laws, the court declared that it cannot invalidate them, and basically that renewal laws are not subject to judicial review. The HCJ did not accept the critique and reaffirmed its decision in other cases.[46] Hofnung argues that renewal laws have been a convenient temporary solution that came instead of a political and civic decision (2001, 71).

Renewal laws also illustrate Israel's ambiguous legal structure. In some cases, a few administrative emergency orders were renewed in one law,[47] but during the first Knesset's term, it became a custom that the Knesset renew each administrative emergency order separately (Hofnung 2001, 69). The terms of the duration of renewal are inconsistent, and administrative emergency orders can be renewed any number of times without restriction. Some renewal laws have no expiration date, but rather stay in force as long as an SOE continues. Other renewal laws prolong administrative emergency orders for short periods. In addition, some administrative emergency orders are periodically renewed. Administrative emergency orders can also be renewed by a correctional law. Finally, administrative emergency orders, as well as renewal laws, are automatically renewed if they are about to expire in the last two months of the Knesset's term (section 38 of Basic Law: The Knesset). A lack of fixed time frames enables the state to stack emergency powers in Israel's law books and provides an even greater array of options for action. Not only is Israel's law repository piled with emergency enactments, but because of their volume, removing them would create a legal void with no available normative statutes to fill the gap.

Dependent Laws

During emergency situations, the ability to call on a stack of primary laws that are activated only during an SOE keeps the state primed for crisis while also enabling it to stay within the boundaries of the rule of law. But in Israel, because these laws are a layer on top of rather than a replacement for mandatory emergency regulations or administrative emergency orders, and because they are also constantly in force given the continued SOE, Israel's dependent primary laws actually hamper its normative system of governance. The process is self-perpetuating: once Israel's law books accumulate a vast number of dependent enactments, sustaining the SOE becomes a question of maintaining a legal foundation that will enable effective governance. Lifting the SOE would, in effect, create a legal void.

Indeed, the existence of dependent laws (in combination with administrative emergency orders) is a key reason for keeping the SOE in force. The Israeli government, in its reply to a HCJ appeal,[48] admitted that the use of emergency powers is a governmental paradigm. Its officials stated in their reply to an appeal submitted by the Association for Civil Rights in Israel (ACRI) that ending the declaration of emergency would deny the ability of the government to administrate effectively, since several civil laws are conditioned by the declaration of an SOE and the process of replacing them with primary normative laws is still ongoing. Thus, part of the logic to sustain the SOE is to prevent a legal vacuum, rather than simply for security reasons.

As noted above, some dependent laws are explicit in terms of the executive authorities they grant, while others assert a legislative power to the authorized authority to enact regulations according to the discretion of the executing agency or to limitations asserted in the law. Some laws in their entirety depend on the validity of the SOE; in others only sections of laws are conditioned by it.[49]

Among key emergency laws of the former form, in which the laws in their entirety are dependent on the validity of the SOE, we find the Prevention of Terrorism Ordinance of 1948.[50] This ordinance, which is still in use today, was passed by the Provisional Council of State in 1948 as a consequence of the assassination of the United Nations peace talk representative, Count Bernadotte, by the *Lechi* underground (a right-wing underground organization also known as the "Stern Gang"). The Israeli government at the time, headed by Mapai (Labor), moved to outlaw and dismantle this organization, as well as the *Etzel* (*Irgun Tzavai Leumi*), the other and even bigger right-wing organization headed by Menahem Begin, initially with the administrative emergency order Emergency Regulation for the Prevention of Terrorism,[51] which was later replaced by this law. Provision 3 of this law states that membership in an organization that has been declared a terrorist organization is an offense punishable by up to five years imprisonment. Mere membership, regardless of its merit, is sufficient to indict and convict someone under this provision, and does not require direct or indirect involvement in any violent activities. Moreover, provision 4(g) prohibits any act which identifies or sympathizes with a terrorist organization in a public place or a place in public view, and includes "flying a flag or displaying a symbol or slogan or by causing an anthem or slogan to be heard, or any other similar overt act clearly manifesting such identification or sympathy as aforesaid." An individual indicted under this provision "shall be guilty of an offence and shall be liable on conviction to imprisonment for a term not exceeding three years or to a fine up to NIS 22,500." In order to convict, it is not necessary to prove identification with an activity undertaken by a terrorist organization, or to prove that the result of the act led to violence, or public disorder, or clearly endangered public safety.[52] This law was corrected in 1980,[53] and sections 12 and 21 were canceled thereupon the wide authorities previously given to the minister of defense, chief of staff, and military commanders were lifted, and the right to appeal was added. Another addition to this correction was more declarative, asserting an existing felony that forbids meetings with PLO members.[54]

More key dependent laws in their entirety include the Prevention of Infiltration (Offences and Jurisdiction) Law of 1954, which is still in force today and was used recently against African refugees. According to this law, anyone who knowingly and unlawfully enters Israel as a citizen of Lebanon, Syria, Egypt, Trans-Jordan, Saudi Arabia, Iraq, or Yemen will be sentenced to five years' imprisonment. Furthermore, the law imposes a penalty of four years' imprisonment or a fine on any "person who knowingly and unlawfully leaves Israel for Lebanon, Syria, Egypt, Trans-Jordan, Saudi Arabia, Iraq, Yemen or any part of Eretz Israel outside Israel." The Control of Products and Services Law of 1957 is yet another member of this category, which, as we know, replaced a few economy-related mandatory emergency regulations. This law grants government ministers wide discretion during an SOE to interfere in the state's economic affairs, particularly in the production and distribution of products and services. An additional law is the Emergency State Search Authorities Law (Temporary Order), 1969. The title "Temporary Order" here is actually misleading. Along with other Israeli laws that bear this title, this law is in fact permanent. This dependent emergency law allows the state's authorities to conduct searches of persons and their property, without a judicially approved search warrant. The Emergency Powers (Detentions) Law of 1979 completes this partial list.[55] This law replaced mandatory emergency regulations 108, 111 (detention), and 112(b) (deportation). As noted, the law was passed by the Likud party after it came into power in 1977, perhaps because some of its key members were themselves targeted by these mandatory emergency regulations during the British Mandate. This law, however, does not revoke the mandatory emergency regulations altogether; it only replaces these regulations that deal with detention and deportation. The main contribution of this law, other than being primary, is that it delegates the power to the minister of defense, as opposed to any military commander. The law grants the minister of defense broad discretionary power to issue an administrative detention order against an individual who is a citizen of the state, and allows an individual to be held without charge or trial. Under article 2(a), the minister of defense may order a person detained if he "has reasonable cause to believe that reasons of state security or public security require that a particular person be detained." Such an order permits detention for an initial period of six months and may be renewed indefinitely. The administrative detention procedure permits an individual to be held without charge or trial. However, due to this enactment, no Israeli citizen or permanent resident can be deported. As noted, a military order copied the practices of this law onto the OPT, but events in 1985 rolled back the lull; thereafter mandatory emergency regulations 111 and 112 were back in force in the OPT.[56]

These laws, which originated as secondary administrative legislation or as mandatory emergency regulations, were thus reenacted as primary laws. As such, emergency regulations transformed from temporary or foreign arrangements to permanent original ones. Other than the Emergency Powers (Detentions) Law of 1979, which in its incarnation as a primary law to some extent reduced the emergency powers it authorizes, the main block of these laws maintained their power; in fact, being primary, they enhanced the validity of these emergency powers.

Independent Laws

Independent emergency laws, which organize matters related to a time of emergency but are not conditioned by a declared SOE, demonstrate yet another patch in Israel's complex emergency legal structure. If such laws were enacted to replace rather than sit alongside mandatory emergency regulations, they could bring coherence to Israel's complex emergency legal structure. But as additional primary legislation, they add to or simply repeat orders already encompassed by mandatory emergency regulations.

Independent emergency laws often have no unique features that separate them from normative laws. Thus, most cannot be recognized according to their form, but only according to their content. As such, one can only recognize them by considering the historical context in which they were enacted, or by reading their content.[57] To make matters even more complicated, these laws differ in their form and their relationship to emergency. Some have a more clear connection to emergency, while others have a more loose or indirect association.

Some laws—for example, the Carrying and Presenting Identification Law of 1982,[58]—are, for practical purposes ordinary laws, with the exception that they have an additional headline that prevents judicial review. A second group of independent emergency laws consists of laws that allude to an emergency situation, but which have no connection to a declaration of an SOE. While these laws are not conditioned by a declaration of an SOE, at least some sections of them allow going outside the normative instructions in a time of emergency (Hofnung 2001, 75–76). These laws assert independent volumes of emergency (sometimes as a sleeping emergency). In some cases, their legislative powers are bound by a formal separate declaration; thereafter, a minister can issue emergency decrees. Such is the Civil Defense Law of 1951, which is valid during a time when the state is under attack or during combats.[59] In paragraph 21 of this law, there is a whole section of "Stand by State in Civil Defense" that is conditioned by a declaration of the minister of defense.

The third category by and large relates to normative laws, which in their form and title have no reference to emergency, though their rationale is based on emergency conditions and security necessities. For example, sections 44 and 46 of the Evidence Ordinance (New Version) of 1971[60] do not mention emergency, but allow the authorities not to present evidence if it may threaten the security of the state. An additional law of this sort is the Military Service (Consolidated Version) Law of 1986,[61] which again has no connection to a declaration of an SOE, but does organize matters pertaining to emergency and security.

A fourth category of independent emergency laws are laws with dual instructions, both normative and prerogative, for times of emergency. That is to say that, in the body of these laws, each instruction has two versions, one for normative times and another for times of emergency. In other words, these laws are drafted in a way in which the normative desirable arrangement is outlined, followed by the authority to override it in a time of emergency. Among such laws are section 191(b) of the Social Security Law (Consolidated Version), 1968,[62] and section 160 of the Penal Law, 1977.[63] A fifth group of independent emergency laws are laws enacted in order to rehabilitate retroactive actions that took place during emergency times and were legitimized by security necessities (Hofnung 2001, 65). In this category we find the General Amnesty Ordinance of 1949,[64] which pardons those who could be accused of crimes during the war and the Military Government in Jerusalem (Confirmation of Acts) Ordinance of 1949.[65]

Yet in the Israeli law books, there are more laws that authorize emergency powers.[66] These laws are mandatory laws, separate from the mandatory emergency regulations. One of these laws is the Press Ordinance of 1933, a mandatory law that was absorbed with the rest of the British Mandatory enactments into Israeli law. The Press Ordinance has three main features. The first asserts that all newspapers must obtain a press licensing, an unusual request in liberal democracies. Section 4(2) states that no newspaper can be printed without obtaining a permit from the district supervisor. The prerequisite of obtaining a permit authorizes the state to determine who is and is not allowed to have their opinion heard. The second feature of this law regards review of content (i.e., censorship), and the third imposes sanctions against press organizations. Under section 19, the minister of the interior may suspend or entirely stop the publication of a newspaper for any period of time he deems appropriate if the newspaper "poses a danger to the public order." This law overlaps with Regulation 94 of the mandatory emergency regulations.[67]

The origin of Israel's Penal Law is also based on mandatory enactment. The Criminal Law Ordinance of 1936 was consolidated with changes into the general Penal Law of 1977.[68] Chapter seven of this law drafts the penal code with regard to matters of state security, espionage, foreign relations, treason, etc. These orders were originally written into law in 1957 as the Correction to the Penal Law (State Security), 1957.[69] This chapter represents the clearest definitions of what constitutes threats against the state.[70] Further, it defines who is an enemy. As an independent law, it is not conditioned by a SOE. This central bill was only enacted in 1957 due to powerful resistance by the Knesset's opposition. The opposing parties were concerned by the authorities that the proposed bill had granted. In fact some parties considered the statute a direct threat to them.[71]

The version of the statute that was voted into law in 1957 authorized a senior police officer to detain a suspect for up to fifteen days before bringing that person into a court room. The law also allows the trial to be discussed without the presence of the suspect or his or her attorney, for reasons of state security. With the law, the customary practice of a long detention without a court order was revoked, but still, the law allows the proceedings of an arrest, investigation, detention renewals, trial and sentencing without any public notification. Moreover, the law turns on its head the burden of proof, insofar as it is the suspect who needs to prove innocence and not the state having to prove the crime. The law, in its original format, reduced the prosecution's burden of proof, inasmuch as it only needed to show that the factual basis was valid (*actus reus*), but not the criminal intent (*mens rea*). The 1967 correction allows the accused the possibility of explaining his or her act in meeting a foreign agent and explain that there was no motivation to harm the state. However, this procedure is still under the arrangement that places the burden of proof on the defendant. The defendant does not have the right to remain silent. The law does include a review mechanism in which only the attorney general, or with his or her written consent, can issue an indictment.

Finally, in the Basic Law: The Government there is an adjunct section that deals with security matters. Section 35 asserts the right of the government to prevent disclosure of its protocols and its decisions if it concerns state security, foreign affairs or any other matter that the government regards as vital information.

Belligerent Occupation

The OPT: A New Level of Jurisdictional Complexity

The OPT bring jurisdictional complexity to an even higher level. Because the political stakes are higher than they are inside the Green Line, so too is the degree of legal patchwork, structured ambiguity, and fluidity. In the OPT, two populations live side by side but are subject to different legal systems and, thus, live in a complete divide. Despite their residence in a common location, Palestinians are governed by a military regime, whereas Jewish settlers are governed by Israeli law.

Formally speaking, the OPT is under a state of *belligerent occupation*: a legal condition that stems from international law. In a belligerent occupation, an occupying state—or a belligerent occupier—is not the sovereign of an occupied territory but temporarily acts as one until sovereignty has been restored. The occupying state is prohibited by international law from annexing the territory or creating another state from it. Still, it may establish military administration over the territory and the population. Further, during the occupation, a military commander simultaneously serves as the legislative, executive, and judicial branches. Belligerent occupation defines a political frame in which every law, regardless of its content, is an emergency law, since an occupation regime parallels an emergency regime. In other words, the belligerent occupation is to the international domain what the emergency regime is to the national arena (Ben-Naftali 2007, 40). Hence, even civil (non-security) acts fall into the emergency category. Moreover, international law provides the belligerent occupier with a set of emergency powers to ensure the "security of the population or [for] imperative military reasons."[72] Thus, according to international law, an occupying force may employ such measures as curfews, control of movement, school closings, restricting free speech, and economic sanctions.

In addition to belligerent occupation, the OPT is governed by other legal sources. According to international law, the law of the occupied territory is still valid and, as such, the Israeli occupying force could use Jordanian law in the West Bank, including Jordanian emergency law. The Israeli occupation force had accepted that the law in force in the OPT prior to June 5, 1967, would remain in force with the caveat that "security enactments take precedence over all law, even if they do not explicitly repeal it."[73] Actually, the Jordanian law can provide rather draconian measures against political unrest or opposition (Dowty 1988, 41–42).

Yet, despite the available emergency powers granted to a belligerent occupier (though they are less expensive than are mandatory emergency regulations) and Jordanian's emergency powers, Israel's authorities have insisted on preserving mandatory emergency regulations in the OPT. As noted, Israeli authorities argue that mandatory emergency regulations are still in force in the OPT because these territories were once part of the British Mandate and had no other valid sovereign power since then. The Jordanians rejected this claim, arguing in return that the mandatory emergency regulations are null in the West Bank. What is at stake here is the validity of the Jordanian sovereignty over the West Bank.[74] The Jordanian government argued that mandatory emergency regulations were in clear contradiction with Jordanian law, and therefore became null. As they saw it, the mandatory emergency regulations became invalidated once the Jordanian military commander of the West Bank during the war of 1948, General Hashim, proclaimed on May 24, 1948, that all laws and regulations in force when the Mandate ended on May 15, 1948, would remain in effect unless they conflicted with any part of the Transjordan Defense Law of 1935 or with the Jordanian Arms and Ammunition Law and the Explosives Law. Moreover, they argue that this procedure was reinforced once more after the war when the Jordanian Government in Amman enacted on December 1, 1949, the Law of Modification of Administrative Procedures in Palestine, which reaffirmed the previous proclamation with regard to laws in force prior to May 15, 1948. Later, on September 16, 1950, the Jordanian government issued the Law Concerning the Laws and Regulations, prevailing on both banks of the Hashemite Kingdom of Jordan. This law asserted that laws and regulations in force on both banks would remain in effect until the national council and the king decided on a new general code, thereby asserting the Jordanian sovereignty.[75] Israel, on the other hand, rejects the Jordanian argument. The Israeli position is that the Jordanian government never enacted a new general code and, as such, all laws and regulations stay in force. According to the Israeli narrative, when Israel took the West Bank on June 7, 1967, General Chaim Herzog, the then-IDF commander of the West Bank, issued a proclamation stating that all previously existing laws and regulations would remain in force, except those that conflicted with the right of the Occupying Power to endure the security of its forces as well as public order, which the Israeli position maintains is in perfect harmony with article 64 of the Fourth Geneva Convention. Accordingly, mandatory emergency regulations are still in force on the OPT. In general, Israel challenges Jordanian sovereignty over the OPT. Israel, therefore, does not recognize the applicability of the Geneva Convention on the OPT since the Jordanian sovereignty over the West Bank was never recognized by the international community.⁷⁶ The Israeli position is that it is not obligated to follow the Geneva Convention, but it nevertheless chose to, out of its own good will. The HCJ holds the position that the Geneva Convention is contractual rather than customary international law, and thus binding only on a country that consents to it. The UN had reviewed the disputed case, and in the Special Committee Report of 1970,⁷⁷ accepted the Jordanian argument.

Conclusion

Israel's governing authorities have maintained a structured ambiguity between various emergency legal mechanisms. This emergency legal system features several overlapping and incoherent legal sources that exist side by side. What might have emerged as a pragmatic and temporary solution during trying times in 1948 quickly became a systemic and permanent mechanism in the hands of the Israeli power holders. Next, I turn to the question of what the political purpose of maintaining such a complex and convoluted legal structure is.

4

PRACTICING FLUIDITY I

The Complementary Relationship between Israel's Emergency Legal Sources

As I demonstrated in the previous chapter, Israel's governing authorities have maintained a structured ambiguity between multiple emergency legal sources. The fact that Israel's emergency legal system is complex and convoluted is often ignored, but it is concerted, not arbitrary. Margit Cohn (1998) similarly defines Israel's overarching emergency legal structure as a complex one that "patches together" various legal authorities. But Cohn never explores why the system is structured this way. To understand the reason for the fluidity between various legal sources, we must recognize the political benefits that this loose structure accords.

Indeed, regardless of security threats, emergency powers should still be based on an original, unified, and coherent legal source. In fact, one can argue that a unified, original, and coherent system of emergency laws should consolidate the sovereignty of the state and simplify the application of these laws. But in Israel, the opposite is true: legal ambiguity enhances sovereign power.

The objective of this chapter is to demonstrate what I term the "dynamics of law" in which legal manipulation extends the already powerful jurisdiction of emergency regulations. My argument in is that Israel's complex system of emergency enactment is a "legal patchwork" of sorts and has cobbled together various overlapping emergency legal mechanisms that complement one another. With these emergency legal mechanisms available, Israel's governing authorities can move freely from one legal mechanism to the next to serve their desired ends. If one legal mechanism might be challenged or meet the limits of its authority, another is available instead. Moreover, Israel's governing officials can mix and match discrete emergency laws and use one legal source to validate the authority of another legal order. As a result, this flexibility enables the state to extend its sovereign power and achieve political ends that would otherwise be impossible. All the while, the state maintains a degree of legitimacy by operating behind a veil of legality.

To demonstrate my argument about the benefits of maintaining a fluid jurisprudence, I outline examples in which the Israeli authorities capitalized on the complementary relationship between different emergency legal sources. I recognize the duplicity of provisions and complementary relationships as the validation of one mechanism by another or as instances of "legal metaphor," the term I use to describe the process in which two emergency legal sources are patched together in order to significantly extend the authority of their original provisions. Unlike the examples discussed in the following chapter that deal with more mundane policies, in this chapter I review examples with ambitious political objectives. In this respect, I examine land expropriation and governing techniques used to establish civil settlements and separate different groups in the Occupied Palestinian Territories. I will also consider the High Court of Justice's fluid juridical stance in a case pertaining to questions of political representation and the Palestinians' ability to participate in policymaking.

Analytical Framework

To articulate the benefits of a multiple, complex and ambiguous legal structure, I rely on the work of various scholars who study the application of law in colonial context, sometimes known as legal imperialism. Their work analyzes domains of jurisdictional complexity in a political context in which emergency plays a dominant role. These studies offer an analytical framework that points to the political advantages of a fluid system that sustains a complementary relationship between various legal sources.

Specifically I draw on the work of Lauren Benton. In *Law and Colonial Cultures: Legal Regimes in World History, 1400–1900,* Benton analyzes domains of jurisdictional complexity in a political context in which emergency plays a dominant role. Benton argues that the interaction of law, property, power, and culture in the charged interaction between the colonizers and the colonized shaped multiple systems of law and complex, ambiguous jurisdictions. The interplay of various cultures fostered legal pluralism. As she refers to it, legal pluralism promotes a "stacked" legal system and culture in which the boundaries are not fixed. While the relationship of law and culture is beyond the scope of discussion here, Benton's concept of legal patchwork helps frame Israel's similarly "stacked" emergency legal mechanisms, which create a fluid structure as well.

As Benton describes, conquerors retained parts of the local law alongside their new legal system as a compromise, of sorts. "Conquest and colonization created conditions that pulled at the boundaries of legal order and often enhanced jurisdictional fluidity" (2002, 81). Thus, instead of forcing their own original legal system on the colonized as the only valid law of the land, the colonizers accepted separate—and often overlapping and conflicting—jurisdictions. In the pursuit of control and in the course of struggles over authority and property, the colonizers were not monolithic in their application of law. In the Iberian Peninsula after the Christian conquest, for example, sections of Muslim law existed alongside the new legal system, which was not itself monolithic (it included canon and secular law), and together they established a plural legal order. These overlapping authorities jockeyed for jurisdiction between secular and religious law as well as between local and centralized law (2002, 33–45). Israel's integration of mandatory emergency regulations is similar to colonizers maintaining local law. In both cases, these clusters of laws represent the token of an old regime, which the new, established authority wanted to remove completely. And yet, in both cases, the new authority retained sections of existing law. As it is, jockeying between separate jurisdictions paid tribute to the old regime while still establishing control and appropriating property. Hence, Benton puts forward a guiding framework for studying complex legal structures.

Duplicity of Provisions

One result of the presence of multiple legal sources is duplicity of provisions and it generates system fluidity by allowing multiple ways to execute political will. Such a condition creates redundancy since several legal sources empower similar authorities. Moreover, this condition enables authorities to move easily from one legal mechanism to the next for convenience. As noted, if one legal mechanism might be challenged or might meet the limits of its authority, another is available instead. In this chapter, however, I only mention the two most significant forms of duplicity of provisions pertaining to emergency laws. My focus is on additional complementary relationships, which,, I discuss in greater detail.

If we remember from the last chapter, chapter seven of the Penal Law of 1977[1] articulates the punitive code with regard to matters of state security. Almost every felony addressed by mandatory emergency regulations has a counterpart in this law. In fact, in limited cases, their penalties are more severe than those imposed by mandatory emergency regulations. This duplication provides an opportunity to revoke mandatory emergency regulations (Tzor 1999), but the state has not seized this opportunity. On the contrary, as confusing add-ons, they only exacerbate an already convoluted system.

As previously noted, jurisdictional complexity is greater in the OPT than inside the Green Line. Since the OPT is under a state of belligerent occupation, several legal systems are in force at the same time. As noted, the Israeli occupation force had accepted, according to international law, that the law in force in the OPT prior to June 5, 1967, would remain so unless it contradicted the occupation military law. Thus, for example, sections of the Ottoman law and the Jordanian law are valid in the OPT. Moreover, as also discussed in the previous chapter, despite the available emergency powers granted to a belligerent occupier and the available Jordanian emergency law, the Israeli authorities insisted that mandatory emergency regulations are still in force in the OPT. These versions of legal structure sometimes overlap but more importantly they also complement one another and grant governing flexibility and ultimately greater political power.

Thus, because various emergency legal foundations apply simultaneously, the OPT's legal system is immensely convoluted. Indeed, similar emergency ordinances are defined and redefined by different jurisdictions. Thus, for example, we find emergency power, demolition of houses, in Jordanian law, in international law (article 53 of the Geneva Convention), and in mandatory emergency regulations (Regulation 119).

In other cases, for example, the overlapping authority of these powers granted to a belligerent occupier, and mandatory emergency regulations are patched together into one decree; this kind of jurisdictional jockeying pulls at the boundaries of legal orders (Benton, 2002, 81). The following excerpt of a decree demonstrates this perfectly: "By the power vested in me as the military commander of the region and according to regulation 86 of the Emergency (Defense) Regulations, 1945 . . . " In this decree, two sources of authority exist alongside each other. The first refers to the authority given to a military commander in a state of a belligerent occupation by international law, while the latter rests on the mandatory emergency regulations.

Complementary Relationship

In this chapter, I focus on additional forms of complementary relationships, particularly how the overlap of these legal sources enables the extension of each one's authority. Specifically, I concentrate on the complementary relationship between the mandatory emergency regulations and the administrative emergency orders, which together form an all-powerful legal tool.

The Israeli Supreme Court, in all of its rulings, never took a stand against Israel's complex emergency legal foundations. Even when the court's judicial stance became more active, it did not review the convoluted structure of the system, only whether the authorized agency acted reasonably.

In its formalistic years, the court avoided disqualifying emergency enactments based on the fact that an alternative emergency bill existed. Moreover, in Klofer-Nave v. the Minister of Culture and Education (1984), the court explicitly ruled that even having an alternative non-emergency arrangement does not revoke the validity of the emergency enactment.[2] During the 1990s, when the court, on limited occasions, applied judicial review and considered the existence of an alternative emergency enactment, it did so only with regard to the administrative authority's discretions and not the actual convoluted legal structure.

Moreover, the court did not use judicial review when the case pertained to a security necessity.[3]

If we recall, shortly after, the court organized the relationship between Israel's two main overlapping emergency legal mechanisms: the mandatory emergency regulations and administrative emergency orders. The court ruled that the administrative emergency orders, which stem from section 9 of the LAO do not, in fact, override or contradict mandatory emergency regulations. The court further decided that new emergency powers will be regulated by administrative emergency orders, but that all the previous emergency decrees that were issued through mandatory emergency regulations—unless explicitly revoked—remained valid. Thus, the HCJ approved this legal patchwork and affirmed the complexity of Israel's emergency enactment. Further complications came with the HCJ's decision in Michlin v. the Minister of Health (HC 70/50). In that case, the HCJ approved that an administrative emergency order can cancel mandatory emergency regulations. Klinghoffer argued that there was a contradiction between the two verdicts (1962, 120–121).

All in all, the court sanctioned a highly flexible legal mechanism that preserves explicit power in mandatory emergency regulations and coupled it with the legislative power of administrative emergency orders to issue new emergency regulations.

Extending the Authority of the Law: One Legal Source Validates and Extends Another Legal Source

Early on it was clear that mandatory emergency regulations complemented administrative emergency orders because they are not conditioned by a declaration of an SOE or limited by a predefined time period (here I refer to the Mandatory Defense Regulation of 1945). But soon enough the government realized that administrative emergency orders can also complement mandatory emergency regulations, they can be used, for example, to validate decrees promulgated by mandatory emergency regulations.

In 1951 the military governor of Galilee, by his authority according to Mandatory Regulation 125 (Closed Areas), declared thirteen Palestinian villages to be closed areas. This action was part of a greater project to expropriate and secure most of the land in Israel under

Jewish control. I elaborate on this project below. For now, it is interesting to note that the Palestinians appealed to the HCJ on procedural grounds and that it proved effective. They argued that the government abused due process because the decree was not published. The court ruled in the Palestinians' favor, asserting that an unpublished decree is invalid.[4] In return, the government, which feared that other unpublished decrees in use, which were issued by virtue of the mandatory emergency regulations, would swiftly be invalidated, issued an Administrative emergency order: the Emergency Regulation (Continuance in Force of Validity of Provisions), 1951,[5] which retroactively legalized all mandatory emergency regulations that were issued since the establishment of the state. Later, this secondary legislation was replaced by a primary enactment: the Law and Administration Ordinance (Amendment No. 2) Law, 1952.[6] In this case, primary Knesset legislation retroactively validated mandatory emergency regulations.

Around this time, administrative emergency orders, together with primary laws, were again used to validate other mandatory emergency regulations. Unlike the Mandatory Emergency Defense Regulations of 1945, which had no expiration date, the mandatory emergency regulations, which pertained to economic policies, were valid only until the year 1950. These emergency regulations include Defense Regulations, 1939; Defense Regulations (Finance), 1941; Defence Regulations (Food Supervision), 1942 and Defense Regulations (Prevention of Price Expropriation), 1944. These orders were kept valid by different legal mechanisms. Important parts of the legislation were either copied into new administrative emergency orders, or renewed by administrative emergency orders[7] or renewal laws.[8] Finally, after a series of renewal laws that continued in force, the Defence Regulations of 1939 and the Defence Regulations (Finance) of 1941 were replaced by primary laws (i.e. laws enacted by the Knesset as primary legislation). The first was replaced with another emergency law dependent on a formal SOE: the Control of Products and Services Law of 1957.[9] The latter, Defense Regulations (Finance) of 1941, was replaced only two decades later with the Currency Supervision Law of 1978.[10] I shall mention these sets of regulations and laws in the next chapter, which deals with the use of emergency powers to implement economic policies. All in all, Israel's authorities have used different legal sources to validate mandatory emergency regulations. By conveniently drawing on different legal systems as needed, Israel's authorities can extend their power.

The OPT: A Double Patchwork

As noted, the OPT heightens jurisdictional complexity even further. By exploiting flexibility in law, Israeli authorities can achieve desired political ends—in this case, maintaining dual, unequal legal systems. More specifically, the legal structure in the OPT enables Israeli authorities to jockey between various sources to suit desired outcomes. With this convoluted legal base, Israel's occupying authorities have managed not only to maintain a long-standing occupation but also to establish civil settlements and govern Israeli citizens who reside in the OPT according to Israeli law. Indeed, what is unique about the Israeli occupation in the OPT is that Israel's authorities have refused to fully acknowledge the occupation. Thus, on the one hand, the 1967 occupation has turned the Palestinian residents of the OPT into an occupied population living under military rule, and never officially annexed the territory; but on the other hand, the Israeli authorities have shown in word and deed over the years that they do not consider the OPT to be occupied land. The Jewish settlement project is based on this refusal to acknowledge that Israel is an occupying force that cannot, under international law, settle civilians on that land. As a result, as the Jewish settlement project expanded over the years, the lives of Palestinians in the OPT have worsened. They lost 60 percent of their land, were forced into small enclaves, and their freedom of movement was restricted.[11] Now, in terms of the Israeli authorities, maneuvering between a military regime and a civilian-settlement project demands a fluid governing system. I turn to explore the legal mechanism that supports the Israeli regime in the OPT.

International law and mandatory emergency regulations highlight a complementary relationship that extends the power of the Israeli authorities. As noted in the last chapter, despite the fact that Israeli officials insisted that mandatory emergency regulations were in force in the OPT, they used military orders to affirm their validity there. Thus military orders, which stem from the authority given to a military commander in a state of a belligerent occupation, have been used to reassert the validity of mandatory emergency regulations in the OPT.[12] These practices echo the use of administrative emergency orders by the Israeli government to validate retroactively mandatory emergency regulations that were not public. In fact, this legal maneuver with military orders is not restricted to mandatory emergency regulations, but is used in general to insert Israel's state law into the OPT. This is one of two mechanisms by which Israel's authorities govern settlers in the OPT.

The empowering dynamic is dual. From one perspective, this is a case in which international law (belligerent occupation) extends the authority of and essentially morphs into regular Israeli state law. And, from another perspective, this is a case in which an emergency legal mechanism (again, belligerent occupation) extends the authority of and validates regular Israeli state law.

Because Israel is a belligerent occupier in the OPT, its own laws do not directly apply in the territories. Hence, governing Jewish settlers in the OPT presents a problem: How can authorities apply Israel's state laws only to Jewish settlers in the OPT? Israel's innovative solution—which some would simply deem illegal—is based on two legal mechanisms that serve as a bridge between the Israeli legal system and the OPT. Both—one directly and one indirectly—are based on the administration of personal law. This legal device was common under colonial rule.

In focusing on the legal administration over Jewish settlers in the OPT, I obviously skip important and contested aspects of the occupation, namely the legality—or rather the illegality—of the settlement project, which required that land be taken control of. Today, 59 percent of the West Bank is controlled by Israel. These areas include settlements, military bases, highways, and the Security Fence. I allow myself to skip these rather essential elements since my objective here is to illuminate the way fluid jurisprudence empowers the authorities; particularly, how one emergency legal mechanism validates, in this instance, normative state law outside its jurisdiction. This political end that strikes a major unequal divide between the population was enabled by the fact that the Israeli authorities can capitalize on legal complexity.

With the increasing entrenchment of Jewish settlements, Israel's authorities have inserted Israeli state law into the OPT as an extension of personal law. In the colonial world, this practice was well established. As Lauren Benton writes in her review of the Iberian Peninsula and the Atlantic world, "In the narrow sense, surely, the Iberian empires were imposing state law; in a broader sense, they were formulating state law as an extension of personal law" (2002, 49).

Israel's authorities, too, have used personal law to apply Israel's state law in the OPT. Thus, for example, an amendment to the Israeli

Income Tax Ordinance in 1980 asserted that income tax from settlers will be collected and used by the State of Israel. The most crucial enactment in this respect was the correction (and extension) of the Criminal Jurisdiction and Legal Aid Law (section 6[b]) in 1984. Accordingly, the minister of justice, upon the approval of the Knesset's Constitution Committee, but not by vote, was authorized to insert any Israeli law onto the OPT. It also explicitly applied a list of nine Israeli laws[13] on settlers by extending the meaning of 'Israeli resident' to include 'any person whose place of residence is in the region and who is an Israeli citizen or entitled to acquire Israeli citizenship pursuant to the Law of Return, 1950".[14] Hence, as a result, services and obligations such as military service, population registration, social security, health care and more[15] were applied to the settlers. An additional amendment enables settlers to vote for the Israeli Knesset from within the OPT despite the fact that Israel never annexed the territories.,[16] It is a further manifestation of the legal abuses of this mechanism: the exterritorial administration of personal law on settlers. This is rather remarkable because, unlike other countries, Israel does not allow its citizens to vote from outside the borders of the state.

The application of these laws is based on an extraterritorial administration of personal law to settlers; these laws apply to individuals, not to the territory as a whole. Figuratively speaking, this setup means that settlers carry on their backs Israel's state laws and are protected by a "shield" of sorts that isolates them from the legal system of the territory in which they reside. Thus, Israeli law protects settlers.

The second mechanism that extends Israeli law to apply to Jewish settlers exemplifies how this jockeying between legal sources enables the implementation of political will. By using military orders, which stem from the authority given to a military commander in a state of a belligerent occupation, the Israeli authorities copied Israeli state laws regarding, for example, budgets, urban planning and infrastructure, education, and applied them in the OPT.

The two principal military orders that established the settlements, and not just settlers, as territories which are governed by the Israeli law were military order 783 (administering regional councils), and military orders 892 (administering local councils), which established regional and local municipalities respectively. These decrees copied Israeli law regarding elections, budgets, urban planning and infrastructure, education, local courts and published it as military order. In 1988 the

Knesset included the settlements under the urban and infrastructure civil code.[17] In particular, Military Order 892 extended the Israeli court system into the OPT. This regulation opens the path for the court to employ its jurisdiction on offenses according to the Israeli law (as opposed to just against Jordanian law as the law of territory) without the need to publish new regulations that copy the Israeli law.[18]

These military orders do not pertain to a security need,[19] but rather serve as a bridge between Israel and the OPT; that is, as a mechanism to apply Israeli law to the OPT. Stemming from the legal framework of belligerent occupation, their status equals that of primary laws, and they are not subject to judicial review. In general, this mechanism is based on territorial law. Because it applies only to Jews, it functions as personal law as well.

But in addition to this personal application of Israel law, Israeli authorities have now created territorial enclaves of Israeli law in the OPT and extended the validity of some laws beyond the territory of Israel. Thus, the territory of the settlements—and not just the settlers as individuals, as discussed previously—are governed by Israeli law. Like the shield of personal law that applies to individual settlers, these settlements, too, are governed by a shield that separates them from the laws that govern the rest of the territory. To ensure that this domain is governed solely under Israeli law, these military orders explicitly assert that Jordanian law is not in force in their designated territories.

Enabled by the structured ambiguity and fluidity of the legal system, these mechanisms establish a wide, unequal gulf between settlers and Palestinians in the OPT. Whereas Jewish settlers enjoy the protection of the Israeli law, Palestinians live under military occupation. In colonial rule, this practice has a long history. In the essay "Codification and the Rule of Colonial Difference," Elizabeth Kolsky (2005) joins Hussain (2003) in illustrating how the British colonial regime in India fused its discriminatory policies into law to justify its own unequal administration. Both describe the application of personal law to a select populace (Kolsky 2005, 673 and 677; Husain 2003, 79). As they demonstrate, this legal mechanism helped separate Europeans from natives. With personal law applying only to Europeans, this group was exempt from the legal system that governed the territory in which Europeans resided.

A principal element of the "Englishman's personal law" was that it disallowed European felons from being brought to trial in courts administered by Indian magistrates. As in colonial India, Jewish settlers are not tried for criminal offences in local courts (in the OPT, these are military courts), but rather in Israeli courts. In fact, this was the first implemented policy of the Israeli occupying forces. As early as July 2, 1967, even before the extensive development of settlements, the minister of justice enacted the administrative emergency order Emergency Regulation (Areas held by the Defence Army of Israel–Criminal Jurisdiction and Legal Aid), 1967.[20] This emergency regulation enabled the Israeli court to try anyone for any act that took place in any region and that was considered an offence under Israeli law. However, section 2(c) excludes persons who at the time of the act or omission were residents of the region. Thus, this section of the regulation applies only to Israelis, not Palestinians.

This case of the OPT demonstrates how jockeying between various legal systems fuels the governing authority's use of exceptional legal mechanisms to extend legal flexibility and enables it to use preferential treatment or achieve other desired ends. Some may deem the application of Israeli law to only Jewish settlers as simply illegal, but this allegation is beside the point. What is significant for this discussion is that Israel's authorities have worked hard to remain within the realm of law. In fact, they insisted on implementing their political will through legal channels, however awkward or roundabout they may seem.

Legal Metaphors: Extending the Authority of the Law

This next dynamic, which is based on a hybrid between two emergency legal mechanisms and compiled into what I term a legal metaphor, takes us back to the example with which I open the book. I began by explaining how two separate emergency sources were the main venues by which a major reform in Israel's foreign exchange policy was executed. Such a hybrid functions exactly as a metaphorical figure of speech (e.g., a "broken heart"). Each word on its own has one meaning, but together they produce an alternative meaning. In the same way, as I demonstrate, each emergency regulation has its own discrete meaning, that is, the authority it grants, but together they produce a different meaning, which represents a much more ambitious objective.

And it should be noted that such a legal metaphor extends the power of the already very powerful emergency regulations.

Land Expropriation by Emergency Legal Metaphors

When different emergency powers have been patched together the combination is an all-powerful political mechanism. While each of the emergency regulations, on its own, is limited and established to organize a more specific task, these restrictions dissolve when the regulations are put together. In other words, the inner boundaries between discrete juridical orders are basically being lifted, and as a result is the extension of the power of the authorities.

For the State of Israel, governing through emergency hybrids that form legal metaphors has yielded tangible gains, including property acquisition (particularly land) in the first decade of the state. At the time of the state's inception, the Jewish population owned—together with territories taken from the British Mandate—about 13.5 percent of the land inside the Green Line. By the early 1960s, however, 93 percent of all the land in Israel had come under Jewish ownership or control (Kedar 2001, 946).[21] The process, by which the state's authorities expropriated land, was to a significant extent completed through emergency regulation, some of which was later replaced by primary law, seamlessly turning emergency temporal arrangements into normative and enduring policy. Broadly speaking, to secure permanently what started as temporary reallocation of land, a series of emergency regulations and formal statutes were issued and enacted from the end of 1948 until 1958. The outcome was a complex array of laws and emergency regulations that were made available to government agencies to secure Jewish ownership and control.[22] This important historical episode is outside the scope of this discussion. I shall only note that, to a significant extent, this course of events is a major part of the Palestinian *nakba*, the catastrophe, as Palestinians refer to the horrible outcomes of the 1948 war, more than seven hundred thousand refugees and the loss of more than six hundred and fifty villages. Keep in mind that the continued loss of land I discuss took place after the war ended; that is, not during the mayhem and the atrocities of war, but after the security threat subsided. At any rate, my objective is to catalog landmark apparatuses in which the state has used emergency hybrids to capture unclaimed or Palestinian-owned land and secure it under Jewish control.

Such emergency hybrid between mandatory emergency regulations and administrative emergency orders stood as the legal foundation for the military government on selected territories of the state during the period between 1948 and 1966. It has long been recognized that the military government was also politically motivated, and one of the main motivations was land expropriation.[23] Administrative emergency orders and mandatory emergency regulations sat side by side as the hybrid legal pillars of this emergency regime. This legal patchwork thus became an all-powerful emergency mechanism.

In April 1949, the military government attained its first legal foundation for securing territory in the OPT through the enactment of an administrative emergency order: Emergency (Security Zones) Regulation.[24] This regulation delineated secured territories ten kilometers wide at the northern border and twenty-five kilometers wide at the southern border. It was forbidden for all people to enter or leave these territories without a permit issued by a military commander ranked colonel or higher.[25] The main three areas included in these security zones were Galilee (the Military Government Northern Area), in which about one hundred and thirty thousand Palestinians were living at the time in sixty-five villages; the Triangle (the Military Government Central Area), in which about fifty thousand Palestinians were living at the time in twenty-seven villages; and the Negev (the Military Government Southern Area), in which there were about twenty thousand nomad Bedouins of about eighteen tribes.[26] Thus, the map of the security zones included as many Palestinian communities as possible,[27] but some Jewish citizens were included as well. While the application of the order was universal in theory, in practice it was enforced almost solely on Palestinians.[28]

The administrative emergency order Security Zones, however, did not authorize the restriction of movement inside the territories. It only delineated restrictions on the movement of those traveling in and out of them. Thus, in January 1950, to control movement inside these security zones as well, military governors were appointed as military commanders in accordance with mandatory emergency regulations. Hence, together, the administrative emergency order and mandatory emergency regulations provided a legal framework to control the Palestinians' movement, speech (press), association, and so on.

Legal patchwork between administrative emergency orders and mandatory emergency regulations were used further in the process of expropriating land. Already during the war of 1948 and shortly after, an emergency legal cluster was used to validate the appropriation of different types of property, such as land, buildings, and more. These acquisitions, if legally sustained whatsoever, were done through military orders, which were based on mandatory emergency regulations (Regulations 48, 72, and 114–118) and administrative emergency order Emergency Regulation (Requisition of Property) 1948.[29] This emergency legal hybrid enabled the authorities to issue certificates that retroactively validated the activities performed during the war.[30]

But this legal patchwork was not the last emergency hybrid used to appropriate Palestinian lands. What followed was the most overt abuse of power, based on a legal cluster between administrative emergency orders and mandatory emergency regulations, to wrest land from Palestinians. In 1949, the minister of agriculture issued the following administrative emergency order: Emergency (Exploitation of Uncultivated Lands) Regulation, 1949. This order authorized the minister to capture land that had been declared uncultivated. This enactment is puzzling because a previous administrative emergency order, Emergency (Absentees' Property) Regulation, 1949,[31] had already addressed abandoned land. But the political motivation for this new administrative emergency order was different.

Indeed the uncultivated land emergency regulation remained in force for five years because it suited state ends. When it was combined with Mandatory Emergency Regulation 125 (Closed Areas), it became an effective mechanism for expropriating additional Palestinian land (that, land which had not been abandoned). Under Mandatory Emergency Regulation 125, Palestinians were denied access to their land. Since Palestinians were prevented from accessing and cultivating their land, such property then qualified as 'uncultivated.' Thereafter, under the Exploitation of Uncultivated Lands regulation, Israeli administrators could expropriate this fallow land. Since the regulation established a review committee with no other options for appeals, this procedure was never evaluated by the HCJ. As it were, the review committees were occupied by the same people who made the decision to capture the land in the first place (Hofnung 2001, 167). The result was that these lands were turned over to neighboring Jewish settlements.

Israeli officials commented on this mechanism in public speeches and in writing, connecting the political objective, namely land expropriation, with the power imparted by these emergency mechanisms. Yehoshua Palmon, an Arab affairs adviser, warned in 1952 that the Mandatory Emergency Regulation 125 was all that prevented the owners of 250,000 dunams[32] of appropriated land from reclaiming it in court.[33] Shimon Peres, the former president of the State of Israel, declared at the time, "It is by making use of the mandatory emergency regulation 125, on which the Military Government is to a great extent based, that we can directly continue the struggle for Jewish settlements and Jewish immigration" (Peres 1962).[34]

Thus, by fusing administrative emergency order and mandatory emergency regulations into legal metaphors, the Israeli authorities expanded their power. Each regulation, which on its own was already powerful, was still limited and set to achieve, by and large, a logical end, but put together, they became an extremely powerful political tool. In this way Israeli authorities capitalized on Israel's fluid emergency legal system. This chain of events reflects Benton's notion of the politically enabling effect of fluid jurisprudence: fluid legal boundaries became a tool to "structure the division of resources and constituted a framework of the 'articulation' of different ways of organizing labor and property" (2002, 22).

Fluid Jurisprudence: Political Representation and Policymaking

The Supreme Court also exhibited political flexibility in switching its judicial philosophy. If the Israeli Supreme Court's judicial approach was consistently formalistic,[35] in the case in question the court turned to embrace natural law philosophy. Thus, in previous cases pertaining to administrative activities against Palestinians, such as the case of the Absentees' Property enactment,[36] the court claimed that it had no competence in the matter and therefore could not provide any legal remedy, the court did intervene in the reviewed case, the Al-Ard case, and ruled against this Palestinian organization.[37]

Given the massive expropriation of Palestinian land, it is unsurprising that the first independent Palestinian faction called itself

Al-Ard (the Land). Indeed, the group was organized at roughly the same time that the appropriation process ended.

Until 1965, Palestinians had only two options for a political base—a Zionist party or the Communist Party,[38] which was co-managed by Jews and Palestinians. The emergence of Al-Ard was a watershed in the relationship between the State of Israel and its Palestinian citizens. For the first time, an independent group of Palestinians sought to associate politically and eventually to run for election to public office. But through various emergency-based measures and rational, the state has quashed Palestinian efforts to participate in public life and block Palestinians from full civic participation.[39] By denying Palestinians the right to full political representation, the state has further solidified Jewish supremacy. Palestinians are thus denied full citizenship rights, not only because they lack access to state resources but also because they are prevented from challenging this doctrine through legitimate democratic institutions. This creates a catch-22 of sorts where Palestinians are subject to land appropriation without avenues to redress their situation.

Further, Palestinian attempts to organize have been quashed. Israel's authorities denied nearly all Al-Ard's attempts to organize. As its first step, the movement sought a permit to publish a newspaper. Al-Ard failed to gain the permit. In fact, throughout the life of the Al-Ard movement, its only success was in obtaining the right to register itself as a company (*khevrah*). This moral victory was short-lived. The next attempt to establish an association (*agudah*) failed, and the denial was reasserted by the court. From that time, any attempt by Al-Ard members to establish themselves as a viable political group was denied.[40]

The Haifa district commissioner denied Al-Ard's request to form an association, arguing that the group posed a threat to the state's safety and security. The Haifa district court approved the commissioner's decision, believing that the group aimed to harm the State of Israel. Al-Ard appealed to the HCJ, arguing among other things that there was nothing in the goals of the organization that could be interpreted as posing a threat to the state. The HCJ, however, upheld the Haifa district court's decision, and Al-Ard's appeal was denied. The court held that Al-Ard was an "unlawful association, because its promoters deny the integrity of the State of Israel and its very existence" (Kretzmer 1990, 24; Peled 1992, 436).[41] This was a sweeping void of Al-Ard's right to associate.

Al-Ard's next step forced the state to deal directly with the question of independent Palestinian participation in electoral politics. Al-Ard ran for the 1965 Knesset elections as a political party. Since the organization had been declared unlawful, however, it ran under the name of the Arab Socialist List. The Israeli authorities responded by having the military governor banish four Al-Ard candidates for "provocative activities against the state" (Jiryis 1969, 327; Zureik 1979, 174).

Despite this pressure, however, the party was not discouraged from running. Eventually, its bid to participate in the elections was denied by the Central Election Commission (CEC), despite the fact that at the time the CEC lacked the statutory authority to deny the participation of parties that met the procedural criteria based on their platform. Such a statute was enacted in 1985.[42]

In its capacity as the Arab-Socialist List, Al-Ard challenged the ban against independent Palestinian political organizations in court but failed. The Arab-Socialist List appealed to the Supreme Court. However, despite the lack of legal foundation for its disqualification, the appeal was denied in one of the court's canonical decisions, the *Yardor* precedent.

At the time, according to the Basic Law: The Knesset (1959), the election committee had to approve the Al-Ard party, running as the Arab Socialist List. Section 23 of the law stated that any petition for candidates' list that was properly submitted would be approved. Yet the court, which at that time was overwhelmingly formalistic in its judicial approach, decided that the matter at hand justified its departure from its judicial doctrine, and the majority of justices embraced natural law philosophy instead.

In this case, Justice Shimon Agranat, the then-president of the Supreme Court of Israel, stepped outside the court's conventional formalist jurisprudence by stating that the law should be interpreted based on the constitutional fact, as it was asserted in the Declaration of Independence (DOI), that Israel was established as a Jewish state. Agranat was one of the presiding common-law trained justices and was not the most ardent formalist on the bench. Already, in the Kol-Haam case (HC 73/53), he used the same legal reasoning in affirming that while the DOI did not have formal legal standing, its values, nonetheless, should guide the court in interpreting cases. This, however, was not true with regard to the second majority justice, Yoel Zosman. Zosman, one of the most formalistic justices on the bench, denied Al-Ard's right to run for elections by asserting the doctrine of "defensive democracy." Relying on the history of the Weimar Republic, Zosman abandoned his formalistic judicial stance and embraced natural law. In doing so, Zosman enhanced the blur between a SOE as part of the positive law and a SOE based on natural law.[43]

Moreover, in this upside-down case, the court's lone dissenter, Justice Haim Cohn, who commonly stepped outside the court's formalism, adhered to a formalist reading of the law, noting that the court had no legal base to disapprove the Arab Socialist List.[44]

As a result of the *Yardor* decision, all political and legal avenues to achieve an effective Palestinian political voice were closed. With the failure of Al-Ard to bring about changes in Israel's political structure, Palestinians had no legitimate means to challenge Jewish dominance. No independent Palestinian party ran for election until 1988, and even then its ability to participate in policy making was denied.

This decision signifies the fluidity of the court's judicial doctrine. Obviously, I am not putting the court's judicial mannerism in comparative perspective, however, with the fluidity of Israel's legal structure as a whole, and in particular with respect to its emergency legal structure, it adds to a flexible legal-political framework.

Conclusions

This chapter demonstrates that the Israeli authorities have amply capitalized on Israel's fluid emergency jurisprudence. Israel's governing administrators use the state's emergency legal structure as a tool to create flexibility in the application of law. Without probing into the intentions of Israel's governing authorities in using emergency powers, we can establish that Israel's authorities have maintained and exploited the emergency regime's structured ambiguity and fluidity to achieve political ends that were otherwise impossible. The Israeli authorities' manipulation of the state's ambiguous emergency jurisprudence has proved effective and not too costly in terms of Israel's legitimacy as a rule-of-law nation. When discriminatory and even oppressive political ends are administrated by legal mechanisms—however awkward—the administration can maintain its character as a government by law. Thus, as it turns out, this unstable and frantic apparatus is in fact a source of the relative stability of Israel's political regime.

A more general conclusion is that a stacked legal system and fluid jurisprudence enable governing flexibility. The ability to jockey with different legal sources extends the power of the authorities, since the inner boundaries between discrete juridical orders can easily be lifted. While each of the regulations on its own is limited and established to organize a more specific task, the restrictions dissolve when the regulations are put together. In addition, one emergency legal authority can extend the validity of another legal enactment, or simply be activated when the alternative has met its limits. Thus, we can conclude that complexity, rather than a focused clear authority, is the source of greater sovereign power. With legal fluidity and structured ambiguity, the sovereign can switch freely from one juridical order to the next rather than be hemmed in by a well-defined legal structure.

In the final analysis, this chapter has shown not the exclusiveness of law and emergency, but rather their entanglement, mutuality, and co-constitution. Thus, the legal exception has been institutionalized into law, thereby justifying its own unequal administration.

5

PRACTICING FLUIDITY II

Emergency Powers for Economic and Financial Ends

This chapter begins by revisiting the event with which the book opens, namely, the use of emergency mechanisms to execute the 1977 regulatory reform of foreign exchange. But rather than focusing on the dynamics of law (i.e., the complementary relationships) that allow for the extension of sovereign power, I analyze situations where emergency legal tools have been used for objectives other than the protection of the state and its people during a time of imminent threat: specifically when emergency powers have been used to achieve desired economic ends. As we shall see, examples of these economic objectives include recurring administrative economic functions such as implementing fiscal or monetary policies and settling labor disputes.

This account again indicates the fluidity of the system, but from a different perspective than in the previous chapter. It describes a fluid framework in which either the governing structure is ambiguously defined (that is, it lacks set authority) or the governing culture exploits the framework's fluidity to bypass authority or violate due process. Ultimately, this framework offers multiple venues for a governing party to execute its political will. Analytically, this type of fluidity is related to the dynamics of law described in the last chapter because it deals with the basic objective of finding "space" within the legal order to create governing flexibility. However, in this case, fluidity enables an interpretation of legal authority that extends emergency powers or simply uses them beyond their intended scope.

The case described in this chapter is a clear example of a government setting where emergency powers become a perpetual aspect of normal political rule, a part of the system of political management, and the normal state of affairs for the administration of the political regime. In this respect, I review how emergency powers were used for routine economic regulation. While this was a constant throughout the years, this chapter focuses on the period from 1974 to 1985. During this period, there was a sharp increase in the use of administrative emergency orders applied for socioeconomic ends. This substantial increase is without precedent in the history of Israel. Moreover, politically, this decade features leadership by both Labor, Likud and a mix, so it demonstrates that whether on the right or the left, the authorities applied extreme measures.

Strangely enough, the use of emergency powers for economic ends has gone almost unnoticed. This reflects a general trend, in which the emergency regulations for economic objectives have received far less attention than their "more" political uses in the context of the "war on terror." To date, short of one article in Hebrew by Mordechai Mironi (1986)[1] that focuses on the use of emergency regulations to resolve labor disputes, no focused research has evaluated this process in full. Indeed, as far as I was able to find, the role of emergency powers prior to the State Economic Regularization Emergency Law of 1985—*Hok Hahesderim* in its original format—has not even been acknowledged. Because the use of the emergency regulations analyzed in this chapter drastically declined after 1984, and because the State Economic Regularization Emergency Law, which enforced deep economic restructuring, received far more public attention and has already been acknowledged in academic research, I end my review with its enactment.

The first objective here is to document and unpack the emergency legal apparatus with which Israeli governments applied emergency powers to regulate the economy. The legal mechanism utilized by these governments to execute economic regulations is still available today in Israel, despite the fact that it has been used significantly less in recent years. The second objective is to demonstrate the significance of this use for Israel's governance and point to the centrality of economic regulation to any analysis of emergency powers in Israel and perhaps in general. Overall, I illustrate that emergency powers are so profoundly entrenched in Israel's governance that the distinction between normative and exceptional modes of governing blurs.

After a brief background discussion, the chapter reviews a general history of economic regulation via emergency powers in Israel. It then moves on to discuss in detail two of the most common emergency regulations: Emergency (Essential Work Services) Regulations and Emergency (Procedures following Changes in Currency Rates) Regulations. I present their legal mechanism and how they were applied. The analysis is limited, as mentioned, to the period between 1974 and 1985.

While the chapter provides a general historical context in which these emergency regulations were put into practice, I do not analyze the reasons for executing economic programs with emergency regulations. Moreover, the context for using the emergency regulation is not in any way presented in order to justify the practice. I spend more time discussing Emergency (Procedures following Changes in Currency Rates) Regulations, because unlike the Emergency (Essential Work Services) Regulations, this regulation never received meaningful documentation. In addition, its use was more limited, thus allowing me to review all instances of its enactment. Before ending my review with Emergency (State Economic Regularization) Regulation of 1985, I document a few additional emergency regulations that were used between 1983 and 1985, because, similar to Emergency (Procedures following Changes in Currency Rates) Regulations, they were essentially never acknowledged.

Background

Most academic studies of SOE powers neglect to consider their use to achieve economic objectives. Yet their use in this context is characteristic of many liberal democracies (Scheuerman 1999, 1870). In general, economic-financial states of emergency (EFSE) have played a major role in the history of emergency powers. In recent years, a vast body of scholarship on emergency powers has emerged,[2] but mostly in the context of the "war on terror" and violations of human rights. But the history of EFSEs is crucial to understanding the role emergency powers have played, particularly that their use is far from exceptional;

on the contrary, they are an aspect of normal political rule and have been used to politically manage the normal state of affairs of modern capitalist states (ibid., 198). The history of EFSEs provides multiple examples in which the line between actual emergencies and the political use of emergency powers has been crossed. In this respect, emergency powers have been used, for example, in controlling labor and managing industrial unrest (Scheuerman 2000).

Ernst Fraenkel (1941) provides an analytical explanation of the phenomenon by which emergency powers are used for achieving economic ends. The Prerogative State is important to the success of the economic policies of the government, he writes (1941, 186). To this end, the Dual State fuses authoritarian tools with rational market operations. In other words, arbitrary power is embedded with rational calculation since the capitalist economy demands this hybrid mechanism (Jayasuriya 2001, 119). Together, as a hybrid, this authoritarian legalism (ibid.) provides powerful tools for policymakers while depoliticising the use of emergency powers–an essential element of the dual state identified by Fraenkel.

Rebecca Kahan argues that ultimately, the most dangerous progenitor of constitutional expansion is the use of emergency powers in response to an economic crisis (2005, 1281). As she writes, emergency powers enacted initially in reaction to an economic crisis are more likely to provoke long-term extra-constitutional powers than violent crises (ibid.).[3] Kahan explains that extra-constitutional responses to economic crises are more likely to cause constitutional sag, while reactions to violent crises have greater potential to lead to "snap back," meaning that constitutional powers return to their pre-crisis position. As she argues, "When constitutional interpretation sags, the loose space between its original position and its stretched position is gradually filled" (ibid.). Extra-constitutional powers that fill the gap become non-crisis powers.

In Israel, the use of emergency powers for economic ends initially began in response to an emergency crisis. Yet rather quickly these powers sagged and stretched the existing law.

In practice, the division between economic crises and violent crises is not that clear. Using emergency powers for economic ends often begins as an accessory to more "common" emergency powers in a time of war or political turmoil ("political" in the narrow sense), and then becomes a habitual administrative tool. In Israel, the use of emergency powers for economic purposes began during an actual time of crisis—the 1948 War of Independenc—but even after the war concluded, emergency powers were used for economic objectives. Moreover, both left- and right-wing governments have applied emergency economic powers to execute a variety of economic policies (ibid., 1873). Israel offers an explicit example of how both sides of the political spectrum use emergency powers to advance their ideological agenda—by the left to foster a centralized economy and by the right to institute neoliberal reform. As we shall see, until October 1977, Emergency (Procedures following Changes in Currency Rates) Regulations was used to maintain the government-controlled economy. The same regulation was then used as part of the reform to liberalize the Israeli economy.

As I discussed in the introduction to this book, defining what constitutes a threat is an ambiguous matter. While certain groups may regard a particular situation as an emergency, others may not. Thus it is difficult to coordinate the legal execution of emergency powers with an objective threat; this difficulty often leads to the political abuse of emergency powers. Despite this problem, we can agree that emergency powers should be used only under extreme conditions that result from clear and imminent threats to the well-being of the state and its people. Usually these extreme conditions stem from war, rebellion, natural disaster or epidemic. But such conditions can also result from severe economic crises that threaten to generate economic meltdowns.

In this chapter, however, I examine distinct cases in which emergency powers were used without the presence of any immediate threat and without the economic objective of allocating resources to a population in need during a time of crisis. Instead, in these cases emergency powers were used to regulate labor disputes or control fiscal and monetary policies. Moreover, unlike the previous chapter where I discuss the use of emergency powers for ambitious political objectives, here I review uses of emergency powers for rather routine economic objectives.[4]

This begs the question of why Israeli authorities chose to apply emergency powers instead of proper legislative channels. As I argued in chapter two, the degree of executive power in Israel is excessive. Israel's fluid legal-political structure allows for substantial governing flexibility. If we recall, the system of government in Israel is parliamentary in which the Knesset is made up of only one house controlled by the government. Moreover, in addition to the governing flexibility generated by constitutional fluidity, administrative legislation (secondary legislation), which is the dominant form of governance executed by government members, operates with limited external control.[5] Thus, the government has curiously chosen to use extreme tools even when it has the power to execute policy through normative channels, though normal channels can be a longer process and require greater political effort. I raise this question not to explain why Israeli policymakers abuse their power, but to point to the embeddedness of emergency powers within Israel's governance. This embeddedness obscures the dubious origins of these powers and allows them to become nothing more than an additional venue for executing policy.

One can argue that emergency powers that appear in the statute books, regardless of how they arrived there, are pieces of "ordinary" legislation. In this respect, applying emergency powers to implement economic regulations are similar to other legal mechanisms, such as executive privilege in the United States, which extend administrative and executive power and operate with little to no oversight. But, this interpretation derogates from the rule of law principles. While the rationale behind such governing tools is to increase, for example, the governing power of the executive branch, the rationale behind emergency powers is fundamentally different, and extending governing power is a means to a totally different end, namely, the protection of the state and its people. In other words, what sets emergency powers apart is that their legitimacy relies on necessity in a time of real and imminent threat, and as such they are different from other governing tools whose rationale is to increase executive power.

Overall, from a liberal interpretation of the rule of law, emergency powers are categorically different from other legal mechanisms that extend administrative and executive power. Such a conception, of course, separates normalcy and crisis, rule and exception. This book, illustrates that the separation is unfounded. Nevertheless, from a rule-of-law perspective, even if emergency powers are used according to the authority granted by law, any regulation executed via emergency powers still violates the fundamental principles of the rule of law, such as the principle of majority rule, the principle of participation, the publicity principle and the principle of equality. Moreover, they often violate protected civil rights. Using emergency powers is based on the recognition that these rule-of-law principles are violated. Ideally, the justification for using them is that extreme conditions warrant extreme tools of governance. If we recall, the argument to rationalize their use is that the rule of law must be suspended to protect the state and its people; in other words, we must violate the law in order to protect the law. But, when emergency powers are used during a state of normality, they not only violate the rule of law and democratic principles, but it is also becomes impossible to make a valid argument supporting their legitimate use.

Generally speaking, policy makers are motivated to use emergency powers because they offer an obvious advantage; they are the most expedient way to execute policy. Emergency enactments allow ministers and administrators to avoid outside scrutiny. Israel, as we know, has been under a legal SOE since the inception of the state. This situation has provided the perfect platform for policy makers to extend the authority of the law via emergency powers. In many cases, government members and administrators were within their legal rights to use emergency powers due to the permanent legal SOE in Israel and the fact that the Mandatory Emergency Regulations are constantly in power. But, from a rule-of-law perspective, applying these powers is in clear violation of the rule of law because, although Israel is under a legal SOE, they have not been applied during an emergency, nor have they been applied for emergency objectives. In the same way that the Israeli parliament (the Knesset) lacks the authority to declare that Israel is no longer a democracy, even if such a decision was reached through the proper legislative process, the Knesset cannot delegate emergency powers for purposes other than dealing with an imminent threat.

Emergency Legal Sources: A Short Recap

As outlined in chapter three, within the Green Line the Israeli government has three main emergency legal sources at its disposal: mandatory emergency defence regulations (mandatory regulations), administrative emergency orders, and primary emergency laws. As I demonstrate, all these emergency enactments were used to regulate non-emergency economic policies. This chapter focuses on administrative emergency orders because they are the most commonly enacted emergency legal source for such objectives. Here I need to make a distinction between the enactment of emergency regulations and decrees promulgated by these enactments. When I argue that administrative emergency orders were the most commonly enacted, I refer to the former and not the latter. In other words, my focus is on the process of enactment rather than the impact of decrees. Israeli law contains few primary emergency laws with economic objectives, and the mandatory emergency regulations are preexisting sets of orders from which no additional enactments are promulgated. Hence, compared to the two other emergency legal sources, administrative emergency orders had the greatest impact on legislation. Once again, this is significant not in terms of the programs that were executed (decrees from all sources have played a crucial role in implementing policies), but in terms of the legislative process. The legislative process is important insofar as it is the only phase where a level of control, albeit a limited one, is present. Decrees, on the other hand, are already a byproduct of the initial emergency legislation and are often never made public, because on a practical level it is understood that publishing every decree is impossible.

If we recall, while mandatory emergency regulations has the status of primary legislation and formal laws are the direct product of primary legislation, administrative emergency orders are a form of secondary legislation. Yet, their status as secondary legislation does not diminish their power because they take precedence over primary law. Moreover, as I discuss in chapter three, the restrictions on administrative emergency orders are limited and mostly theoretical. Since the State of Israel has been under a continuous SOE since its establishment, most government members have the authority to issue administrative emergency orders at any time, provided that the government approves them. Another reason administrative emergency orders are used to economic ends is related to the Law and Administration Ordinance, 1948,[6] which stipulates that they may also be used for the "maintenance of supplies and essential services." Thus it is difficult to argue that administrative emergency orders that were enacted with economic ends exceed their granted authority. Finally, even the crucial three-month restriction—which maintains that unless administrative emergency orders are brought to the Knesset and voted on, they remain valid for a duration of three-months from their date of enactment—has been ignored time and again, as demonstrated in chapter three and as will be illustrated again in this chapter. These limited restrictions, I argue, are the foundation that enables administrative emergency orders to take on an abusive role, given, of course, the political will to use them beyond the protection of the state and its people.

From a rule of law perspective, using administrative emergency orders instead of regular forms of secondary legislation constitutes a clear violation of the rule of law. Unlike normal secondary legislation, which in terms of implementation orders usurps its authority from the legislative branch, either *juxta legem* (according to law) or even *praeter legem* (outside of the law),[7] emergency regulations (*contra legem*: contrary to the law)[8] simply bypass the legislative brunch and thus violate the principles of the democratic process of enactment (the principles of participation, publicity and majority rule). It therefore challenges the sovereignty of the legislative branch and violates the separation of power. As noted in chapter two, their use by Israeli government members is surprising given the government's extensive power, particularly with respect to secondary legislation, which operates under little supervision or control. Moreover, the process by which administrative emergency orders are used to enact policies that should be enacted through primary legislation constitutes a serious violation of democratic due process of legislation (Medina, 2012).

Executive-Dominated Emergency Economic Regulations[9] in Israel: A General Review

The use of emergency powers to enact non-crisis economic regulation began in the early days of the state and has continued since then. In fact, the number of emergency regulations used to implement economic policies far exceeds the number of emergency powers used for objectives pertaining to national security inside the Green Line.

As we know, the State of Israel was indeed founded in a moment of crisis amidst the War of 1948. At this time, Israel's emerging leadership implemented emergency measures, some of which were used to implement economic policies. This practice, however, continued well after the war ended and has continued ever since.

Quickly after the inception of the state, and even before the War of 1948 was over, emergency regulations were used to execute non-emergency economic objectives. This is further empirical evidence to support Kahan's argument (2005) regarding constitutional sag by which extra-constitutional powers become non-crisis powers. In the early days of the state, Israel's economic emergency codex was based on the mandatory emergency regulations. The bulk of these orders were enforced though a cluster of legal tools and, in one way or another, are still valid today. These emergency regulations, if we recall, include: Defence Regulations, 1939; Defence Regulations (Food Supervision), 1942, Defence Regulations (Prevention of Price Expropriation), 1944 and Defence Regulations (Finance), 1941. Eventually, these were more or less replaced by primary laws (that is, laws enacted by the Knesset as primary legislation). The first three were replaced with an emergency primary law, which is dependent on a formal SOE: the Control of Products and Services Law of 1957.[10] Defence Regulations (Finance) of 1941, was replaced two decades later with the Currency Supervision Law of 1978.[11]

Israel used the Mandatory Defence Regulations to establish its financial institutions by allowing the intuitions created in the British Mandate period to continue their operation in the newly established state. First, the minister of finance, Eliezer Kaplan, invoked Defence Regulations (Finance) of 1941 to appoint a foreign exchange controller,[12] who then issued a decree drawing on the same emergency to establish continuity in the financial institution.[13] At that moment, Defence Regulations (Finance) of 1941 was also used to appoint David Horowitz to the position of managing director of the Ministry of Finance (he later became the first governor of Israel's central bank), giving him the authority to freeze the assets of persons who no longer resided in Israel.[14] This authority targeted the assets of Palestinians.

The authority of the Defence Regulations of 1939 was initially channeled through an original administrative emergency order that consisted of a patchwork of two emergency legal sources. Hence the Emergency Regulation (Compulsory Payments) or 1952,[15] which introduced a type of tax on holders of certain goods, referenced specific sections of the original mandatory emergency regulations. These references can be found in the definition of authorized agency and the section that asserts the penalty. Based on this administrative emergency order at least 442 decrees were issued since the establishment of the state and the early 1990s.[16]

But not only the Mandatory Defence Regulations and administrative emergency orders were used to regulate the economy. Primary emergency laws were used as well. For example, the Control of Products and Services Law was used to promulgate some 4,000 supervision decrees over goods and services from the period beginning with the law's enactment in 1957[17] until 2012.[18] This law, which depends on a declared SOE, grants ministers legislative powers (that is, the power to issue decrees) at their own discretion without having to obtain the approval of the Knesset or consult any additional body. For example, section 6 of the law authorizes a minister to issue orders to set the maximum price of a commodity, the maximum profit from the sale of that commodity, and the maximum salary for a service. Many of these decrees bypass primary law and thus many regulations that should be enacted by primary laws, or at least by normative secondary legislation, are not. In 1996, the Knesset enacted the Supervision over Commodities and Products Law.[19] This law replaced and eliminated several provisions of the Control of Products and Services Law, 1957. New instructions no longer depend on the existence of an SOE, and they no longer have precedence over ordinary legislation.

Generally speaking, the High Court of Justice was more willing to intervene in cases in which emergency powers were used to execute economic policies, but overall the court was still rather restrained. In such cases the HCJ reviewed the policymakers' discretion rather than the authority to use emergency powers.[20] At any rate, already in 1963,[21] the court asked the legislator to use normative laws for issues that do not directly concern an emergency, particularly with respect to section 46 of the Control of Products and Services Law, 1957, which, as we know, granted ministers far-reaching authority. But after the legislator ignored the court's wishes, the court succumbed and followed the available law.[22] Later, in the late 1980s, the court disqualified two administrative emergency orders, which were enacted by the power of section 46 of this law. In both cases, the court did not rule against the validity of the power granted by the law.[23]

Executive-Dominated Emergency Economic Regulations in Israel: 1974–1985

As stated, during the decade between 1974 and 1984, Israel's governments enacted an unprecedented number of administrative emergency orders. The Labor government headed by Yitzhak Rabin, in his first term as prime minister, followed by the Likud government, after its political transformation in 1977, promulgated a great number of emergency regulations, significantly more than had been enacted before. These emergency regulations were not declared in order to allocate resources in a time of war or crisis, or to help a population in need; rather, their purpose was to regulate labor disputes and fiscal and monetary policies. The two dominant administrative emergency orders were Emergency (Essential Work Services) Regulations and Emergency (Procedures following Changes in Currency Rates) Regulations. During this time period, almost two of these emergency regulations were enacted per month. Emergency (Essential Work Services) Regulations continues to be used, but at a significantly lower rate. Emergency (Procedures following Changes in Currency Rates) Regulations, was last used in 1983. The new foreign currency exchange policy and the Currency Supervision Law of 1978[24] made this emergency regulation superfluous in many situations. As noted, I extend my review until July 1985 in order to highlight a few more administrative emergency orders that have gone unnoticed.

Figure 2 displays the use of Emergency (Essential Work Services) Regulations and Emergency (Procedures following Changes in Currency Rates) Regulations beginning with the inception of the State of Israel in 1948 until 2012. It demonstrates a significant increase in their rate of application between 1974 and 1984.

Despite the fact that these two emergency regulations were used for different purposes, they share a similar section that grants further legislative power. In addition to being based on the same emergency legal source as administrative emergency orders, both, as I shall soon elaborate, are used to authorize provisions that enable further emergency legislation of decrees. This process is significant because it does not require authorization by any other legislative or administrative body and, moreover, in most cases there is no legal obligation to make these decrees public.

Emergency (Essential Work Services) Regulations

Emergency (Essential Work Services) Regulations is the most commonly used administrative emergency order. They were based on emergency regulations that were used to recruit manpower during the Arab-Israeli War of 1948 (Mironi 1986, 351–352). Their use for non-crisis economic ends is testimony to Kahan's account of how extra-constitutional powers become non-crisis powers and stretch law.

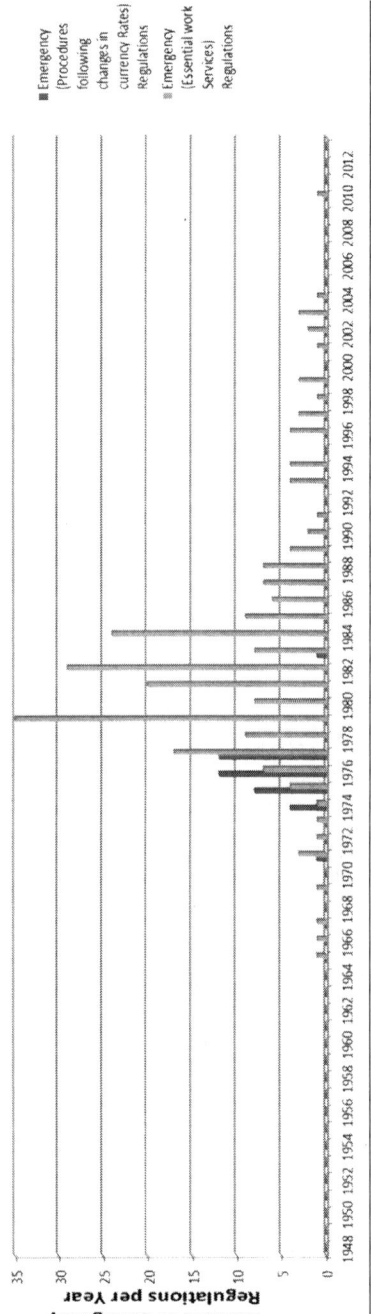

Figure 2. Output of Emergency Regulations: *Procedures following Changes in Currency Rates and Essential Work Services*, 1948–2012

* Methodology: including corrections to the regulations because it may increase the authority of the decree

Essentially, this emergency regulation prevents the worker's right to strike. Emergency (Essential Work Services) Regulations has been used so often it is impossible to imagine that it was only used during states of emergency, unless of course we are to assume that Israel was under conditions parallel to those experienced, for example, in Europe during the Thirty Years' War. Thus, even without going into detail, simply due to the fact that Israel did not suffer a constant state of a war, rebellion or other major crisis from 1974 to 1984, we can conclude that emergency powers were used for political gains and, in the process, prevented the worker's fundamental right to strike. Thus, it would not be unreasonable to assume that emergency powers were used as an assault on organized labor.

In an article from 1986, Mordechai Mironi describes the context, the legal framework and the enactment process of the Emergency (Essential Work Services) Regulations. Moreover, in the second part of the article, Mironi offers a normative assessment of performance—dealing with the tension between the public's right to receive the service and the right of workers to strike—and a functional assessment that uses the concept of the "narcotic" effect, which assumes that every tool which is constantly used loses its effectiveness. Finally, Maroni, applying the concept of acceptability, calls for a reform in the process by which administrative emergency orders are enacted. In his opinion, more oversight should be added, the use of such emergency regulations should be removed and the parties directly involved in the (labor) dispute should not be allowed to use such force. Yet Maroni does not address the bigger question of what this phenomenon means with regard to the Israeli regime and democracy as a whole, or what can we assume about the relationship between law and emergency.

Emergency (Essential Work Services) Regulations have been enacted so often, it is virtually impossible to document every instance. Thus, my objective is twofold; first, I will dissect and analyze this extreme legal tool and then I will describe how a tool reserved for emergency situations became a conventional tool of governance, thus blurring any meaningful division between extreme governing apparatuses and proper forms of governance.

Emergency (Essential Work Services) Regulations basically commission authorized agents to issue confinement decrees,[25] which are basically "back to work" orders. By confining employees to their work, the right to strike is thus prevented. These decrees should not be confused with *prevention* decrees that are issued by the court (as opposed to the government) against labor unions if they fail to follow due process before going on strike (this usually occurs when a union does not give sufficient notice before going on strike). In fact, Emergency (Essential Work Services) Regulations were often used immediately, despite this less severe measure's availability (Mironi 1986, 353, 382). Perhaps the reason for preferring this extreme mechanism is that it is controlled by the government and does not rely on the discretion of an alternative institution, i.e. the court.

Comparatively, around this time, the Nixon administration was also using emergency powers against unions in the USA; specifically, they were used against the American Postal Workers Union. Approximately a decade later we find similar actions in the UK. During the tenure of Margaret Thatcher in the 1980s, emergency powers were used against miners and railway workers (Golan, 2008, 287).

In this respect, one can locate the Israeli episode within the general effort to reduce organized labor's power in order to produce a more dynamic market. According to Johnathan Nitzan and Shimshon Bichler, in the late 1960s an emerging capitalist social bloc, primarily representing the private sector but also a managerial stratum of government or *Histadrut* (Israel's organization of trade unions), with the support of the Labor Party pushed for this restructuring (2002, 104, 155). The post-1967 French weapons embargo resulted in a growing security industry in Israel, which continued to expand, particularly after the 1973 war.[26] The capitalist social bloc was frustrated with the structure of the labor market, which was heavily unionized. Their objective, in their own words, was to make the labor market more dynamic. The fact that certain people from within the Histadrut were part of this coalition should not be surprising. The Histadrut suffered from severely conflicting interests; on top of being Israel's largest institution representing workers, it was also one of the biggest employers in Israel and owned many industries. Overall, this growing coalition, with the support of the Labor government, aspired to reform the labor market.

Considering the context in which Emergency (Essential Work Services) Regulations were enacted after 1974, it is logical to assume that these measurements were taken as part of a focused policy to restructure the labor market. The significant rise in the use of these emergency regulations actually took place at a time when the number of labor disputes was on the decline; there were more strikes between 1960 and 1972 (Mironi 1986, 350–351, 364). Moreover, the process of enacting the Emergency (Essential Work Services) Regulations did not reflect a state of urgency either. In most cases the ministers were not called to a special meeting in order to approve the emergency measures and in many events the votes were postponed until the next weekly meeting (ibid., 371). Furthermore, the work sectors targeted by this emergency regulation—public broadcast (not during a time of war), banks, energy (oil exploration), transportation (again not during a time of war), education, agriculture, and so on—do not indicate imperativeness with relation to a SOE.

In addition, the way the Emergency (Essential Work Services) Regulations were applied indicates that the motivation to use them was to limit collective bargaining rather than to ensure the smooth continuation of an essential service. At times, these emergency regulations denied non-essential workers, such as secretaries or drivers, the right to strike. Moreover, these emergency regulations applied to private companies and not just government industries. In other instances, the emergency regulations were enacted, but no decrees were issued because both sides reached an agreement (Mironi 1986, 380). Furthermore, sometimes the government would deny workers the right to strike but would not intervene when the employer, for example El Al airlines, stopped providing its services.

In 1986, shortly after the period examined in this chapter, the Attorney General clearly stated that it is improper to use Emergency (Essential Work Services) Regulations to deal with labor disputes during routine times.[27] This statement coming from such an eminent legal authority signifies the extensive abuses committed by governments on both the left and right of the political spectrum.

The Legal Process

The Emergency (Essential Work Services) Regulations are enacted in two steps. The initial emergency enactment is general in scope and targets any sector declared essential by the minister and approved by the government. First, ministers enact the administrative emergency order: a minister issues the emergency regulation and then the government must approve it. This initial enactment acts as a sort of primary legislation. In this respect, the decrees issued by the authority and promulgated by the initial regulation are a sort of secondary implementation order. Indeed, many ministers have enacted this emergency regulation, including the minister of defense, the minister of finance, the minister of energy and infrastructure, the transport minister, and the ministers of communications and education. In most cases, the ministers' involvement in the process only goes as far as the initial enactment of the administrative emergency order. Then, authorized agents empowered by the emergency regulation issue the decrees, basically according to their own discretion.

In the early 1970s, the ministers' power increased after the procedure for enacting this administrative emergency order was modified. Until 1970, the minister of labor issued the absolute majority of the Emergency (Essential Work Services) Regulations. Under this procedure, other ministers had to petition the minister of labor to enact this emergency regulation, and the minister of labor reserved the right to decline the petition, which occurred on limited occasions. With growing pressure from ministers, the procedure was changed; thereafter each minister had the sovereignty to issue Emergency (Essential Work Services) Regulations. Ministers had a great incentive to use this extreme measure since they were responsible for the services that, if workers were to go on strike, might be denied.

As noted, once the Emergency (Essential Work Services) Regulations is enacted, an authorized agent, usually the general manager, can issue confinement decrees to force employees back to work. This means that a party in the dispute, the actual employer, is empowered with the authority to prevent the strike (Mironi 1986, 368). Sections 1 and 2 of the Emergency (Essential Work Services) Regulations provide the general manager or "any person s/he may commission," with the power to issue decrees that force workers to go back to work.

The general manager, however, does not have to issue decrees. In some cases, no decrees were issued after the emergency regulation was enacted, which leads one to conclude that there was a lack of urgency behind the emergency regulation's enactment. In addition, it is not necessary to issue the confinement decree at the same time as the Emergency (Essential Work Services) Regulations' enactment; the decree can be issued as long as the regulation is in force. Authorized agents can issue as many decrees as they deem necessary, but when the emergency regulation expires or is revoked, all the decrees are nullified.

Some confinement decrees were general and included the entire work sector, but others were personal and were given to specific workers.

Emergency (Essential Work Services) Regulations impose various sanctions on workers who refuse to go back to work. These sanction range in severity from fines to imprisonment, or even layoffs without compensation. A later addition of the regulation asserted that the sanctions would even apply to workers who resigned to avoid complying with the decree.

At times, the Israeli government, in order to extend the power of its authority, would evade the renewal process in the Knesset after three months had passed from the day the emergency regulation was enacted. The majority of Emergency (Essential Work Services) Regulations (51 percent) expire by themselves after three months, and ministers revoked 42 percent of the regulations before their expiration date (Mironi 1986, 366). As for the rest, the government simply reissued them as new and bypassed the Knesset. As noted, this practice was more common with respect to Emergency (Procedures following Changes in Currency Rates) Regulations. This procedure is generally regarded as side stepping the renewal protocol.

Evading the renewal process is puzzling given that the government controls the Knesset (the coalition forms a majority). With regard to this regulation, the Knesset only denied its renewal on one rare occasion. There was no ongoing labor dispute at the time of the refusal (1981), but the minister of energy petitioned that the regulation be renewed for a year because, as he claimed, he expected that a labor dispute with workers of the electricity company would emerge.

Another way to extend the authority of the government is to enact a correction to the regulation. The correction extends the regulation's authority, not its duration. For example, in 1983, during a medical doctors' strike, the Emergency (Essential Work Services) Regulations was corrected to prevent doctors from resigning. It is generally understood that this procedure is allowed but that the corrected emergency regulation is only valid for the duration of the original enactment. (Mironi 1986, 359).

Finally, a key factor that extends the power of Emergency (Essential Work Services) Regulations is that many of the decrees issued with their authority are not made public. In this respect, public officials argue that, from a practical perspective, publicizing all the decrees is simply impossible due to the fact that many decrees target limited groups or specific individuals rather than the public at large. On the other hand, not publishing the decrees helps to obscure the fact that emergency powers were seemingly used to restructure the labor market during peaceful times. Because they are not published, there is no record documenting the decrees and their objectives.

Emergency (Procedures following Changes in Currency Rates) Regulations

During the decade from 1974 to 1985, the Israeli government also enacted a significant number of administrative emergency orders, particularly Emergency (Procedures following Changes in Currency Rates) Regulations, which was part of a routine economic regulation as well as a key contributor to a major structural reform in Israel's foreign exchange policy. Thus, the use of this emergency regulation signifies an additional and significant deviation from the basic principles of the rule of law. In this respect, Israeli governments ignored proper forms of governance by which fiscal and monetary regulations, or any other major economic reform for that matter, should be enacted either through primary legislation or at the very least through secondary legislation that was commissioned by the legislature. Hence, this episode is further confirmation of the commingling between law and emergency by which extra-constitutional powers become non-crisis powers (Kahan 2005).

Background: The 1970s Economic Crisis

As stated, this chapter does not attempt to answer why the Israeli authorities chose to use emergency powers instead of the regular forms of regulation available to them. Having said that, it seems rather clear that the economic turmoil of the 1970s is related to this development. Still, by providing a short background of the historical context in which Emergency (Procedures following Changes in Currency Rates) Regulations was used, I by no means offer any justification. As I argued, according to the rule of law perspective, short of an immediate profound crisis in which the state (including its economic institutions) and its people are in real jeopardy, the use of emergency powers is a direct offense to the rule of law and the democratic character of the state.

The 1970s was a period when many countries, including the USA, experienced economic stagnation, soaring inflation, high rates of unemployment, and an energy shortage. Israel's economy, particularly after the war in 1973, was in turmoil. Rising defense expenses and energy costs led to increasing inflation, worsening terms of trade, and a rising import surplus. This collection of variables signified a growing deficit in Israel's balance of payments (BOP).

From the establishment of the state in 1948 until 1972, there were only two years, 1966 and 1967, when the Israeli economy did not enjoy impressive growth relative to other countries. The Israeli market grew at a rate of about 10 percent per year. However, from 1973 until 1984, Israel's growth fell to about a third of its previous rate to an average of 3.4 percent per year. At the same time, inflation rates jumped from 12 percent in 1972 to an average of 42 percent in the years from 1974 to 1978. Then, from 1979 to 1982, inflation soared to 119.3 percent per year and continued to increase to 190.7 percent in 1983, and finally 444.9 percent in 1984 (Zilberfarb 2005, 16).

The crisis was also reflected in Israel's growing deficit. This was mainly a result of the rise in defense expenditures. Thus, the budget deficit grew from an average of about $1 billion between the years 1970 and 1972 to $2.3 billion in 1973, and then to $3.3 billion in 1974 (Rivlin 1992, 19).[28]

As I explore, Emergency (Procedures following Changes in Currency Rates) Regulations were used as part of a regulatory policy to deflate the Israeli currency—called the Israeli Lira[29] at the time—in an attempt to counter the growing deficit in Israel's BOP. Until October 1977, the government controlled foreign exchange, putting limitations on both the private and business sectors in terms of the amount of money they could hold and the number of foreign currency transactions they were allowed. Israel's foreign exchange policy was based on the mandatory emergency regulatio Defense (Finance) Regulation of 1941, which prohibited all foreign-exchange transactions, except those that were specifically permitted. Gradually, over the years, more and more permits were given. This emergency based regulation was only changed in 1978 by a new law, the Currency Supervision Law of 1978, which was enacted as a part of the liberalization process (Michaeli 2007, 76). Yet the relaxation of foreign exchange continued until 1998, when the policy was turned on its head: all foreign exchange was allowed unless it was specifically prohibited.

The rationale behind Israel's foreign exchange policy was explained by the overwhelming shortage of foreign currency in Israel during the early years. In order to protect Israel's domestic manufacturing, from time to time, the government devalued the Israeli Lira. Michael Michaeli refers to this policy as "imports without payment," or "imports without allocation of foreign exchange" (2007, 72). The idea behind this program was to improve Israel's BOP: lowering the prices of Israeli exports while at the same time reducing the demand on imports. With time, only imported products that competed with domestic products were protected (Ibid: 76). It should be noted that Israel's inflation far exceeded that of most of its trade partners and devaluation was a way to maintain Israel's competiveness (Rivlin 1992, 13).

Emergency Regulations following Devaluations

As noted, Emergency (Procedures following Changes in Currency Rates) Regulations had been used as part of a regulatory policy to devalue the Israeli currency. Specifically, it followed the actual act of currency devaluation in order to prevent profiting from the act, mainly by people who held American dollars prior to the time that the regulation took effect. This emergency regulation also granted the minister of finance almost unlimited power to issue more decrees (section 17, henceforth, the "authorizing paragraph").[30] This regulation's rather mundane objective contributes to the question of why the Israeli authorities chose emergency regulation as the preferred means of action.

In 1962, the government devaluated the Lira by 67 percent. At that time, however, the regulation to prevent any gains was carried out with a different emergency enactment: the Emergency (Compulsory Payments) Regulation[31] that was turned into law in 1958. A secondary objective behind this devaluation was to balance the BOP, but it primarily was an attempt to compensate the elimination of export subsidies and to lift quantitative restrictions on imports, leaving tariffs as the only means of protecting domestic manufacturing (Michaeli 2007, 76).

The Emergency (Procedures following Changes in Currency Rates) Regulations were used for the first time after a 20 percent devaluation on August 22, 1971.³² It most likely came as a response to the end of the gold standard in the USA. Just a few days before, on August 15, 1971, President Nixon shocked the global economy when he officially ended the international convertibility of US dollars to gold, thereby bringing an official end to the Bretton Woods arrangement.³³

The excessive use of the Emergency (Procedures following Changes in Currency Rates) Regulations started in November of 1974. Since then, it was enacted in two forms, a long version, which included a tariff on top of the exchange rate tax, and a shorter version that included only the latter. The tax payment went to the state's treasury. In the long version the tariff payments include a levee on stock, import tax, port service fees and stevedoring fees. The penalty for non-compliance in both versions is three years imprisonment or a penalty of up to 100,000 Liras. Both versions contain a provision allowing the competent authority to conduct inspections at anytime and anywhere in order to "catch anything that might serve as evidence in court." Moreover, as previously mentioned, both versions enclose a paragraph that authorizes the minister of finance to further enact regulations "on any matter relating to the implementation of these provisions." A broad interpretation of this paragraph, as we shall see, grants the minister of finance legislative power, which is free from any form of control.

On November 10, 1974, after a 43 percent devaluation, which came together with a import surcharge and export subsidies, the minister of finance issued a long version of the Emergency (Procedures following Changes in Currency Rates) Regulations.³⁴ As an anecdote which deserves a full account itself, this regulation and others that followed were copied by military orders and issued in the occupied territories.³⁵ At any rate, from this moment until a few months after the October 1977 political upset when the Likud took over the government, this emergency regulation had been used frequently for routine currency exchange regulations.

The next phase represents highly abusive uses of the Emergency (Procedures following Changes in Currency Rates) Regulations. These abuses stem from the regulations being enacted as part of a preplanned program consisting of the crude execution of a series of reissued regulations. On June 1975, the Labor government headed by Prime Minister Rabin and his minister of finance, Joshua Rabinovitz, introduced a new policy: crawling peg devaluation. Accordingly, the government devalued the Israeli currency by 2 percent each month. This program, which basically lasted until October 1977, continued the effort to improve the BOP, but with an additional objective: to eliminate the prospect of currency speculations. Retrospectively, the crawling peg system did not stop the inflationary effect of the devaluations. At any rate, once a month between June 1975 and October 1977, following each currency devaluation (twenty-eight in total), new Emergency (Procedures following Changes in Currency Rates) Regulations were enacted.[36] Although each emergency regulation was enacted to prevent gains pertaining to a specific devaluation date, the exact same regulation was enacted each time. This means that the government renewed the same emergency regulation without ever seeking the Knesset's approval. Thus, in doing so, the government deviated from the principle of the sovereignty of the Knesset twice. The first deviation is attributed to using an emergency regulation instead of a normative regulatory process and the second to bypassing the Knesset by reenacting the same emergency regulation instead of wining its approval. Overall, this whole chain of events is a clear affront to the rule of law and democratic forms of government. It is evident that this program was preplanned and thus divorced from a SOE. Hence, a routine economic program was executed with an extreme tool, which once again demonstrates the fluid relationship between law and emergency.

From Crawling Peg to Floating Rate

The final uses of Emergency (Procedures following Changes in Currency Rates) Regulations take us back again to the event that opens the book, namely, the reform in foreign exchange that took place in October 1977. This time, this emergency regulation was not only used to implement a preplanned program, but to execute a major economic restructuring. In this respect, this emergency regulation was part of the foundation used to execute a major reform in foreign exchange policies, or at the very least an attempt to execute the reform (Zilberfarb 2005, 15; Rivlin 1992, 16) while bypassing the use of primary legislation.

In October 1977, the newly elected rightwing Likud party, now in control of the government, introduced a program, which became known as the "The Ehrlich Liberalization" after Minister of Finance Simcha Ehrlich, to relax foreign exchange. The plan had three main objectives: the relaxation of foreign-exchange controls; the implementation of a new exchange rate system; and the creation of a new agency, the Bank of Israel, to control exchange rates instead of the Ministry of Finance. The first two objectives were implemented with emergency powers, including, of course, Emergency (Procedures following Changes in Currency Rates) Regulations. Despite the fact that this is a major episode in Israel's economic history, scholars who have written about this development have failed to acknowledge the legal means by which it was executed.[37]

On October 28, 1977, the government devalued the Israeli Lira by 47 percent, and as before, issued the Emergency (Procedures following Changes in Currency Rates) Regulations[38] to prevent any possible profiting. But this application was not the only use of this regulation. This time, policymakers made use of the authorizing paragraph. It should be noted that while the enactment process of an administrative emergency order requires an internal review, which must be approved by the government, regulations enacted by the power promulgated by the authorizing paragraph of the Emergency (Procedures following Changes in Currency Rates) Regulations require no additional form of control or review.

The same day, the government moved to relax foreign-exchange controls with two additional emergency regulations.[39] As I argued in chapter 1, the government capitalized on Israel's multiple and complementary emergency legal sources. At any rate, these emergency regulations eased control on payments for goods and services, particularly for foreign travel. Travel taxes and taxes on income capital movements were abolished. External borrowing, long and short term, was deregulated and Israeli residents who conducted business with the outside world could hold external deposits. Moreover, Israeli citizens were permitted to buy assets linked to foreign currencies, which were previously protected by the government against devaluation—before, only people who were directly involved in foreign trade, for example those in the banking sector, were allowed to do so (Rivlin 1992, 15). Finally, for the first time, Israeli residents were permitted to buy up to $3,000 for foreign travel.

Two days after, on October 30, 1977, as part of the implementation of the new exchange rate system, the authorizing paragraph of the Emergency (Procedures following Changes in Currency Rates) Regulations was put to use. According to section 37 of this regulation, and by the authority granted to him be the minister of finance, the governor of the Bank of Israel promulgated an additional regulation: the Limitation on Bank Credit Orders.[40] This regulation made an executive in the Bank of Israel, and not the Ministry of Finance, the controller of foreign exchange.[41]

Thus, emergency powers, including Emergency (Procedures following Changes in Currency Rates) Regulations, were the main mechanisms in a program to restructure the Israeli economy. At a certain point, it seems, they ceased to be a tool reserved for emergency situations and simply became one more normal and available enactment mechanism.

The Aftermath of the 1977 Reform

The liberalization program was hindered by a growing economic crisis. The new plan came with a rise in inflation, from 28 percent in the first three quarters of 1977 to over 53 percent in the last quarter (Michaeli 2007, 79). According to Michael Michaeli, the reason for the failure was that the new program was not accompanied by adjustments in the financial system. The liberals were not the biggest faction within the Likud party; the biggest faction was *Herut*, which had a populist and nationalist agenda. As a result, government expenditure actually grew, mainly thanks to spending on defense and settlements. Thus, while the liberals called to reduce the cost of government, the members of the nationalist-populist Herut established a welfare state in the occupied territories. The outcome was a growing deficit and unbridled inflation. The liberals, however, continued with their plan, but soon had to rollback their efforts. On March 30, 1978, the government passed the Currency Supervision Law in the Knesset. This law finally replaced the mandatory regulation as the source of foreign exchange policy. Already, in February 1979, by the authority of this law, the Bank of Israel banned companies and households from taking short or medium term credit in foreign exchange.

This move away from emergency powers to regular law, however, did not end the government's use of hyper-regulations for other economic policies. In February 1980, the government replaced Israel's official currency, the Lira, with the Shekel (not the current New Shekel in use today) by enacting the Emergency (Shekel) Regulation (KT 4095, February 24, 1980). It is unclear why this policy should have been issued as an emergency enactment. Moreover, the Likud government continued to use emergency regulations to enact fiscal and monetary policies, regulations such as the Emergency (Foreign Currency Acquisition Tax) Regulations (KT 4479, April 6, 1983) and the Emergency (Procedures following Changes in Currency Rates—Import Tax) Regulations (KT 4543, October 12, 1983)—this represents the last use of this emergency regulation. But the list goes on to include: Emergency (Imported Services Tax) Regulations (KT 4672, July 24, 1984), and Emergency (Foreign Tourist Services Deposit) Regulations (KT 4710, October 4, 1984).

This point in the chronology brings us closer to the economic recovery plan that was executed by the administrative emergency order State Economic Regularization Emergency Law of 1985 (*Hok Hahesderim*) in its original format in July 1985. This emergency regulation enforced deep economic restructuring: subsidies were drastically reduced, taxes were steeply increased and a new monetary policy was introduced. Yet, unlike the emergency regulations I mentioned thus far, this emergency regulation, which later turned into law, received far more public attention and has been discussed in academic research (Golan 2008; Nachmias and Klain, 1999). Therefore, my review will end here. I will, however, document one more administrative emergency order that played a leading role in the economic recovery plan, despite being less recognized than State Economic Regularization Emergency Law.

Amidst the backdrop of the growing economic crisis, the first war in Lebanon and a state of political deadlock, Likud and Labor formed a national unity government with the objective of stabilizing the economy. What is striking about the national unity government's use of emergency powers is that despite its overwhelming control of the Knesset and its national pact with the Histadrut, which essentially meant that there was no real opposition in the Knesset or in civil society, the Israeli authorities found it prudent to use emergency powers instead of normal regulations. Indeed, the national unity government and the Histadrut signed a three-month wage and price freeze in November 1984, which was later renewed until January 1985. The wage and price freeze was regulated with emergency powers that the government issued twice via the Emergency (Products and Services Price Stability) Regulations.[42] With such a wide consensus, it is puzzling why the government chose to use such extreme and antidemocratic measures when they could presumably have passed their agenda through primary legislation and with little opposition. This is also an additional case of reissuing what is basically the same regulation before the first expires and doing so without seeking the Knesset's approval. This emergency regulation was issued again on July 1, 1985,[43] the same day that the State Economic Regularization Emergency Law was issued.

In September 1985, two months after the economic stabilization program was first introduced, this emergency regulation was replaced by a temporary law, the Law for Stability of Products and Services Price (Temporary Order) of 1985, which was extended by the Knesset until 1996. Following this legislation, approximately 1,400 decrees were issued by the minister of industry and trade and the minister of finance.[44]

Conclusion

Overall, we can also conclude that it is crucial to consider the application of emergency powers for economic ends in order to fully appreciate the robust link between emergency and what is taken as normative law. Specifically, this episode in Israel's economic regulatory history represents the embeddedness of emergency powers in the system of governance. As we saw, during the decade between 1974 and 1985, Israel's governments, regardless of their political affiliations, routinely used emergency powers to implement economic policies. Standard matters (e.g., currency exchange) and major reforms (e.g., the effort to reorganize the labor market and the introduction of a new foreign exchange rate policy), which had nothing to do with allocating resources in a time of war or crises or helping a population in need, were enacted by the use of emergency regulations.

The aforementioned episode stands as empirical evidence demonstrating the way emergency powers, which usually begin as a reaction to a crisis, become non-crisis regulatory apparatuses. It also points to the entanglement between emergency and law, or in Ernst Fraenkel's terms, the commingling between the Prerogative State and the

Normative State. Emergency regulations are powerful tools for achieving particular economic interests; however, when used for standard economic objectives they become depoliticized.

We can also conclude from these findings that the ongoing SOE in Israel has not only affected minority populations but has had a far greater impact on the general populace than previously thought. This impact exceeds what is normally understood about the SOE's role, namely, as a security measure used in the struggle with the Palestinians. Moreover, the government behavior reviewed here indicates not only the way in which the executive branch of government has intensified its power at the expense of the legislature, but also the way in which the difference between emergency powers and democratic forms of government has been obscured. In Israel, it seems that convenience, flexibility, speed and efficiency take precedent over the principle of participation, transparency, monitoring and due process. It marks a political culture in which the ends justify the means. Taken together, this political culture with the availability of emergency laws and the habit of using them turn emergency powers into the governing tool of choice at the expense of other legislative or executive solutions. To practice this governing culture, one has to extend the power of the law, and this can be achieved with emergency powers. As I mentioned, all emergency mechanisms used between 1974 and 1985 are still valid today and can be activated at any time.

In addition, it would be interesting to thoroughly consider the role of emergency powers in the neoliberal transformation of Israel. In light of the criticism of the Attorney General on the use of emergency powers in labor disputes, we can conclude that they were used to reshape the labor market. Also, as documented in this chapter, between 1977 and 1985 emergency regulations were used to reduce government involvement in the foreign exchange market and then, in July 1985, a deep systemic economic change was executed. Thus, these events put into question the perceived link between free market economy and democracy, particularly in the context of neoliberal politics.

In any case, with respect to Israel, the claim that economic liberalization is the result of a withdrawal of the state is not credible in light of the evidence presented in this chapter. In this respect, the case before us affirms the paradox of neoliberal deregulation. Although ideologically neoliberalism is synonymous with deregulation, in practice the neoliberal transformation was executed with an "unprecedented number" of regulations (Jordana and Levi-Faur 2004, 1). Specifically, in the case documented in this chapter, neoliberal reform in Israel was carried out with heavy government involvement and executed with extreme measures.

6

CONCLUSION

As this book has illustrated, Israel's legal-political structure is based on a sustained and mutually reinforcing composition of rule-of-law applications and emergency powers, which together make up its governing system. Side by side, these apparatuses form an enduring government composition built on these synergistic tools. They establish a flexible and empowering interdependency. This methodology has helped execute a significant array of policies in Israel that range from a military government to routine monetary and fiscal policies.

In the final analysis, this study shows that relationship between law and emergency is not one of exclusivity, but rather entanglement, mutuality, and co-constitution. On the one hand, legal exceptions have been institutionalized into law, thereby justifying the unequal administration of law. In Fraenkel's terms, emergency powers put powerful tools in the hands of policymakers, while their use by law depoliticizes them. On the other hand, legal tools extend the power of emergency regulations. As a result, Israel's regime, which houses contradictions, is stable and largely able to sustain its legitimacy.

There are several implications of the evidence presented here about the role of emergency powers in the Israeli regime and about the Israeli political system in general. The evidence indicates that emergency powers in Israel have played a much bigger role than their principal function of protecting the state and its people in times of imminent threat. What may have emerged as a pragmatic temporary solution during trying times in 1948 became a systemic and permanent mechanism of control in the hands of the Israeli authorities and used for various political and economic ends. Without probing into the intentions of Israel's governing authorities in using emergency powers, we can establish that Israel's authorities have used the emergency regime's structured ambiguity to achieve political ends otherwise impossible. Hence, this book points to a profoundly different conclusion from the prevailing conception among public and academic scholarship. The dominant conception asserts that Israel's state of emergency is an unfortunate reaction to a constant security threat, despite derogations from the rule of law over the years. Accordingly, Israel's emergency regime is classified as an exception to the rule. (Bracha 1978; Dowty 1988; Hofnung 2001). But the evidence presented in this book debunks such notions. The book clearly demonstrates the deep embeddedness of emergency powers in Israel's "regular" system of governance.

As shown, Israel's authorities have used emergency powers for various political and economic ends. In part, these measures have been applied in order to enforce policies against Palestinians. This book focuses on two major program objectives inside the Green Line: the allocation of land, and the limiting of both the political representation of Palestinians and their ability to partake in policy-making. In the OPT, as discussed, emergency tools have created and sustained two unequal and separated legal systems. But as discussed in chapter 5, emergency powers were also routinely used to implement economic policies both in standard matters, such as limiting immediate profits in currency exchange, and also in major reforms, such as the effort to reorganize the labor market and the introduction of a new foreign-exchange-rate policy.

We can therefore conclude that the ongoing SOE in Israel has had a far greater impact on the general populace than previously thought. As a constituting part of the Israeli regime, the role emergency powers goes beyond what is commonly understood as security measures used in the struggle against the Palestinians. Such objectives, and even political abuses that have taken place in this context, are often silently accepted by the Jewish majority. But the execution of economic policies with emergency powers clearly demonstrates that emergency powers have had an impact on every Israeli resident. Ultimately, the general impact of emergency powers is a direct result of their use as a governing system to the extent that the difference between them and democratic forms of government are obscured.

As demonstrated in chapter 2, Israel's legal and political systems in general operate in a fluid structure. Israeli law is constructed by multiple layers of legal traditions. Moreover, due to the Harrari Resolution and the way in which it has been executed over the years, Israel's constitutional framework has considerable gaps. Significant human rights do not enjoy legislated entrenchment, the functions and relationship between Israel's political branches are unresolved, and there is no constitutional law that formally defines the hierarchy between its laws and the process for making constitutional amendments.

Perhaps the most crucial aspects of Israel's general legal-political fluidity is the fact that the Knesset acts simultaneously as a legislative branch and as a constituent assembly, or to put it differently, the Knesset functions as an eternal constituent assembly. On top of the fact that Israel's government is powerful because it controls the single house of the Knesset,[1] due to lack of binding controls the Israeli government often operates without transparency and outside the Knesset's review altogether. Thus I argue, with respect to the formal power to execute political will, Israel does not have a governability crisis, but rather the opposite. In terms of legal authority, Israel's policy makers have sufficient power to operate almost free from formal barriers.

But despite the empowering volatility of Israel's general legal-political fluidity, Israel's emergency legal foundation holds even greater potential for extending sovereign power. While Israel's main emergency legal sources are more than sufficient to stand on their own, they have instead been allowed to sit side by side, creating a legal patchwork of sorts. Israel's complex system of emergency enactment has cobbled together various emergency legal mechanisms that sometimes overlap and sometimes complement one another. As I demonstrate, maintaining such a complex legal structure serves the Israeli leadership's political purposes. By manipulating dynamics of law that are based on a stacked legal system, Israel's power holders gain flexibility in the application of law and ultimately greater sovereign power. The dynamics of law extend the already powerful jurisdiction of emergency powers.

As I have argued, with these various emergency legal mechanisms available, Israel's governing authorities can move freely from one legal mechanism to the next to serve desired ends. If one legal mechanism might be challenged or meet the limits of its authority, another can be used instead. Moreover, Israel's governing officials can mix and match discrete emergency laws. While each of the regulations, on its own, is limited, these restrictions dissolve when combined into a legal metaphor, thereby empowering the government with the ability to execute a much ambitious political objective. Power holders can also use one legal source to validate the authority of another legal order, sometimes even retroactively. As a result, this flexibility enables the state to extend its sovereign power and achieve political ends otherwise impossible. All the while, the state maintains a degree of legitimacy by operating behind a veil of legality.

Indeed, making use of Israel's ambiguous emergency jurisprudence proved effective and not too costly in terms of Israel's legitimacy as a rule-of-law nation. In mobilizing the fluidity of the system, Israel's authorities managed to bridge what appeared to be an intrinsic contradiction: a government by law and systemic discriminatory policies, particularly against Palestinians. When discriminatory and even oppressive political ends are administrated by legal mechanisms—however awkward—the administration can maintain its character as a government by law. Hence, as it turns out, this unstable, chaotic apparatus is arguably the source of the relative stability of Israel's political regime.

Some of the assertions made here about the nature of governance and authority in Israel, therefore, could benefit from further research in other countries. It may help bolster the assertion here that the dichotomy between the rule of law and emergency powers is false. The two can fuel and embolden each other.

Thus this book, which is an in-depth study of the State of Israel, compliments additional scholarship in asserting the profoundly entangled relationship between law and emergency (Scheuerman 1999–2000; Neocleous 2006; Lazar 2013). It has been empirically demonstrated that this commingling has been the rule in most countries regardless of the continent on which they are located for a continuous duration in modern history. And, as noted, this phenomenon takes place not just in totalitarian or developing states, but in liberal democracies as well. In broad brushstrokes, I will now offer a short survey of states other than Israel where the comingling of law and emergency has occurred. From 1922 to 1998, Northern Ireland, for example, was under a state of emergency, albeit in different capacities. Indeed, Northern Ireland is a good example of a perpetual SOE. In this respect, the Emergency Power Act of 1973 was renewed in 1978, 1987, 1991 and once again in 1996.[2] Multiple countries across the African continent, from Egypt to South Africa also function as good examples.[3] Many South and Central American countries have experienced prolonged durations of governance under emergency powers which has enabled far-reaching powers to become general governmental apparatuses.[4] This is true for Chile, Argentina, Uruguay and El Salvador, amongst others countries; they all have experienced long periods of institutionalized states of emergency under military regimes according to The Despouy Report. Columbia is one particular example where a state of emergency,[5] in various forms, has been enforced almost uninterruptedly for some 40 years.[6] Moreover, Colombia's perennial SOE became a constitutional norm approved by the Constitutional Court (Volcansek and Stack 2011, 199–223). The perpetually commingled relationship between law and emergency also appears in Asia, where Israel, of course, is located. Other states in Asia where this relationship exists include, to name only a few, Pakistan, Sri Lanka and India, where the commingling has "enabled illicit constitutional engineering" (Huq 2006, 99). The same applies to Southeast Asia (ibid.). Kanishka Jayasuriya indicates that in many South Asian states, emergency powers were enabled within the constitutional order (2001, 109). In fact, he adds, in countries such as Singapore, these "regimes of exception have become the norm" (ibid., 110). But, as mentioned, this condition applies to developed democracies as well as developing countries. For example, four national emergencies were declared in the United States between 1933 and 1972. Thus, creating a stretch of over forty years where the commingled relationship between law and emergency was the rule (Gross and Aoláin 2006, 175–176).[7]

In this respect, the theoretical contribution of this book is relevant to many other states outside Israel and should be tested by further empirical research. First, the co-constitutive model offers an analytical tool to reconsider governing regimes without first having to define them as democratic, rule-of-law regimes or as a prerogative, emergency-based governing systems. This book shifts the focus from the question of whether emergency power can conform to the rule of law to an exploration of how the two coexist. Indeed, most of the relevant scholarship has centered on the ways in which law can be made to control and maintain emergency powers, if it is indeed possible at all. Moreover, this question has been considered vis-à-vis various crises. Such attention is based on a perspective shared by both liberals and radical skeptics—the emergency paradigm—that separates law and emergency. Hence, both liberal and radical skeptics, who otherwise do not agree on anything, divide "normal" times and "normal" order of government from "exceptional" times of emergency and "exceptional" order of government. But as I have demonstrated, such a perspective is unfounded when considering the case of Israel, as well as when considering other countries around the world. This study of Israel's emergency jurisprudence is further proof that the binary conception that separates law from emergency is a political myth (Neocleous 2006, 204),[8] and moreover, that emergencies should not be treated as temporary conditions. Considering the Israeli case, the argument that the war on terror, which was declared following 9/11, is a new phenomenon is simply false.

The co-constitutive model, instead, offers an analytical tool to examine political systems that are similar to Israel's and where emergency powers and the rule of law are profoundly commingled and have been for a long period of time. The co-constitutive model, therefore, can illuminate governing dynamics that extend sovereign power and, moreover, can open additional venues to understand the structure and operation of political regimes.

The mutual relationship between the rule of law and emergency powers, over significant periods of time, should not be surprising. On the one hand, the rule of law is the best source of governing legitimacy, and, on the other hand, emergency powers are arguably the most effective tool to break through the cracks of the rule of law to assert sovereign will.

Thus, they complete each other and together they form a sustaining affiliation. Such a long-term relationship was recorded by Ernst Frankel regarding the Nazi regime in Germany and by students of colonial (or imperial) regimes. But I argue, and have demonstrated through the Israeli case, this co-constitutive relationship prevails in other and less extreme political environments.

The co-constitution model points to several phenomena that we need to understand in studying states of emergencies and uses of emergency powers. First, and as argued by Nasser Hussain in his hyperlegality model (2007), the use of emergency powers represents the extension of law, not the withdrawal of it. In this context, it is the extension of law, not the curtailment of law, which extends power. This is crucial if we want to understand the role of emergency powers. In the Israeli case, the dynamics of law extend law (and thus sovereign power) from within; that is, without stepping outside the legal realm. As a result, the regime can maintain legitimacy to a degree. Overall, with emphasis on dynamics of law, we can look beyond the emergency powers' externalities, or their incorporation into the juridical order to achieve political goals.

An additional conclusion that emerges from the Israeli case is how we understand the concept of sovereignty. With the dynamics of law discussed in the book, we can conclude that complexity rather than a focused, clear authority is the source of greater sovereign power. With legal fluidity and structured ambiguity, the sovereign can switch freely from one juridical order to the next rather than be hemmed in by a well-defined legal structure.

This realization about complexity rather than a focused clear authority as the bedrock of sovereign power has already been articulated in different capacities, particularly in the Schmittian concept of sovereignty. Carl Schmitt argues that the sovereign is not the rule maker, but the one who determines the exception to the rule (1985, 36). According to Schmitt, the entire political system is based on this dynamic. On the one hand, there is the exclusion of crisis from the political realm in order to establish "normalcy," but on the other hand, there is the ever-present ability to go outside the constitutional order.[9]

Schmitt goes on to argue that "if the space of the exception is limitless, then so too sovereign power".[10] With the blurring of the border between the legal and the extra-legal, the sovereign is inside and outside the juridical order (ideally, in an SOE, law is suspended *by* law in order to save law) and thus possess infinite power. In the same fashion, this study demonstrates that sovereignty should be understood not just by the ability to assert one's original legal system, but, even more so, by the capacity to move from one legal system to the next at will and to choose which legal authority to apply and when. Adi Ophir's definition of sovereignty captures this dynamic. For him, "sovereignty is, at the same time, the authority to decide at any given moment what is the governing law" (2003, 360).[11] Hence, in the same way as the suspension of law is a sign of sovereignty, so too are contradicting and overlapping legal authorities are manifestations of sovereignty.

This book complements this understanding of sovereignty by showing that sovereign power, in many respects, is a question of flexibility.[12] In Israel, governmental flexibility has gone beyond the use of emergency powers as legal exceptions; it was also based on juridical complexity that created space within the juridical order and thus opportunities for the regime. As illustrated, jockeying between separate jurisdictions proved highly effective in establishing control and in appropriating property. Overall, in all of the paradigms I reviewed, exceptions, juridical complexity and lack of borders are facets of sovereignty. That is, the ability to play on both sides of the juridical border, between legal authorities and across different territories, is, in fact, the core that extends sovereign power. In the final analysis, thus, a nonunified legal foundation proves more enabling in extending sovereign power.

An additional contribution of the co-constitutive model to the discussion of states of emergencies and uses of emergency powers is the alternative use of emergency powers for nonsecurity purposes such as the shaping of political economy. As we know, in recent years a vast body of scholarship has covered emergency powers, but mostly in the context of the war on terror and violation of human rights. The co-constitutive model offers a window into the relationship between emergency and law, and power and law from the perspective of political economy. It is only by considering the use of emergency powers for economic ends that were unrelated to security or wartime conditions, that we can see the embeddedness of emergency in Israel's general legal-political system. Understanding the application of emergency powers for economic ends truly illustrates the robust link between emergency and what is taken as normative law.

Finally, we have to ask what this discussion ultimately means. How should we understand this commingling of law and emergency? First, we should accept the reality that law and emergency are not separated from each other in regimes like Israel. They are inextricable because emergency powers are effective in breaking through the constraints of the rule of law to assert sovereign will. And to make their application even more effective, law itself is often used to extend the power of emergency apparatuses. In fact, this dynamism, as demonstrated in chapter 2, exists in a less extreme context such as criminal and civil procedures. Criminal law, for example, "is a codified regime of rights derogations in the service of order" (Lazar 2013, 162). Here too, fluidity and blurring of the lines between the rule of law and public order are often the default. Emergency is one extreme mode of this commingling between rational law and sovereign power.

Law itself is an instrument of political rule. Therefore, we must accept the fact that law never rules on its own (Lazar 2013, 162; Darian-Smith and Fitzpatrick 2008, 3). At times, law is part of governing mechanisms that derogate rule-of-law principles. One conclusion is that legal pluralism (based on multiple, fluid, and ambiguous laws working together) can deny political pluralism, such as is the case with the Palestinians' limited political representation and policy-making. The Israeli case also indicates that such a regime can be quite comfortable when law and emergency commingle.

To sum up: first, considering the empirical evidence, our premise should be that law and emergency are not at odds with each other. Second, we should also study emergency and emergency powers absent crisis. Israel is a perfect example in this respect. Studying its emergency regime vis-à-vis a crisis has led to the invalid conclusion that emergency powers are an exception to the standard method of governance. In fact, as was demonstrated in the book, they are an integral part of Israel's governing methodology. And finally, we should consider that law is partly responsible for the derogation of the rule of law.

With these realities established, we can move to the difficult task of addressing political regimes that are based on mutually enforcing modes of government: law and emergency. Indeed, there are no simple solutions and at times we stand powerless against this phenomenon. But when we face such a reality, we must turn away from the question, how to better apply emergency powers in a time of crisis? Instead of placing the crisis and emergency powers at the center of our thinking, we should reflect on sovereign power and how it operates to extend itself. The commingling of law and emergency is not an accident that stems from the use of emergency powers in a time of crisis. Rather, it is the outcome of particular governmental entities explicitly seeking to exert their power.

Fighting against this condition will probably take a cluster of actions, partly legal, partly through supportive political institutions and agencies and partly through a mobilized civil society. These actions should be a result of the understanding that we sometimes need to protect the rule of law *from* law to prevent it from being undercut. We should concentrate on the way power works and about the political project it aims to serve. It is clear that in Israel, for example, upon its political project vis-à-vis the Palestinians, the regime would seek to extend its power and use the mutual reinforcing dynamics between law and emergency for that end.

Final Note

The co-constitution of law and emergency as a governing tool is here to stay—and not just in Israel. This unambiguous statement is based on the recognition in the dynamics between law and power. To be sure, law can restrain power, but for law to rule and be relevant, it must also be ever responsive to power.

I do not argue that emergency apparatuses are consistent everywhere; while some forms of legal fluidity is most likely to be present in any regime, its magnitude varies from state to state. Thus, in some regimes the use of fluid dynamics of law can be relatively limited. It depends, first, on how easy it is to use them and second, on whether or not a political project seeks to empower one social group or class at the expense of another.

In light of this, Israel's co-constitution of law and emergency is not about to disappear. The availability of emergency tools in Israel and considering its political circumstances and project makes this fluid governing mechanism common and most valuable. In fact, it is the only way the Israeli regime can sustain itself in its current operation. Israel's juridical complexity was shaped by a political conflict and ultimately came to serve political purposes, including, of course, economic ends. This governing flexibility, in turn, has served Israel's separatist policies toward Palestinians within and outside the Green Line as well as different economic policies.

For this reason, recent aspirations to explicitly and formally apply Israeli law in the OPT have quickly vaporized. This process has been dubbed "legal annexation" of the OPT. The position of the Israeli legal elite is unequivocally against this prospect. They understand all too well that such actions would deeply diminish Israel's power by eliminating its ability to maneuver between establishing Jewish supremacy and continuing to have some adherence to law. Without legal fluidity and ambiguity, Israel either will declaratively be a Jewish supremacy, non-democratic regime and lose whatever international credibility it still has, or, have to share equality with Palestinians. For this reason, for example, Israel's settlers' party, the Jewish Home party, withdraw from its initiative to apply Israeli labor law in the OPT.[13] They discovered that Palestinian workers will then enjoy similar rights as Jewish settlers.

Thus, I see no end in the near future to the political use—or, more accurately, abuse—of Israel's complex emergency jurisprudence. As long as Israel's political condition remains the same, both within and outside the Green Line, we should not expect this outcome anytime soon. Only revamping Israel's political structure and project will allow for such a development.

NOTES

Chapter 1

1. The original declaration of the state of emergency was pronounced by the Provisional Government on May 19, 1948, and approved by the Provisional Council of the State, and came into force on May 21. "The Prime Minister, David Ben-Gurion, proposed that the following proclamation be promulgated: 'By virtue of Section 9(a) of the Law and Administration Ordinance 1948, the Provisional Council of State hereby proclaims that a state of emergency is in force in the State.' A vote was taken and the proposition was adopted." *Provisional Council of State Minutes*, Session B, May 19, 1948, 10. The declaration was published on May 21, 1948. IR, no. 2, 6.
2. Transactions in Foreign Currency Decree, KT 3775.
3. KT 3774.
4. KT 3775.
5. In a state of siege, one promulgates legal measures that anticipate an emergency crisis. For a good review, see Gross and Aoláin 2006, 26–30.
6. Whereas a state of siege is the instrument used in civil law countries, martial law is typical of common law systems. Martial law grants a commander non-statutory, extraordinary powers, with the use of military tribunals, while ordinary law is suspended. For a good review, see Gross and Aoláin 2006, 30–35.

7. John Locke, *The Second Treatise*.
8. See Ackermann 2004; Dyzenhaus 2006; Ferejohn and Pasquino 2004; Gross 2003, 2013; Oraa 1992; Scheuerman 2006; and Tushnet 2005a and 2005b.
9. Oraa 1992; for a good review, see Gross and Aoláin 2006, 245–364.
10. For Schmitt, the failure of liberalism lies at the moment (which for him is unavoidable) that the regime has to decide between suspension of the legal order and its destruction.
11. See also Fisken 2004, 15.
12. Models of accommodation have been structured into international law as well. In this respect, certain human rights treaties such as the European Convention on Human Rights and Fundamental Freedoms of 1950 and the International Covenant on Civil and Political Rights of 1966, have a derogation clause. This derogation clause establishes a legal regime to regulate states of emergency. Still, nearly half the states in the international community are not parties to treaties of this kind. On the other hand, certain emergent principles of the derogation clause are *general international law*, meaning that they stand as customary international law and apply to all states, even those that are not parties to the treaties.
13. For a good review see Gross and Aoláin 2006, 17–26; and Ferejohn and Pasquino, 2004.
14. Posner applies a utilitarian consideration: "A constitutional right should be modified when channeled circumstances indicate that the right no longer strikes a sensible balance between personal liberty and public safety." Posner 2006, 147.
15. Yoo advocates an interpretation that grants the president all the executive powers that have not been explicitly given to Congress by the constitution (2005); see also Arato, 2006: 546–547.
16. For a good review see Gross and Aoláin 2006, 66–72.
17. I borrow this term from Andrew Arato 2006.
18. According to the extra-legal measures model, public officials may use extra-legal tools "when they believe that such action is necessary for protecting the nation and the public in the face of calamity, provided that they openly and publicly acknowledge the nature of their actions" (Gross 2003, 1023).
19. Sometimes also titled "orthodox advocates" or "legal traditionalists." Arato 2006.
20. Quoted from Justice Jackson's dissent in *Korematsu v. United*

States, 323 U.S. 214, 246 (1944). See also Posner and Vermeule 2005, 57–59.

21. There is also a call to turn to and enforce international law as a way to ensure that the court will hold true to its responsibility to uphold the rule of law. Saito 2007, 12.
22. See also Neocleous 2006, 204.
23. Even for Schmitt it is the ever-present potential for crisis—the "nearness of crisis" (Fisken 2004, 17)—that is the general feature of modern (Western) political systems of government. For a brief time, Carl Schmitt appeared to endorse this position through the analytical prism of the commissarial dictatorship (*kommissarische Diktatur*). Later he abandoned this view when he wrote *Political Theology* (Zuckerman 2006, 528).
24. Hussain calls the recent antiterrorism legislation in the UK "hyperlegality," by which he means that it represents the opposite process of a withdrawal of law. This extension of law is based on "increasing use of classifications of persons in the law," and "the use of special tribunals and commissions" (2007: 516).
25. See also Hussain 2007, 519.
26. See Benton 2002; Hussain 2003, 2007; Kolsky 2005; Darian-Smith and Fitzpatrick 1999.
27. In *The Jurisprudence of Emergency: Colonialism and the Rule of Law* (2003), Nasser Hussain notes that in colonial India, under British rule, emergency was an elastic category and exceptional emergency powers became the governing norm. He describes the ever-present state of emergency, which suspended law and enabled colonizers to exert their political will through legal channels.
28. The Israeli state existed without an official military government for only half a year, between December 1966 and June 1967.
29. See the list in Cohn 1998, 625–626.
30. On the other hand, during the Second Lebanon War in the summer of 2006, when there was a great need to declare a state of emergency in order to allocate special funds and provide for Israel's northern residents who had suffered an ongoing bombardment, the country that lives in a constant state of emergency did not officially declare one. Later it was discovered that a neoliberal rationale was behind this decision. Israel's government at the time did not want to harm the country's credit rating. See Azulai 2007.
31. Other scholars who support this definition include Gavizon (1999)

and Dowty (1999). Others offer alternative definitions, such as an "illiberal democracy" (Sàdi 2002; Peleg 2004) and "majoritarian" (Navot 2002).
32. The OPT includes the West Bank and, until 2005, the Gaza Strip. The Palestinians residents of the OPT have lived under Israeli military control since June 1967.
33. The Green Line was defined by the Rhodes 1949 Armistice Agreements and represents the territory of the pre-1967 state of Israel.
34. For Lustick (1980, 77), this system is based on three elements: segmentation, co-option, and dependency.
35. Yet Rouhana's analysis remains at the level of ideology. He does not describe the actual emergency mechanisms by which the Jewish majority gains ethnic dominance over the Palestinians. Others argue that Jewish national hegemony simply takes precedence over universal democratic values (Bishara 1993; Azoulay and Ophir 2008).
36. Gad Barzulai's study of national consensus and dissent also indirectly demonstrates how conflicting conceptions have shaped Israel's sociopolitical order fairly sustainably so far (1996).
37. See also Gad Barzilai (1996, 185–189), who differentiates a "state under siege" and a "garrison state". Barzilai argues that while Israel has been a state under siege since its inception, it has never been a garrison state.

Chapter 2

1. See also Barak-Erez 2012, 501–503.
2. See, for example, Zubida and Mekelberg 2008.
3. In addition, neither Israel's borders nor the scope of its citizenry are securely defined. In certain circumstances, the world Jewry has priority over non-Jewish citizens. See, for example, Bernet 2009.
4. In 1994, as part of an amendment to the basic laws that were enacted in 1992, an introductory paragraph was added, which for the first time codified the connection between the DOI and the basic laws. The paragraph states that the rights proclaimed by Israeli law shall be respected in the "spirit of the DOI."
5. The 1992 enactments of two basic laws restrict Knesset legislation

to some extent. On November 22, 2010, the Knesset enacted the "Referendum Law" by a regular vote. This law challenges the principle of the supremacy of the Knesset. The Referendum Law pertains to whether the Knesset had the authority to withdraw Israel's sovereignty from East Jerusalem and the Golan Heights as a result of a peace agreement. This law can be overridden by a regular law, and Israel's Supreme Court has yet to speak on the matter.
6. Justice Barak, CA 6821/93.
7. There was a strong German influence in the establishment of Israel's legal system, particularly on the judiciary. Many of the key figures were German immigrants; among them, for example, were Pinchas Rosen, the first and most influential minister of justice, and his partner in a legal firm, Justice Moshe Zamora, the first president of the Supreme Court of Israel. See Salzberger and Oz-Salzberger 1999.
8. During the Yishuv's period, the World Zionist Organization held periodic elections.
9. Even the territorial application of the Israeli law is unsettled. At first, it was established that the law would apply within Israel's territory (section 1 of the Territorial Jurisdiction and Authorities Order, 1948). It was then decided that Israel's territory would be anywhere Israeli law was applied (in the Absentee Law of 1950, among other places). Then the state asserted its sovereignty over a territory (East Jerusalem, 1967) by proclaiming that Israeli law applied there, and finally, the state applied its law on a territory beyond its borders (Golan Heights). (This is without discussing the complex relationship of the State of Israel to the OPT; for more, see Rubin 1995, *Mishpatim* 25, 215–239).
10. British Mandatory legal influence can be found, for example, in criminal law and tort.
11. IR no. 2, supplement 1 (May 21, 1948): 1; LSI vol. 1 (1948): 7.
12. IR 5708: 1; LSI vol. 1 (1948): 7.
13. *Provisional Council of State Minutes*, Session A, May 16, 1948, 8; see also Hofnung 2001, 54.
14. Section 46 in the King-in-Council asserted that in the event of lacuna, the courts in Israel should follow the British common law and the British equity principles.
15. See Shapira and Baracha 1978, 14–5.
16. The *Tanzimat* was based on the French civil code and existed side

by side with the *Shari`ah* Islamic law. As part of the reform, new secular courts called *nizame* were also established. For the influence of Ottoman law on Israeli law, see Baron 2008 (Hebrew.)

17. The *Majalla* was an Ottoman project that codified part of the Muslim Sharia-based law in the late 19th century.
18. SH, no. 978 (July 31, 1980).
19. See note 3; HC 7/48; HC 10/48; there are some who see the fact that the DOI has no formal legal standing as a historic mistake, a missed opportunity. See Sofer 2012, 32–33.
20. Yet in 2010, the proposal to add the phrase "in the spirit of the Declaration of Independence" was rejected during the debates on the wording of Israel's "declaration of loyalty," the oath taken when receiving Israeli citizenship.
21. *Kol HaAm v. Minister of Interior*, HC 73/53, 7 PD, 871 (October 16, 1953); an appeal issued by the communist newspaper *Kol HaAm* in 1953 against the decision of the minister of the interior to close the paper for fifteen days due to a controversial article on the Korean War.
22. "Eretz Yisrael" often refers to the geo-political territory defined by the British Mandate, which is different from both the biblical State of Israel and the current acknowledged political borders of the State of Israel.
23. SH, no. 1 (February 19, 1949): 1; LSI vol. 3: 3.
24. See, for example, CA 6821/93.
25. Quoted in Hirschl 2009, 483.
26. This decision was supported by almost all members of Mapai, the most prominent party at the time, the party of Ben-Gurion, which later merged into the Labor party. See Negbi 1987, 31.
27. DK vol. 5 (June 13, 1950): 1743.
28. See also Friedmann 2012.
29. The Law of Return grants Jews and their third degree relatives the right to be an Israeli citizen. It is a major component of Israel's citizenship law and ultimately defines Israel's citizenry borders.
30. For more on this topic, see Sofer 2012.
31. *Bergman v. Minister of Finance*, HC 231/73, 23 (1) PD, 693 (Henceforth "Bergman.")
32. Bergman; see Sofer 2012, 46.
33. HC 107/73; other cases that validated this approach are HC 148/73 and HC 60/77.

34. See also Fridman 2012, 122–123.
35. For a detailed account of the voting process, see Rubinstein 1999.
36. Amnon Rubinstein (2012) reminds us that the enactment of these basic laws coincided with the change to direct election of the prime minister—a change that overshadowed the laws' enactment. A few years later Israel went back to its old electoral system.
37. See Landue 1996, 701. This is the reason that he and others reject the Supreme Court's broad interpretation, by which these rights are considered protected. According to Landue, what was taken out through the front door cannot be taken in through the window.
38. HC 4676/94.
39. The overcoming clause was borrowed from the Canadian Charter by Chief Justice Barak.
40. DK 136, 5439, 1994.
41. Moreover, an additional introductory paragraph, which should function as an introduction to the actual constitution, was added to the two basic laws. It indicates that the objective of these basic laws is to protect the asserted civil liberties according to the "values of the State of Israel as a Jewish and democratic state." This added provision is central in framing Israel's national identity as Jewish, a definition that obviously derogates the civic standing of Palestinians with Israeli citizenship.
42. See also Peled and Navot 2009, 434.
43. See ibid. and Hirschl 2009, 478.
44. *Poraz v. The State of Israel*, HC 1368/94, 57 (5) PD, 913.
45. See Dotan 1997.
46. See Gavizon 1997.
47. Sapir argues that through this arrangement the court makes the missing Basic Law: Legislation redundant. Sapir 2010, 17.
48. Most of the laws in Israel originated from proposals in government bills. This condition speaks directly to Israel's limited separation of powers.
49. See "Custom (in Canon Law)," *The Catholic Encyclopedia*, vol. 4 (New York: Robert Appleton Company, 1908). http://www.newadvent.org/cathen/04576a.htm.
50. Ibid.
51. Ibid.
52. Elef-Shilo 2012.

53. Avital 2013.
54. See Kremnitzer 2000, 181.
55. The Justices Law was enacted in 1953, according to which a nine-member commission is elected with a professional majority: the minister of justice who heads the commission, an additional minister, two KMs, two elected lawyers from the Israel Bar Association, and three justices, including the president of the Supreme Court.
56. The court's understanding of international law, specifically the Geneva Convention, furthers legal fluidity. Although Israel approved the Geneva Convention—in fact, Israel was one of its most ardent supporters, as a reaction to the Holocaust—the HCJ asserts that this general approval does not turn the convention into an integral part of Israeli law, since the Knesset never re-enacted it. Because the Geneva Convention is part of the customary international law (as opposed to the obligatory international law), it does not bind the state of Israel, and Israel only voluntarily applies its humanitarian aspects.
57. The decision to review cases from the OPT was mainly the doing of one person, Meir Shamgar, who later became the president of the Israeli Supreme Court. In his tenure as the IDF's chief military prosecutor and later as the attorney general, he pushed to place the Israeli military government in the West Bank and the Gaza Strip under judicial review. For more, see Hofnung 2001, 322.
58. See, inter alia, Lion Sheleff, who argues that the HCJ's activism stops at the Green-Line (1993). Ronen Shamir (1990) reviewed all of the appeals from the OPT from 1967 to 1986. He concludes that besides a few "landmark cases" that reinforce the legitimacy of the HCJ as both autonomous and independent, in the overwhelming majority of cases the HCJ supported the state's action in the OPT.
59. In fact, it took almost a whole decade before the Law of Jurisdiction was enacted in 1957. Before this enactment, according to Regulation 37 of the Emergency (the Jurisdiction Constitution) Regulations of 1948, all of the court's verdicts needed to be approved by the general chief of staff or the minister of defense. However, this policy was not rigidly enforced. At times, Israel's government and administrative agencies simply ignored the court's

orders. This non-compliance took place not only in the formative years of the state, but even in recent times, specifically in cases pertaining to the OPT.
60. According to Ferejohn and Pasquino (2004), the court acquires extensive authority over legislation when the political system is fragmented.
61. For an argument supporting the court's transition from formalism to activism, see Mautner 1993.
62. The court's critics argue that the "state codification becomes a footnote for the courts' review." Ariel Rosan-Tzvi, quoted in Shamir 2001, 289.
63. Generally speaking, legal activism does not have one certain definition. By legal activism, I mean a judicial approach in which the court diverges from its common legal doctrine and introduces new legal norms. Adi Perush's definition is actually more concise. He defines it as the process in which the court diverges from the common legal norms and new public policies are produced through the decisions of judges (1993, 717–718). Based on a different conceptualization, Ronen Shamir alludes to similar conclusions, namely that the court creates a legal environment in which everything is possible. Shamir argues that what is taken to be the HCJ's legal activism is actually radical legal formalism. Radical formalism maintains that law encompasses all. As in any other formalist doctrine, law is autonomous and supplies judges with tools that maintain their objectivity. The difference is that radical formalism does not direct its attention inward into the legal system and its logic, but outward. Law, in this context, digests everything outside law, making it part of the legal realm (Shamir 2001, 282–283).
64. More particularly, Daniel Friedmann, the previous minister of justice, advocated a reform to limit the power of the Supreme Court to review of the Knesset.
65. For more, see Sapir 2010, 136.
66. Ichener and Zimoki 2013.

Chapter 3

1. These clauses are the following: Section 9(b) of the Law and Administration Ordinance, 1948; Section 39(3) of the Basic Law:

The Government, and Section 46(b) of the Control of Products and Services Law–1957
2. *Palestine Gazette*, no. 675, supp. 2 (1937): 267.
3. *Palestine Gazette*, supp. 2 (1939): 545; and *Palestine Gazette*, supp. 2 (1940): 1118.
4. Defense (Immigration) Regulations, 1940; Defense (Court Appeals) Regulations, 1940; Defense (Closed Areas) Regulations, 1940; Defense (Currency) Regulations, 1941; Defense (Control of Food) Regulations, 1942; and Defense (Prevention of Profiteering) Regulations, 1944. Author's translation.
5. The Yishuv refers to the pre-statehood Jewish political community.
6. *Ha-Praklit, Journal of the Jewish Bar Association of Palestine* 3, no. 1 (1946): 1.
7. The main set of regulations removed by the LAO in 1948 were sections 102–107(c), which dealt with restricting Jewish immigration. In addition, sections 114–118 were replaced by an original Israeli law, the Emergency Land Requisition (Regulation) Law of 1949. In 1950, section 33 on punitive flogging was removed. Section 138 on explosives and section 111(a) were replaced by original laws in 1954 and 1961, respectively.
8. *Palestine Gazette*, supp. 2 (1946): 302.
9. IR, 2 (1947): 1554.
10. The first renewal law was the Order for the Extension of the Validity of Defense Emergency Regulations (Temporary Provision), 1950, SH, 11. The last renewal law was the Order for the Extension of the Validity of Defense Emergency Regulations (Temporary Provision) (No. 13), 1957, SH, 117. I shall return to this set of regulations in chapter 5.
11. The Defense (Currency) Regulations were replaced by section 21 of Control over Currency Law of 1978, SH, 108.
12. 1957, SH, 24. I will further discuss this law in subsequent sections and in chapter 5.
13. 1978, SH, 108.
14. Section 2 and section 6(5).
15. *Cook v. the Minister of Defense*, 1948, and *Levon v. Gubernik*, 1948. See chapter 5.
16. In 1979 the HCJ reasserted that the mandatory regulations were still part of Israeli law, in *Abu Awad v. Commander of the Judea and Samaria Region*, HC 97/79, 33 (3) PD, 309.

17. Menahem Begin's Irgun (Etzel) made an independent arms deal, and the weapons arrived on the *Altalena* cargo ship. The leaders of the forming state, headed by the Labor party, Mapai, and its leader, Ben-Gurion, denied it access. In the crossfire, the ship sank. The army commander at the site was future Prime Minister Yitzhak Rabin.
18. A set of published regulations by the British mandatory administration against the Jewish population in Palestine, mainly forbidding Jewish immigration.
19. In 1979, the HCJ reasserted that mandatory regulations are still part of the Israeli law (*Abu Awad v. Commander of the Judea and Samaria Region*).
20. The main restriction introduced by the court was that before executing mandatory regulation 111(4) (detention), an advisory committee had to be appointed. *El Karbutli v. Minister of Defense* (1948). Advisory committees are required for mandatory regulations 108–110 as well. The HCJ introduced an additional limitation, which involved the commonly used mandatory regulation 125 (Closed Areas). The court asserted that mandatory regulation 125, as opposed to an execution order, is a "regulation having legislative force" and as such has to be published in an official gazette. *Aslan v. Military Governor of Galilee*, HC 220/51, 5 PD, 1480 (1951). I shall address this topic in length in chapter 4.
21. *El Karbutli v. Minister of Defense* (1948).
22. Emergency Defense and Security Law, 1949, HH 13 (June 24, 1949): 117. Author's translation.
23. DK 2 (July 12, 1949): 975–988.
24. SH, 11, 1951. Author's translation.
25. Jellamy is the name of the prison in which they were detained.
26. Moshe Sharett, representing the government. DK 9 (May 21, 1951): 1823.
27. Ibid; When the Likud party, headed by Begin, came into power in 1977, this regulation and part of regulation 112 were replaced by law.
28. DK 9 (May 22, 1951): 1831. Author's translation.
29. DK 9 (1966): 1978. Author's translation.
30. Shimson argued that "the Emergency Regulations, 1945, have no place in our [Israel's] law books." DK 46 (June 13, 1966): 1708.
31. Some of the Likud members were themselves targeted by mandatory regulations, and the memory was perhaps still vivid.

32. A military order copied the practices of this law onto the OPT, but events in 1985 rolled back the provision; thereafter, mandatory regulations 111 and 112 were back in force in the OPT.
33. The Basic Law: The Knesset (only by a special majority of eighty Knesset members or more); the Basic Law: The Government; the Basic Law: The President; and a small number of entrenched paragraphs, including section 3 of the Customs and Excise Duties (Variation of Tariff) Law, 1949; section 11 of the Second Knesset (Transition) Law, 1951; section 20(a) of the Elections (Modes of Propaganda) Law, 1959; section 22 of the Judiciary; section 4 of the Basic Law: Freedom of Occupation, 1992; and section 12 of the Basic Law: Human Dignity and Liberty, 1992.
34. Minister of defense, minister of industry and commerce, minister of finance, minister of agriculture and minister of transportation, IR (June 6, 1948): 16; minister of the interior and minister of immigration, IR (July 30, 1948): 70; prime minister, IR (November 15, 1948): 82; minister of labor, YP (1952): 779; minister of communication, YP (April 1, 1956): 424; minister of development, YP (1967): 1618; minister of justice, YP (1967): 1830; minister of health, YP (1977): 327; minister of energy and infrastructure, YP (1979): 908. See complete list in the Attorney General's Guidelines, no. 60.012, entitled "Subordinate Legislation—Guidelines and Procedures," or in Yitzhak Zamir, "Subordinate Legislation Guidelines and Procedures," (Iyunei Mispat 11, 1986): 339–379).
35. Until the 1970s, administrative orders were used relatively infrequently, and usually in times of war. Since the 1970s, administrative orders have been used more often in the context of economic policies and labor disputes. For more on emergency powers in labor disputes, see Mironi 1986.
36. Later to become the Knesset.
37. The title of formal laws before the establishment of the state.
38. IR 2, supp. 1 (May 21, 1948): 1; LSI vol. 1, 7.
39. For example, the Prevention of Terrorism Ordinance of 1948.
40. For example, the Emergency (Licenses for Firearms—Extension of Validity) Regulations, 1948 (IR 40, suppl. 2 [February 25, 1949]: 97) was extended three times in this way. This procedure became more common in the 1970s with administrative order pertaining to currency control and labor relations. See Hofnung 2001, 55.

41. See also Hofnung 2001, 56–57.
42. Section 18 of the Government's Working Rules; see also Hofnung 2001, 56.
43. Section 54 of the Government's Working Rules.
44. *Poraz v. Government of Israel*.
45. SH, no. 1780 (March 7, 2001): 158.
46. For example, *Goldman v. the Attorney General*, HC 110/52, 7 PD, 694; 485/75, 656; *Osem Food Industry v. the Minister of Commerce and Industry*, HC 37/89, 43 (4) PD, 111; *Goldsmiths v. the Minister of Commerce and Industry*, HC 388/89, 44 (1) PD, 397; *Mipromal v. the Commissioner of the Custom Department*, CA 530/78, 35 (2) PD, 169, 174. See full list in Hofnung 2001, 70.
47. For example, the Extension of Emergency Regulations Law of 1949, SH, 7. Author's translation.
48. *The Association for Civil Rights in Israel v. Israel's Government and Knesset*, HC 3091/99 (not published).
49. For example, section 57 of the Models and Patents Order (author's translation), SH, 105, (canceled in correction no. 9, 2008); section 32 (*Over Time*) of the Annual Vacation Law, 1951 (author's translation); section 5 (*Nightshift*) of the Working and Rest Hours Law, 1951 (author's translation); and section 37 (*Trespassing in a Closed Military Zone*) of the Civil Wrongs Ordinance (Consolidated Version).
50. IR, supp. 1 (1948): 73.
51. IR, supp. 2 (September 20, 1948): 145.
52. See Adalah, the UN Human Rights Committee—Information Sheet no. 1: State of Emergency (22 July 2003).
53. The Prevention of Terrorism (Amendment) Law, 1980, SH, 1980, 187.
54. Section 4(7) of this law; see also Hofnung 2001, 208.
55. More dependent laws include: the Ship Order (Limitation of Transfer and Mortgaging),1948; the Fire Arms Law, 1949; the Absentees' Property Law, 1950, SH, no. 37, 86 (March, 20, 1950); the Extension of Emergency Regulation Law (Legal Administration and Additional Regulations), 1969; the Extension of Emergency Regulations Law, 1973; the Order for the Extension of the Validity of Emergency Regulations (Supervision over Watercrafts) [Consolidated Version], 1973; and Security Service (Consolidated Version), SH, 105, 1986.

56. See Dowty 1988, 43.
57. See also Hofnung 2001, 66, 75–76.
58. SH, 20, 1983 (author's translation). More laws of this sort include the Security Service (Combined Version), 1986, SH, 105; the Term Renewal Law, 1975 (author's translation); and the Emergency Labor Service Law, 1967, SH, 5727, 86.
59. More laws from this category include section 32 of the Annual Vacation Law, 1951, SH, 324 (author's translation); section 6 of the Prohibition of Night Backing, SH, 1951, 61 (author's translation); section 191 of the Social Security Law (Consolidated Version), SH, 1968, 212 (author's translation); sections 103 and 127 of the Penal Law, 1977, SH, 226; and section 29(1) of the Legal Procedure Law (Consolidated Version), 1982, SH, 1982, 43 (which prevents detainees from meeting their lawyers).
60. New Version, 421.
61. Author's translation.
62. SH, 1968, 212. Author's translation.
63. SH, 226.
64. IR, 1949, supp. 1, 173.
65. IR, 1949, supp. 1, 170. Author's translation.
66. The Police Ordinance, 1926, and the Criminal Law Ordinance, 1936, are two more mandatory laws that have connections to emergency powers. These laws hinder the right to protest. Both were corrected in 1960 by a case law and thereafter the procedure granted the authority to disqualify demonstration to the regional police chief and only with reason (*Levi v. the Police Commander of the South Region*, HC 153/83, 38 (2) PD, 393).
67. Regulation 94 states, "The regional supervisor is authorized as he sees fit, and without providing any reasons, to refuse to grant such a permit."
68. SH, 226, 1977.
69. SH, 172, 1957.
70. See also, Hofnung 2001, 109.
71. See more in ibid., 110–114.
72. Article 49 of the Fourth Geneva Convention. As we can see, international law has dual objectives. On the one hand, it seeks to protect the occupied population, but on the other, it allows the belligerent occupier to use emergency powers when it concerns security necessities.

73. Benvenisti 1987, 145.
74. This matter is no longer crucial since Jordan officially declined all claims on the West Bank in 1988.
75. See Goldstein 1978, 36.
76. It was only recognized by the UK and Pakistan, Egypt never claimed to have sovereignty over the Gaza Strip.
77. Palestine International Documents on Human Rights 1948–1972, UN General Assembly, October 26, 1970, report of the special committee to investigate israeli practices affecting human rights of the population of the occupied territories, UN Doc. A/8089, 18–20. Michael Goldstein asserts that the Israeli side's argument has validity because "It does seem rather strange that measures that would be justified under articles of the Fourth Geneva Convention can be declared invalid because they conflict with other articles of the same international agreement" (1978, 37).

Chapter 4

1. SH, 226, 1977.
2. In an additional case, *Social Security Labor Union v. the Minister of Labor and Welfare*, HC 188/79, 35 PD, 449, and in *Niztan v. Shlomo Lahat*, 35 (1) PD, 555, the court rejected the argument that having a special labor court implies that such issues would be handled in this institution. See Cohn 1998, 654.
3. *Mdinovest v. the Health Ministry CEO*, HC 256/88, 44 (1) PD, 19; *H.S.A v. the Minister of Labor and Welfare*, HC 344/89, 44 (1) PD, 456; and *Poraz v. The State of Israel*, HC 2994/90, 44 (3) PD, 317. See Cohn 1998, 652–660.
4. See chapter 3, note 5.
5. KT, no. 226 (December 10, 1951): 286.
6. SH, no. 93, 134 (March 13, 1952); LSI, vol. 6, 39.
7. Emergency Regulation (for the Extension of the Validity of Emergency Regulations), 1951. In this respect, one emergency legal mechanism extends the validity of other emergency source.
8. A series of renewals laws such as the Emergency Regulation (Continuance in Force of Validity of Provisions), 1951 or the Order for the Extension of the Validity of Defence Regulations (Finance).
9. SH, 1957, 24.

10. SH, 1978, 108.
11. There are numerous accounts on the Israeli regime in the OPT. See, for example, Meron 1987; Kretzmer 2002; Galchinsky 2004, Ben-Naftali et al. 2007; Gordon 2008; and Azoulay and Ophir 2008.
12. Military Order 224 (1968) explicitly reaffirms the validity of mandatory regulations in the OPT, and Military Order 378 (1970) repeats the provision concerning administrative detentions.
13. Entry into Israel Law, 1952; Defence Services Law, 1959; Chamber of Advocates Law, 1961; Income Tax—Amendment in 1980; Population Register Law, 1965; Emergency Labor Services Law, 1967; National Insurance (Consolidated Version), 1968; Psychologist Law, 1968; and Emergency Regulations Extension (Registration of Equipment) Law, 1981.
14. Section 6(b), Criminal Jurisdiction and Legal Aid Law. See also Shehada 1985, 66.
15. See B'Tselem, 2002, 50–51
16. Paragraph 147 of the Knesset Election Law, SH, 1969, 103.
17. Section 3(e) of the Law of Cities and Urban Development.
18. See Shehadeh 1993, 42–44, 74–75. In December 1987, the Israeli authorities published Military Order 1213, according to which Jewish settlers were excluded from a previous Military Order (65) prohibiting non-residents from working in the West Bank without permission; hence, it declared Jewish settlers to be residents. See, Shehadeh 1993, 120–121.
19. See also Hofnung 2001, 297.
20. KT 2069, 1967, 2741. Later this administrative order was renewed as a renewal law, the Law for the Correction and the Extension of the Validity of Emergency Regulations (Judea, Samaria and the Gaza Strip, Criminal Jurisdiction and Legal Aid), 1977. As we can see, at that time the title of the occupied territories were changed from "areas held by the Defence Army of Israel" to "Judea, Samaria and the Gaza Strip." This conversion was motivated by a heated debate in the Knesset during this enactment when the question about the legal standing of and relations with the OPT was raised during the deliberations. Since the Oslo Accord, the law has not been valid in area A, which is under Palestinian rule, and in any case, there are no Israeli settlers in that area. An additional administrative order, which was extended by the renewal law, was

the Emergency Regulation (Areas Held by the Defence Army of Israel—Service of Documentation), 1969, (KT, 2482, 460), which helped organize legal procedures among settlers and themselves and between Israeli citizens and Palestinians.
21. Israel's remaining private lands are more or less equally divided between Jews and Palestinians. This "equality," however, is deceptive. Israel's public land is not, in practice, available for Palestinians.
22. See Lustick 1987, 260.
23. The official Israeli justification for these security zones was that Palestinians were considered a hostile population. An armed clash between the parties had just occurred and Israel's officials feared that the Palestinians who lived near the borders might support enemy forces. But it was also politically motivated, namely to prevent the return of Palestinian refugees, to support the ruling Mapai party, and most significantly, for land expropriation. See Jiryis 1969. Moreover, even Israeli officials argued as much. A secret appendix to a report issued by a three-man committee, appointed by Ben-Gurion to review whether the power of the military government could be restricted, asserted that the main reason for the military government was land. See "The Problem of Security Settlement by Jews in the Area of the Military Government," by Y. Salomon, a member of this committee, in his memoir, *In My Own Way,* quoted in Kretzmer 1990, 155, note 2.
24. Though the military regime ended in 1966, these regulations continued to be renewed until 1972.
25. See Korn 2004.
26. Data from Jiryis 1969, 15, 17.
27. In 1949 the security zones presided over 90 percent of the Palestinian population see. Lustick 1987, 176.
28. See the State Comptroller Report no. 9 on the Defense Ministry for 1957–1958, 78; and Kretzmer 1990, 124. For an exception to the case in which a Jewish citizen appealed against the military government, see *Beker v. the Food Supervisor*, HC 44/50, 4 PD, 542.
29. Later, in 1949, the Emergency Regulation (Requisition of Property) was made into law.
30. See also Hofnung 2001, 164–165.
31. IR 37, 59. This regulation later was replaced by a primary law: *Absentees' Property Law* (LSI, vol. 37 [1950]: 86). As a result of

this enactment, no Palestinians were allowed to return, regardless of the reason they had left, even if they simply waited until the battle's end to return to their home. The outcome also included internal absentees, or as the Israeli authorities termed them, present-absentees. This group found themselves inside the territory of the state of Israel, but unable to return to their homes and lands. These lands were either placed under the management of the Development Authority or sold to the Jewish National Fund (JNF), which is a Jewish organization, not a state institution. Moreover, the wording of the absentee enactment gives an incentive to leave the state of emergency in force, since the validity of one's status as an absentee is conditioned by an official declaration of a state of emergency.

32. A unit of area used in the Ottoman Empire: one dunam equals one thousand square meters.
33. See Forman and Kedar 2004, 814.
34. Quoted in Jiryis 1969, 46.
35. One exception was *Kol Haham* (HCJ 73/53).
36. CA, 25/55, *The Custodian of Abandoned Property v. Sammara Al-Rabi*, 209. See also Jiryis 1969, 62. Without the remedy of the court, this law asserted that "the custodian may not be questioned about the information sources which led him to issue a decision by virtue of this law." This certificate serves as a verdict based on the fact that the custodian was his own judge in matters in which he sought favorable verdicts for himself (HC 43/49. 932).
37. The court did rule in favor of Al-Ard's right to form a company, but on formalistic grounds *Qardosh v. The Registrar of Companies*, HC 241/60, 15 PD, 1151 (19 May 1961).
38. Whereas the Israeli authorities from time to time used emergency powers against the Communist party's institutions and members—the most well-known event being *Kol Haham* in 1953 (HCJ 73/53), in which the government attempted to terminate publication of its newspaper—the Communist party, which was jointly operated, was never prevented from partaking in Israel's body politic. Al-Ard, on the other hand, was excluded.
39. Palestinians can have an active role as policymakers only in local municipal government. See Saban 2002, 277–288, 299, 302, and 306–307.
40. Israel's authorities not only denied Al-Ard's right to associate,

but also, using its emergency powers, moved to ban the movement altogether. Three days after the court's decision, in mid-November 1964, three of the movement's leaders were authorized to be arrested under Mandatory Emergency Regulation 84(1)b. According to press accounts, the reason for their arrest was that infiltrators had been captured across the border with orders to contact the leaders of Al-Ard (see Landau 1969, 99). Eventually, in the absence of a formal accusation, all three were released and put under house arrest, also according to a mandatory emergency regulation (see Jiryis 1969, 325; Zureik 1979, 174). Then, on November 23, 1964, under the power granted by the mandatory emergency regulations, the minister of defense published a decree stating, "The group of people known as Al-Ard . . . are an illegal association." *Ylakut ha-Pirsomim* (official state publication), 1134, 1965, 638 (23 November 1964).

41. *Jiryis v. The Haifa District Commissioner*, HC 253/64, 18 (4) PD (11 November 1964). Perhaps it was the unapologetic "celebration" of Palestinian nationalism and the independence of the Al-Ard movement. Al-Ard's true intentions are a matter of some debate. What we do know is that Al-Ard members operated in the public, and at least in their pursuit to establish themselves as an association and later as a political party, did not act violently. I bring here Al-Ard's platform in full.

> The Association will act to achieve the following aims or a part thereof: 1. Raising the educational, scientific, health, economic, and political level of its members. 2. Bringing complete equality and social justice among *all* strata of the people of Israel. 3. Finding a just solution for the Palestinian problem, through its consideration as an *indivisible unit*—in accordance with the wish of the Palestinian Arab people; a solution which meets its interests and desires, restores to it its political existence, ensures its full legal rights, and regards it as the framework of the *supreme wishes of the Arab nation*. 4. Supporting the movement of liberation, unity, and socialism in the Arab world, in all *lawful* ways, while considering as *the deciding power in the Arab world*—a factor which should make *Israel* regard it in a positive manner. 5. Acting to make peace prevail in

the world in general, and in the Middle East in particular.
6. Supporting all movements of progress everywhere in the world, opposing imperialism, and assisting all peoples desirous of freeing themselves from it.

Taken from Landau 1969, 102–103; (emphasis added).

42. Responding to a challenge from both the left and the right that denied the idea that the state of Israel could be at the same time both Jewish and democratic, the Knesset, in 1985, formally enacted into law the doctrine previously defined by the Court in *Yardor* as defensive democracy. Section 7A(1) of the amendment to the Basic Law: The Knesset disqualifies candidates' lists if they deny "the existence of the State of Israel as the state of the Jewish people." Sections 7A(2 and 3) were a direct respond to the attack from the right (the Kach party). These sections disqualify candidates if they reject Israel's democracy or support racism. While this enactment appears to be a moderate compromise against attacks from the radical right and left, its meaning, which became Israel's formal policy, is far from moderate. The rejection of racism does not in any way deny representation; on the contrary, it protects representation. Yet Israel's national identity as the state of the Jews officially asserted under-representation of political views in Israel, meaning that Palestinians who are Israeli citizens ultimately lack the ability to shape political policy. The result is that no political body can push to revoke all formal discrimination, chief among which is land allocation.
43. See also Neiberger 1996, 6.
44. See Peled 1992, 437; Kretzmer 1990, 22–26; and Gavizon 1986.

Chapter 5

1. Additional scholarship that mentions this phenomenon references Mironi's article. See Cohn 1998, 623; and Hofnung 1996, 58–59.
2. See chapter 1, page 000.
3. Kahan argues that this finding is based on the following factors: temporariness, systemization: breadth, entrenchment and opt-out, public awareness and comprehension, special interests, and dialectic of the other.
4. Gadi Algazi (2006), in an article titled "Matrix in Bil'in" (published in English as "Offshore Zionism"), offers a powerful illustration of

the mix between political and capitalist interests that are achieved under the cover of the occupation. As he describes, the state of Israel has used its powers as an occupying force to help software firms and real-estate developers (some are international companies) to build a settlement and a high-tech industry park. This episode accounts for multiple degrees of exploitation and oppression affecting several disadvantaged populations: Orthodox Jews with large families looking for cheap housing, Orthodox Jewish women who are exploited as a source of cheap labor, and the most oppressed population, the Palestinians, whose land is expropriated.
5. See chapter 2, 000–000.
6. In 1992, the Law and Administration Ordinance, 1948 was replaced by Basic Law: The Government as the source for administrative emergency orders. However, our discussion ends before 1992.
7. See "Custom (in Canon Law)," *The Catholic Encyclopedia*. See also chapter 2.
8. See "Custom (in Canon Law)," *The Catholic Encyclopedia*.
9. The title is taken from Scheuerman 1999, 1870.
10. SH, 1957, 24.
11. SH, 1978, 108.
12. IR 9, 48, July 14, 1948.
13. Ibid.
14. Ibid.
15. KT 261, April 11, 754.
16. Source: David Levi-Faur's Database, which is based on Israel's formal legal publication.
17. SH, 1957, 24.
18. Source: David Levi-Faur's Database.
19. SH, 1996, 192.
20. See also Cohn 1999, 658–659.
21. *The Attorney General v. Austriher Cr. A.*, 63\156, 17 PD, 2088.
22. For example, AD 5/80, APA"I *Cooperative Association v. the Minister of Commerce and Tourism*, 24 (3) PD, 277, 280.
23. In the first case (*Medinust v. the CEO of the Minister of Health*, HC 256/88, 44 [1] PD, 19), the court disqualified the use of an administrative emergency order, despite ruling that the administrative emergency order stood the test of the criteria. The court revoked the administrative emergency order based on the authorized-authority rationale regarding the use of the administrative

emergency order. In the second case, (*International Trade Incorporated v. The Minister of Commerce and Industry*, HC344/89, 44 [1] PD, 456), the court invalidated the administrative order because it did not meet the criteria. See also HC 226/68 and HC 2994/90.
24. SH, 108, 1978.
25. The title "confinement decree" is not official and does not appear in the law; rather, it comes from recruitment orders issued during the 1948 War.
26. See Maman 2008, 140.
27. Enacting Emergency Regulations in Coping with Strikes in Essential Services. Attorney General Guidelines, guideline no. 21.588. See also Cohn 1999, 662–663, 683.
28. See also Halevi 1986, 254.
29. Israel's currency later changed to the Shekel, and then to the New Shekel.
30. This section appears in the short version. A similar section appears at the end of the longer versions as well.
31. KT 1261, February 11, 1962
32. KT 2734
33. I could not find anything in the relevant scholarship to support this hypothesis.
34. KT 3246.
35. MO, 564.
36. The short version.
37. See, among others, Halevi 1986; and Zilberfarb 2005.
38. KT 3774.
39. The Transactions in Foreign Currency Decree (KT 3775) was based on the Mandatory Defense (Finance) Regulation, 1941, and Emergency (Cancelation of the Services Import Tax and the Travel Tax, and Correction of the Value Added Tax Law) Regulation (KT 3775).
40. KT 3775.
41. The second enactment used to execute the new plan was executed with an amendment to the Bank of Israel Law, 1954. While this regulation was not an emergency enactment, it still did not require the Knesset's approval.
42. No. 1, November 4, KT 4724, and no. 2, November 27, KT 4734.
43. KT 4826.
44. Source: David Levi-Faur's Database.

Chapter 6

1. The Israeli government, through its control of the Knesset and the lack of a fully legislated binding constitution, has the power to enact any law, even if it contradicts liberal and democratic conventions.
2. See Volcansek and Stack 2011, 72–133.
3. For a good survey, see Hatchard 1993.
4. For a good survey on South America, see Loveman 1994.
5. A state of siege, to be exact.
6. The Despouy Report ends its review in 1997. See also Neocleous 2006, 203.
7. "By the early 1970s, government by emergency declarations had become routine" (Belknap 1983, 68). Belknap quotes Senators Frank Church and Charles Mathias, who declared in 1974, "Emergency government has become the norm." STAFF OF SENATE SPECIAL COMM. ON NATIONAL EMERGENCIES AND DELEGATED EMERGENCY POWERS, 93D CONG., 2D SEss., A BRIEF HISTORY OF EMERGENCY POWERS IN THE UNITED STATES at v (Comm. Print 1974).
8. According to Neocleous, it is "the biggest political myth".
9. See also Fisken 2004, 29.
10. Schmitt 2005; quoted from Hussain 2007, 374.
11. In fact, he argues that even sovereign gaps, which are instances in which the sovereign denies the positive aspect of life management (obviously echoing Foucault), are a sign of sovereignty. Ann Stoler joins Ophir in arguing that "being an effective empire has long been contingent on partial visibility—sustaining the ability to remain an unaccountable one" (2006, 142).
12. Studies of colonial (or imperial) law reflect similar conclusions.
13. Levinson 2015 and Hecht 2015.

BIBLIOGRAPHY

Primary Sources

Official Gazette during the Provisional Council of State.
The State of Israel Official Publication: Laws of the State of Israel—Authorized English Translation of Laws Promulgated by the Knesset.
The State of Israel Official Publication: Protocols of Knesset Proceedings.
The State of Israel Official Publication: Bills Presented to the Knesset.
Fundamental Laws of the State of Israel, edited by Joseph Badi. New York: Twayne Publications, 1961.
The State of Israel Official Publication: Regulations Issued by Ministers of the Government.
The State of Israel Official Publication: Government Notices.
The State of Israel Official Publication: Decisions of the Supreme Court

Court Cases

Cook v. the Minister of Defence, The Law. HC 1–2/48, vol. 3, 307 (1948). Not officially published.
Levon v. Gubernik. HC 5/48, 1 PD, 58 (1948).
El Karbutli v. Minister of Defence. HC 7/48, 2 PD, 2 (January 3, 1949).

Ziv v. Gubernik. HC 10/48, 1 PD, 85 (1948).
Akiva Baron v. the Prime Minister of Israel. HC 16/1948, 1 PD, 109 (December 8, 1948).
Laib and Zvi Abramovitz v. the Competent Authority for Emergency Regulations [Yehoshoa Governik]. HC 29/48, 2 PD, 283 (March 1, 1949).
Aharon Shainan v. the Competent Authority for Emergency Regulations [Yehoshoa Governik]. HC 22/49, 2 PD, 654 (July 22, 1949).
Tanus Ashkar v. the Supervisor over Absentee Property, the Northern District. HC 43/49, 2 PD, 926 (Dec. 6 49).
Naif Salim v. the IDF General Chief of Staff. HC 95/49, 4 PD, 34 (February 2, 1950).
Subhi El-Ayubi v. the Minister of Defence. HC 46/50, 4 PD, 222 (May 26, 1950).
Michlin v. the Minister of Health. HC 70/50, 4 PD, 319 (June 1, 1950).
Mavda Hana Daud v. the Minister of Defence. HC 64/51, 5 PD, 1117 (July 31, 1951).
Aslan v. Military Governor of Galilee. HC 220/51, 5 PD, 1480 (November 30, 1951)
Mavda Hana Daud v. the Security Zones Appeal Committee, the Office of the Military Governor of the Galilee. HC 239/51, 6 PD, 229 (February 25, 1952).
Bilar v. the Minister of Finance. HC 243/52, 7 PD, 424 (April 9, 1953).
Mustafa Saad Badar v. the Minister of the Interior. HC 8/52, 7 PD, 366 (February 19, 1953).
Haya Kaufman v. the Minister of the Interior. HC 111/53, 7 PD, 534 (June 9, 1953).
Nahmud Rashid Abu Josh v. Yitzhak Rabin, the Military Commander of the Region of Jerusalem. HC 118/53, 7 PD, 941 (November 10, 1953).
Jamal Mahmud Atzlan v. the Military Governor of the Galilee. HC 288/51, HC 33/52, 9 PD, 689 (April 28 1955).
Mantzur Tufik Kardush v. the Public Associations Registrar. HC 241/60, 16 PD, 1151 (May 19, 1961).
Yaakov Yardor v. The Chairman of the Election Central Committee. EA 1/65, 19(3) PD, 365.
Azmi Ibrahim Mrar v. the Minister of Defence. HC 17/71, 25a PD, 141 (January 20, 1971).
Negev Automobile Service Station Ltd v. State of Israel. HC 107/73, 28(1) PD 640.

Klofer-Nave v. The Minister of Culture & Education. HC 372/84, 35(3) PD, 233.
Poraz v. Government of Israel. HC 2994/90, 44(3) PD, 317.
Bank Mizrachi v. Migdal. CA 6821/93, 49(4) PD, 221.
Meatreal Ltd v. Knesset. HC 4676/94, 50(5) PD, 15, 28.
The Association for Civil Rights in Israel v. Israel's Government and Knesset. HC 3091/99 (not published).
Ajuri v. IDF Commander. HC 7015/02, 56(6) PD, 352.
Herut National Movement v. Chairman of Central Elections Committee. HC 212/03, 57 (1) PD, 750.
Adalah: Legal Center for Arab Minority Rights in Israel and 15 others v. the Minister *of the Interior and 4 Others.* HC 7052/03, 61(2) PD, 202.
Beit Sourik Village Council v. The Government of Israel and the Commander of the *IDF Forces in the West Bank.* HC 2056/04, 58(5) PD, 807
The Gaza Coast Regional Council v. the Knesset. HC 1661/05, 59(2) PD, 481.

Statutes

Palestine (Defence) Order in Council of 1937. *Palestine Gazette*, no. 675, supp. 2 (1937): 267.
Emergency Powers (Defence of the Colonies) Order in Council of 1939. *Palestine Gazette*, supp. 2, 545 (1939); and *Palestine Gazette*, supp. 2 (1940): 1118
Emergency (Defence) Regulations of 1945. *Palestine Gazette*, no. 1422, supp. 2 (1945): 1055–1098.
Law and Administration Ordinance. 1948. IR, 5708, 1; LSI 1, 7 (1948).
Prevention of Terrorism Ordinance, 1948. IR, 73 (1948).
Emergency (Security Zones) Regulations. 1949. KT 11 (April 4, 1949): 169.
General Amnesty Ordinance. IR, supp. 1 (1949): 173.
Emergency Regulation (Continuance in Force of Validity of Provisions). KT 226 (December 10, 1951): 286.
Civil Defence Law. SH, 78 (1951).
Evidence Ordinance (New Version). LSI, 421 (1971).
The Penal Law. SH, 226 (1977).

Emergency Powers (Detention) Law, 1979.
Carrying and Presenting Identification Law, 1982. SH, 20 (1983).
Basic Law: The Government. SH, no. 1780, 158. (March 7, 2001).

Books and Articles

Ackermann, Bruce. "The Emergency Constitution." *The Yale Law Journal*, Volume 113, no. 5 (2004): 1029–1091.

Acktzin, Benjamin. "Bilar Precedent and the Israeli Legal System." *Hapraklit* 10, 1953. (Hebrew.)

Agamben, Giorgio. *Home Sacer*. Stanford University Press, 1998.

———. *State of Exception*. Chicago: University of Chicago Press, 2005.

Alavi, Hamza. "The State in Post-Colonial Societies: Pakistan and Bangladesh." *New Left Review* I/74 (July–August 1972).

Algazi, Gadi. "Matrix in Bil'in: A Story of Colonial Capitalism in Current Israel." *Theory and Criticism* 29 (2006): 173–192. (Hebrew.)

Arato, Andrew. "Politics of Emergency: The Bush Tribunals and the Specter of Dictatorship." *Constellations* 9, no. 4 (2002): 457–476.

———. "Their Creative Thinking and Ours: Ackerman's *Emergency Constitution* after *Hamdan*." *Constellations* 13, no. 4 (2006): 546–572.

———. "Constituent Power in War Time: Ten Theses." Lecture at the Democratic Citizenship and War Workshop, Tel Aviv University, 2007.

Arendt, Hanna. *The Origins of Totalitarianism*. New York: Harcourt Brace Jovanovich, 1994.

Avital, Tomer. "This Is the Way Information Is Concealed: Beyond Closed Doors, Secret Protocols and Secret Envelops." *Kalkalist*, June 16, 2013.

Azoulay, Ariella, and Adi Ophir. *This Regime Which Is Not One: Occupation and Democracy Between the Sea and the River (1967–)*. Tel Aviv: Resling Publishing, 2008. (Hebrew.)

Barak, Aharon. "The Constitutional Revolution: Protected Human Rights." *Mishpat VeMimshal* A9 (1992): 29–30. (Hebrew.)

———. *The Judge in a Democracy*. Princeton, NJ: Princeton University Press, 2006.

Barak-Erez, Daphne. *Milestone Judgments of the Israeli Supreme Court*. Israel: Ministry of Defence, 2006. (Hebrew.)

———. "Governmental Instability in Israel: Is It All the Fault of the Electoral System?" *The Law & Business Journal* (IDC Law Review), 2012: 493–509.

Barzilai, Gad. *Wars, Internal Conflicts and Political Order: A Jewish Democracy in the Middle East*. Albany: State University of New York Press, 1996.

———. "Political Institutions and Conflict Resolution—The Israeli Supreme Court and the Peace Process." In *The Middle East Peace Process: Interdisciplinary Perspectives*, edited by Ilan Peleg. Albany: State University of New York Press, 1998. 87–105.

Belknap, Michal R. "The New Deal and the Emergency Powers Doctrine." *Texas Law Review* 62 (1983): 67–109.

Ben-Eliezer, Uri. *The Making of Israeli Militarism*. Bloomington: Indiana University Press, 1998.

Ben-Naftali, Orna, Miri Sharon, and Aeyal M. Gross. "Reflections on the Legal Structure of the Occupation Regime." *Theory and Criticism* 31 (2007): 205–218. (Hebrew)

Benjamin, Walter. *Illuminations: Essays and Reflections*. New York: Harourt Brace Jovanovich, 1968.

———. "On the Concept of History." Translated by Harry Zohn. In *Selected Writings, Vol. 4: 1938–1940*, edited by Howard Eiland and Michael W. Jennings. Cambridge, MA: Belknap Press, 2003.

Benton, Lauren. *Law and Colonial Cultures: Legal Regimes in World History, 1400–1900*. New York: Cambridge University Press, 2002.

———. *A Search for Sovereignty: Law and Geography in European Empire*. New York: Cambridge University Press, 2010.

Benvenisti, Meron. *The West Bank Handbook: A Political Lexicon*. Jerusalem: The West Bank Data Project and the Jerusalem Post, 1987.

Bernet, Moshe. *A Nation Like Any Nation: Towards the Establishment of an Israeli Republic*. Jerusalem: Carmel, 2009. (Hebrew)

Bishara, Azmi. "The Arab Minority in Israel." *Theory and Criticism* 3 (1993): 20–27. (Hebrew)

Bracha, Baruch. "Restriction of Personal Freedom without Due Process of Law According to the Defence (Emergency) Regulations, 1945." *Israel Yearbook on Human Rights* 8 (1973): 296–323.

Chatterjee, Partha. *The Nation and Its Fragments: Colonial and Postcolonial Histories*. Princeton: Princeton University Press, 1993.

Cohn, Margit. "'The Practice of Patching' in Emergency Legislation," *Mishpatim* 29 (1998): 623–688. (Hebrew.)

Cole, David. "Judging the Next Emergency: Judicial Review and Individual Rights in Times of Crisis." *Michigan Law Review* 101, no. 8 (2003): 2565-2595.

———. "The Priority of Morality: The Emergency Constitution's Blind Spot." *The Yale Law Journal* 113, no. 8 (2004): 1753–1800.

Darian-Smith, Eve, and Peter Fitzpatrick, eds. *Laws of the Postcolonial.* Ann Arbor: University of Michigan Press, 1999.

Dotan, Yoav. "A Constitution for Israel? The Constitutional Dialogue after 'the Constitutional Revolution." *Mishpatim* 27 (1997): 149–209 (Hebrew.)

Dowty, Alan. "The Use of Emergency Powers in Israel." *Middle East Review* 21, no. 1 (1988): 34–46.

———. "Is Israel Democratic? Substance and Semantic in the 'Ethnic Democracy,'" *Israel Studies* 4, no. 1 (1999): 1–15.

Dyzenhaus, David. "Schmitt v. Dicey: Are States of Emergencies Inside or Outside the Legal Order?" Presentation at Columbia University, Fall 2005.

———. *The Constitution of Law: Legality in a Time of Emergency.* Cambridge University Press, 2006.

Elef-Shilo, Michal. "How to Control Secondary Legislation? Analysis of the Control Mechanism Over Secondary Legislation in Israel." MA thesis, Hebrew University, 2012.

Forman, Geremy, and Alexandre (Sandy) Kedar. "From Arab Land to 'Israel Lands': The Legal Dispossession of the Palestinians Displaced by Israel in the Wake of 1948." *Environment and Planning D: Society and Space* 22 (2004): 809–830.

Fraenkel, Ernst. *The Dual State: A Contribution to the Theory of Dictatorship.* Translated by E. A. Shils, in collaboration with Edith Lowenstein and Klaus Knorr. Oxford University Press, 1941.

Ferejohn, John, and Pasquale Pasquino. "The Law of Exception: A Typology of Emergency Powers." *The International Journal of Constitutional Law* 2, no. 2 (2004): 210–239.

Fisken, Tim. "After the Rule of Law: The State and the State of Exception in an Age of Globalization." *Critical Sense* 12, no. 1 (2004): 11–40.

Friedmann, Daniel. "Does Israel Have a Constitution and Who Wrote it?" *The Law and Business Journal* (IDC Law Review) (2012): 117–153.

Gal-Nor, Yitzak. "The 1984 Election's Result and the Uncertainty that Follows." *State, Government and International Relations* 25 (1985): 34–45. (Hebrew.)

Galchinsky, Michael. "The Jewish Settlements in the West Bank: International Law and Israeli Jurisprudence." *Israel Studies* 9, no. 3 (2005): 115–136.

Gavison, Ruth. "The Constitutional Revolution: Reality or Self-Fulfilling Prophecy?" *Mishpatim* 27 (1997): 23–147. (Hebrew.).

———. "Jewish and Democratic? A Rejoinder to the Ethnic Democracy Debate." *Israel Studies* 4, no. 1 (1999): 44–72.

Gavison, Ruth, Mordechai Kremnitzer, and Yoav Dotan. *Judicial Activism: For and Against, the Role of the High Court of Justice in Israeli Society*. Jerusalem: Magnes Press, 2000. (Hebrew.)

Gazit, Shlomo. *The Carrot and the Stick: Israel's Policy in Judea and Samaria, 1967–68*. Washington, DC: B'nai Brith Books, 1995.

Golan, Tal. "The Democratic Deficit of the State Economic Regularization Emergency Law (Hok Hahesderim) and the Decline of the Israeli Welfare State." *Law and Government* (Mishpat VeMimshal) 11 (2008); 243 (Hebrew.).

Goldstein, Michael. "Israeli Security Measures in the Occupied Territories: Administrative Detention." *Middle East Journal* 32, no. 1 (Winter 1978): 35–44

Gordon, Neve. *Israel's Occupation*. California: University of California Press, 2008.

Gross, Aeyal M. "The Politics of Rights in Israeli Constitutional Law." *Israel Studies* 3, no. 2 (1998): 80–118.

Gross, Oren. "Chaos and Rules: Should Responses to Violent Crises Always Be Constitutional?" *The Yale Law Journal* 112, no. 5 (2003): 1011-1134.

———. "The Prohibition on Torture and the Limits of Law." In *Torture: A Collection*, edited by S. Levinson. Oxford University Press, 2004. 229–256.

———. "Constitutions and Emergency Regimes." In *Comparative Constitutional Law*, edited by Tom Ginsburg and Rosalind Dixon. Edward Elgar Pub, 2013. 334–355.

Gross, Oren, and Fionnuala Ní Aoláin. *Law in Times of Crisis: Emergency Powers in Theory and Practice*. New York: Cambridge University Press, 2006.

Greene, Alan. "Separating Normalcy from Emergency: The Jurisprudence of Article 15 of the European Convention on Human Rights." *German Law Journal* 12, no. 10 (2011): 1764-1785.

Halevi, Nadav. "Perspectives on the Balance of Payments." In *The Israeli Economy: Maturing through Crises*, edited by Yoram Ben-Porath. Cambridge, MA: Harvard University Press, 2003: 241–263.

Hatchard, John. "States of Siege/Emergency in Africa" *Journal of African Law* 37, no. 1 (1993): 104–108

Harris, Ron. "Arab Politics in a Jewish State: El-Ard Movement and the Supreme Court." *Plilim, the Multi- Disciplinary Journal of Public Law, Society and Culture* Vol. 10 (2001): 107–155. (Hebrew.).

Hecht, Ravit. "Bennett's Withdrawal" *Haaretz*, http://www.haaretz.co.il/opinions/.premium-1.2689027 (accessed 29 July 2015) (Hebrew.)

Hirschl, Ran. "The Socio-Political Origins of Israel's Juristocracy." *Constellations* 16, no. 3 (2009): 476–492.

Hofnung, Menahem. *Democracy, Law and National Security in Israel*. Dartmouth Publishing Company, 1996.

———. *Israel: Security Needs vs. the Rule of Law*. Jerusalem: Navo Publishing, 2001. (Hebrew.)

Horbitz, Dan, and Moshe Lisk. "Democracy and National Security in an Ongoing Conflict." *Contemporary Judaism* 4 (1988): 27–34.

———. "Forty Years to the Pinal Code." *Mishpatim* 19, no. 4 (1990): 703–723. (Hebrew.)

Horwitz, Morton. "The Rule of Law: An Unqualified Human Good?" *The Yale Law Journal* 86, no. 3 (1977): 561–566.

Huq, Z. Aziz. "Uncertain Law in Uncertain Times: Emergency Powers and Lessons from South Asia." *Constellations* 13, no. 1 (2006): 89–107.

Hussain, Nasser *The Jurisprudence of Emergency: Colonialism and the Rule of Law*. Ann Arbor: University of Michigan Press, 2003.

———. "Beyond Norm and Exception: Guantanamo." *Critical Inquiry* 33, no. 4 (2007): 734–753.

Ichener, Itamar, and Tova Zimoki. "Undermining the Court" Yediot Ahronoth, October 10, 2013.

Jamal, Amal. "The Contradictions of State-Minority Relations in Israel: The Search for Clarifications." *Constellations* 16, no. 3 (2009): 493–508.

Jayasuriya, Kanishka. "The Exception Becomes the Norm: Law and

Regimes of Exception in East Asia" *Asian-Pacific Law & Policy Journal,* 2:1 (Winter 2001), pp. 108-124.

Jiryis, Sabri. *The Arabs in Israel 1948–1966*. Beirut: the Institute for Palestine Studies, 1969.

Jordana, Jacint, and David Levi-Faur, eds. *The Politics of Regulations: Institutions and Regulatory Reforms for the Age of Governance*. Cheltenham, UK: Edward Elgar Publications, 2004.

Kahan, Rebecca M. "Constitutional Stretch, Snap-Back, and Sag: Why Blaisdell Was a Harsher Blow to Liberty than Korematsu." *Northwestern Law Review* 99, 1279–1313.

Kedar, Alexander (Sandy). "The Legal Transformation of Ethnic Geography: Israeli Law and the Palestinian Landholder 1948–1967." *NYU Journal of International Law and Politics* 33, no. 4 (2001): 997–1044.

Kelsen, Hans. *General Theory of Law and State*. New Jersey: the Lawbook Exchange, 1999.

Kimmerling, Baruch. *Zionism and Territory: The Socio-Territorial Dimensions of Zionist Politics*. Berkeley Institute of International Studies: University of California, 1983.

———. "Boundaries and Frontiers of the Israeli Control System: Analytical Conclusions." In *The Israeli State and Society*, edited by Baruch Kimmerling. Albany: State University of New York Press, 1989.

———. "Militarism in Israeli Society." In *Theory and Criticism* 4 (1993): 123–141. (Hebrew.)

Klinghoffer, Hans Y. "On Emergency Regulation in Israel." In *Sefer Yovel Le-Pinhas Rozen*, edited by Haim Cohen. Jerusalem, 1962. (Hebrew.)

Kolsky, Elizabeth. "Codification and the Rule of Colonial Difference: Criminal Procedure in British India." *Law and History Review* 23, no. 2 (2005): 631–683.

Korn, Alina. "Military Government, Political Control and Crime: The Case of Israeli Arabs." *Crime, Law and Social Change* 34, no. 2 (2000): 159–182.

———. "Political Control and Crime: The Use of Defense (Emergency) Regulations during the Military Government." *Adalah's Review* 4: *In The Name of Security* (Spring 2004): 23–32.

Kretzmer, David. *The Legal Status of the Arabs in Israel*. Boulder, CO: Westview Press, 1990.

———. "The HCJ's Review of House Demolitions and Sealing in the Occupied Territories." In *Klinghoffer's Book on Civil Law*. Jerusalem: Hebrew University Press, 1993. 305–357. (Hebrew.)

———. *The Occupation of Justice: The Supreme Court of Israel and the Occupied Territories*. Albany: State University of New York Press, 2002.

Krishna, Sankaran. *Globalization and Postcolonialism: Hegemony and Resistance in the Twenty-First Century*. Rowman & Littlefield, 2008.

Lahav, Pnina. "Rights and Democracy: The Court's Performance." In *Israeli Democracy Under Stress*, edited by Ehud Sprinzak and Larry Diamond. Boulder: Lynne Rienner Publications, 1993. 125–52.

———. *Judgment in Jerusalem: Chief Justice Simon Agranat and the Zionist Century*. Tel Aviv: Am Oved Publishers, 1999. (Hebrew.)

Landau M. Jacob. *The Arabs in Israel: A Political Study*. NY: Oxford University Press, 1969.

Landau, Moshe. "Constituting a Constitution via Court Decisions." *Law and Government* (*Mimshal VeMishpat*, University of Haifa Law Journal), 3, 1996: 697–705.

Lazar, Nomi Claire. *States of Emergency in Liberal Democracies*. New York: Cambridge University Press, 2013.

Levinson, Chaim. "Under Pressure from the Farmers of the Jordan Valley: Bennett Withdrew the Application of Labor laws in the Territories." *Haaretz*. http://www.haaretz.co.il/news/politi/.premium-1.2688436 (accessed 29 July 2015) (Hebrew.)

Levitsky, Nomi. *The Supremes: Inside the Supreme Court*. Bnei Brak, Israel: Hakibutz Hamehuad Publication, 2006. (Hebrew.)

Locke, John. *The Second Treatise on Civil Government*. Edited by Peter Laslett. Cambridge: Cambridge University Press, 1988.

Loveman, Brian. *The Constitution of Tyranny: Regimes of Exception in Spanish America*. Pittsburgh: University of Pittsburgh Press, 1994.

Lustick, Ian. "Arabs in the Jewish State: A Study in the Effective Control of a Minority Population." PhD dissertation. University of California, Berkeley, 1978.

———. *Arabs in the Jewish State: Israel's Control of a National Minority*. Austin, TX: University of Texas Press, 1980.

Mann, Michael. *The Dark Side of Democracy: Explaining Ethnic Cleansing*. New York, NY: Cambridge University Press, 2005.

Maoz, Asher. "The System of Government in Israel." *Tel Aviv University Studies in Law* 8 (1988): 9

Maravall, M. Jose. and Adam Przeworski, eds. *Democracy and the Rule of Law*. New York, NY: Cambridge University Press, 2003.

Massad, Joseph A. "The 'Post-Colonial' Colony: Time, Space, and Bodies in Palestine/Israel" in *The Persistence of the Palestinian Question, Essays on Zionism and the Palestinians*, edited by Joseph A. Massad. New York: Routledge, 2006: 13–40.

Mautner, Menachem. *The Decline of Formalism and the Rise of Values in Israeli Law*. Tel Aviv: Ma'adaley Daat, 1993. (Hebrew.)

———. *Laws and Culture in Israel at the Threshold of the Twenty First Century*. Tel Aviv: Am Oved Publishers, 2008. (Hebrew.)

Medina, Barak. "Four Myths about Judicial Review (in Response to Robert Bork and Richard Posner articles on Justice Aharon Barak's Judicial Activism)." In *Din VeDvarim*, C (2007): 399–427. (Hebrew.)

———. "The Constitutional Principle for Legislating Primary Arrangements: A Response to Yoav Dotan and Gideon Sapir."*Mishpatim* 42 (2012): 449. (Hebrew.)

Mironi, Mordechai. "Back-to-Work Emergency Orders: Government Intervention in Labor Disputes in Essential Services." *Mishpatim* 15 (1986): 350–388. (Hebrew.)

Michaeli, Michael. "The Liberalization of Israel's Foreign-Exchange Market, 1950–2002." In *The Bank of Israel* vol. 2, *Selected Topics in Israel's Monetary Policy*. Edited by Haim Baraki and Nissan Liviatan. Oxford University Press, 2007. 67–97.

Nachmias, David, and Eran Klain. "The State Economic Regularization Emergency Law (Hok Hahesderim): Between Politics and Economy." Position paper. Israel: The Israel Democracy Institute Publication, 1999 (Hebrew).

Navot, Doron. "Is the State of Israel Democratic? The Question of Israel's Democratic State in the Wake of October Events." MA Thesis. Tel Aviv University, 2002. (Hebrew.)

Negbi, Moshe. *Above the Law: The Constitutional Crisis in Israel*. Tel Aviv: Am Oved Publishers, 1987. (Hebrew.)

Neiberger, Benjamin. "National Security and Democracy—Tensions and Dilemmas." In *Democracy and National Security in Israel*, edited by B. Neiberger and A. Ben-Ami. Tel Aviv: The Open University, 1996. 7–31. (Hebrew.)

Neocleous, Mark. "The Problem with Normality: Taking Exception to 'Permanent Emergency.'" *Alternatives: Global, Local, Political* 31 (2006): 191–213.

Neumann, Franz. *The Democratic and the Authoritarian State*. London: The Free Press of Glencoe, 1964.

———. *The Rule of Law: Political Theory and the Legal System in Modern Society*. Leamington Spa: Berg, 1986.

Nitzan, Jonathan, and Shimshon Bichler. *The Global Political Economy of Israel*. London: Pluto Press, 2002.

Ophir, Adi. "Between the Sanctification of Life and Their Abandonment: Instead of an Introduction to Homo Sacer." In *Technologies of Justice: Law, Science and Society*, edited by Shai Lavi. Israel: Ramot, Tel Aviv University, 2003. (Hebrew.)

Oraa, Jaime. *Human Rights in States of Emergency in International Law*. Oxford: Clarendon Press, 1992.

Parush, Adi. "Judicial Activism, Natural Law, and Legal Positivism—Judge Barak and 'The Omnipotent Knesset' Doctrine." *Tel Aviv University Law Review* 17, no. 3, special issue: "Judicial Activism in Israel" (1993): 689–715. (Hebrew.)

Peled, Yoav. "Ethnic Democracy and the Legal Construction of Citizenship: Arab Citizens of the Jewish State." *The American Political Science Review* 86, no. 2 (1992): 432–443.

Peled, Yoav, and Adi Ophir, eds. *Israel: From Mobilized to Civil Society?* Bnei Brak: Van Leer Jerusalem Institute, Hakibbutz Hameuchad Publishing House. (Hebrew.)

Peled, Yoav, and Doron Navot. "Ethnic Democracy Revisited: On the State of Democracy in the Jewish State." *Israel Studies Forum* 20, no. 1 (2005): 3–27.

———. "Towards a Constitutional Counter-Revolution in Israel?" *Constellations* 16, no. 3 (2009): 429–444.

Peled, Yoav, and Gershon Shafir. *Being Israeli: The Dynamics of Multiple Citizenship*. Tel Aviv: Tel Aviv University Press, 2005. (Hebrew.)

Peleg, Ilan. "Jewish-Palestinian Relations in Israel: From Hegemony to Equality?" *International Journal of Politics, Culture and Society* 17, no. 3 (2004): 415–437.

Posner, Richard A. *Not a Suicide Pact: The Constitution in a Time of National Emergency*. New York: Oxford University Press, 2006.

Posner, Richard A., and Adrian Vermeule. "Accommodating Emergencies" In *The Constitution in Wartime: Beyond Alarmism and Complacency*, edited by Mark Tushnet. Durham, NC: Duke University Press, 2005.

Ram, Uri. "Issues and Agendas: The Colonization Perspective in Israeli Sociology: Internal and External Perspectives." *The Journal of Historical Sociology* 6, no. 3 (1993): 327–350.

Rodinson, Maxime. *Israel: A Colonial-Settler State?* New York: Monad Press, 1973.

Raz-Krakotzkin, Amnon. "The Six Months State: Israel, the Occupation and the Dual-Nationality Position." *Mahsom*: http://www.arabs48.com/mahsom/article.php?id=5501. Accessed May 5, 2009. (Hebrew.)

Rivlin, Paul. *The Israeli Economy*. Boulder: Westview Press, 1992.

Rossiter, Clinton L. *Constitutional Dictatorship: Crisis Government in the Modern Democracies*. Princeton, NJ: Princeton University Press, 1948.

Rouhana, Nadim. "The Political Transformation of the Palestinians in Israel: From Acquiescence to Challenge." *Journal of Palestine Studies* 18, no. 3 (Spring 1989): 38–59.

———. *Palestinian Citizens in an Ethnic Jewish State: Identities in Conflict*. New Haven, CT: Yale University Press, 1997.

Rubinstein, Amnon. "Mandatory Emergency (Defense) Regulations: The Verdict and Need for Change." *Hapraclit* 28 (1972): 486–499. (Hebrew.)

———. "The Changing Status of the 'Territories': from Trustee Holding to a Hybrid Legal Frame." *Theoretical Inquiries in Law* 11, no. 3 (1986): 439–456. (Hebrew.)

———. *The Constitutional Law of the State of Israel*. Tel Aviv: Schocken Publishing House, 1996. (Hebrew.)

———. "The Knesset and the Human Rights Basic Laws." *Mimshal and Mishpat* 5, no. 1 (1999): 339–358. (Hebrew.)

———. "The Story of the Basic Laws." *The Law & Business Journal*, 2012: 79–109.

Rubinstein, Amnon, and Alexander Yakobson. *Israel and the Family of Nations: The Jewish Nation State and Human Rights*. New York: Routledge, 2009.

Rubinstein, Elyakim. *Country's Justices: The Beginning and Character of the Israeli Supreme Court*. Tel Aviv: Schocken Publishing House, 1980. (Hebrew.)

Saban, Ilan. "After the Barbarism: Security Legislation, Emergency Powers, and Their Implementations in the Morning After." In

The Morning After: The Era of Peace—Not Utopia, edited by Meron Benvenisti. Jerusalem: Carmel Publishing House, 2002. (Hebrew.)

Sàdi, Ahmad H. "The Peculiarities of Israel's Democracy: Some Theoretical and Practical Implications for Jewish-Arab Relations." *International Journal of Intercultural Relations* 12 (2002): 119–133.

Merry, Sally Engle. "Legal Pluralism." *Law & Society Review* 22, no. 5, (1988): 869–896.

Saltman, Michael. "The Use of the Mandatory Emergency Law by the Israeli Government." *The International Journal of the Sociology of Law* 10 (1982): 385–394.

Salzberger, Eli. "Constituent Authority in Israel." *Law and Government* 3 (1996): 679–696. (Hebrew.)

Salzberger, Eli, and Fania Oz-Salzberger. "The Hidden German Origin of the Israeli Supreme Court." In *Law and History*, edited by Menachem Mautner and Daniel Gutwein. Jerusalem: Zalman Shazar Center for Jewish History, 1999.

Sapir, Gideon. *Constitutional Revolution in Israel: Past, Present and Future*. Tel Aviv: Miskal-Yedioth Ahronoth Books and Chemed Books, Bar-Ilan University Press, and the University of Haifa Press, 2010.

Schauer, Frederick. "Formalism." *The Yale Law Journal* 97, no. 4 (1988): 509–548.

Scheuerman, William E. "The Economic State of Emergency." *Cardozo Law Review* 21 (1999–2000): 1869–1894

———. "Emergency Powers and the Rule of Law after 9/11." *Journal of Political Philosophy* 14, no. 1 (2006): 61–84.

Schmitt, Carl. *The Concept of the Political*. Chicago: University of Chicago Press, 1996.

———. *Nomos of the Earth in the International Law of Jus Publicum Europaeum*. Candor, NY: Telos Press Publishing, 2003.

———. *Political Theology*. Chicago: University of Chicago Press, 2005.

Segal, Zeev. *Standing Rights in the High Court of Justice*. Jerusalem: Shoken, 1988. (Hebrew.)

———. "No More Constitutional Democracy." *Haaretz*, B1 (November 2, 2007). (Hebrew).

Shachar, Yoram. "History and Sources of Israeli Law." In *Introduction to the Law of Israel*, edited by A. Shapira and K. C. De-Witt Arrar. The Hague: Kluwer Law International, 1995.

Shafir, Gershon. *Land, Labor, and the Origins of the Israeli-Palestinian Conflict, 1882–1914*. New York, NY: Cambridge University Press, 1989.

———. "Zionism and Colonialism: A Comparative Approach." In *Israel in Comparative Perspective: Challenging the Conventional Wisdom*, edited by Michael N. Barnett. Albany: State University of New York Press, 1996. 227–242.

Shamir, Ronen. "'Landmark Cases' and the Reproduction of Legitimacy: The Case of Israel's High Court of Justice." *Law & Society Review* 24, no. 3 (1990): 781–806.

——— *The Colonies of Law*. Cambridge: Cambridge University Press, 2000.

———. "The Politics of Reasonableness: Reasonableness as a Juridical Power." In *Israel: From Mobilized to Civil Society*, edited by Yoav Peled and Adi Ophir. Jerusalem: The Van Leer Jerusalem Institute and Hakibbutz Hameuchad, 2001.

Shapira, Amos, and Baruch Baracha. *Basic Principles of Public Law in Israel*. Israel: The Ministry of Defence Publishing House, 1978. (Hebrew.)

Shapiro, Martin. *Courts: A Comparative and Political Analysis*. Chicago: University of Chicago Press, 1981.

Shapiro, Yonatan. *Democracy in Israel*, Tel Aviv: Masada, 1977. (Hebrew)

Shehada, Raja. *Occupier's Law: Israel and the West Bank*. Washington, DC: Institute for Palestine Studies, 1985.

———. *The Law of the Land: Settlements and Land Issues under Israeli Military Occupation*. Jerusalem: PASSIA, 1993.

Sheleff, Lion. "The Green Line Is the Border of Judicial Activism: Queries about Supreme Court Judgment in the Territories." *Tel Aviv University Law Review* 13, no. 3, Special Issue: "Judicial Activism in Israel" (1993): 757–810. (Hebrew.)

Shenhav, Yehouda. "The Imperial History of State of Exception." *Theory and Criticism* 29 (2006): 205–218. (Hebrew.)

Shenhav, Yehouda, and Yael Berda. "The Colonial Foundations of State of Exception: Juxtaposing the Israeli Occupation of Palestinian Territories with Colonial Bureaucratic History." In *Occupation: Israeli Technologies of Rule and Governance in Palestine*, edited by M. Givoni, S. Hanafi, and A. Ophir. New York: Zone Book, 2010.

Shetreet, Shimon. "A Contemporary Model of Emergency Detention Law: An Assessment of the Israeli Law." *Israel Yearbook on Human Rights* 14 (1984): 182–202.

———. "Forty Years to Constitutional Law." *Mishpatim* 19(4) (1990): 573–615. (Hebrew.)

Shohat, Ella. "Notes on the "Post-Colonial." *Social Text* 31/32 (1992): 99–113.

Shprintzak, Heud. *Illegalism in Israeli Society*. Jerusalem: Shocken Publishing House, 1985. (Hebrew.)

Smooha, Sammy. "Minority Status in an Ethnic Democracy: The Status of the Arab Minority in Israel." *Ethnic and Racial Studies* 13, no. 3 (1990):389–413.

Steinmetz, George. *The Devil's Handwriting: Precoloniality and the German Colonial State in Qingdao, Samoa, and Southwest Africa*. Chicago: University of Chicago Press, 2007.

Stoler, Ann. "On Degrees of Imperial Sovereignty." *Public Culture* 18, no. 1 (2006): 125–146.

Taylor Saito, Natsu. *From Chinese Execlusion to Guantanamo Bay: Plenary Power and the Prerogative State*. Boulder: University Press of Colorado. 2007.

Thompson, E. P. *Whigs and Hunters: The Origin of the Black Act*. New York: Pantheon Books, 1975.

Tribe, Laurence H. and Patrick O. Gudridge. "The Anti-Emergency Constitution." *The Yale Law Journal* 113, no. 8 (2004): 1801–1870.

Tushnet, Mark. "Defending Korematsu? Reflections on Civil Liberties in Wartime." *Wisconsin Law Journal* 2 (2005 a): 273–307.

———. "Emergencies and the Idea of Constitutionalism." In *The Constitution in Wartime: Beyond Alarmism and Complacency*, edited by Mark Tushnet. Durham, NC: Duke University Press, 2005.

Tzor, Michal. Position Paper: The Mandatory Defence Emergency Regulations. The Israeli Institute for Democracy, 1999. (Hebrew)

Volcansek, Mary L., and John F. Stack Jr., eds. *Courts and Terrorism: Nine Nations Balance Rights and Security*. New York: Cambridge University Press, 2011.

Weber, Max. *From Max Weber: Essays in Sociology*. Edited by H. H. Gerth and C. Wright Mills. New York: Oxford University Press, 1958.

———. *Economy and Society*, Vol. II. CA: University of California Press.

Wolfgang J. Mommsen. 1984 [1959]. *Max Weber and German Politics, 1890-1920,* Chicago: University of Chicago Press, 1978.

Yiftachel, Oren. *Ethnocracy: Land and Identity Politics in Israel/Palestine.* Philadelphia: University of Pennsylvania Press, 2006.

Yoo, John. *The Powers of War and Peace.* Chicago: University of Chicago Press, 2005.

Zakaria, Fareed. "The Rise of Illiberal Democracy." *Foreign Affairs* 76, no. 6 (1997): 22–43.

———. "Civil Law—Revolution or Development." *Mishpatim* 19, no. 4 (1990): 563–571. (Hebrew.)

Zilberfarb, Ben-Zion. "From Socialism to Free Market—the Israeli Economy, 1943-2003." *Israel Affairs,* (2005) 11:1. 12-22.

Zubida, Hani and David Mekelberg. "The Israeli Political System: Between Governance and Collapse", Israel: Israeli Political Science Association, 2008. (Hebrew)

Zuckerman, Ian. "One Law for War and Peace? Judicial Review and Emergency Powers between the Norm and the Exception" in *Constellations* Vol. 13, Issue 4 (2006): 522-545.

Zureik, T. Elia. *The Palestinians in Israel: A Study in Internal Colonialism.* Boston: Routledge & Kegan Paul, 1979.

INDEX

1977 regulatory reform of foreign exchange, 103
1992 constitutional reform, 28, 38, 45, 48
1992 constitutional revolution, 38, 40, 41, 172, 174–175, 182
1994 amendment, 40, 41

Absentee Law of 1950, 149
Abu Awad v. Commander of the Judea and Samaria Region, 154–155
Ackermann, Bruce, 6, 146, 172
Acktzin, Benjamin, 72, 172
Administrative
  emergency orders, 54–56, 58, 64–74, 87–90, 96–79, 104, 109–114, 116, 121, 165
  legislation, 43, 76, 108
Administration of personal law, 16, 91–92
Agamben, Giorgio, 5, 11, 172
Agranat, Shimon, 33, 100, 178
Al-Ard, 98–101, 162–163
Algazi, Gadi, 165, 172
Allocation of land, 95, 134

Allocation of resources, 22
Altalena, 60, 155
Amendment, 29, 39–41, 68, 70, 89, 91–92, 135, 148, 157, 160, 164, 166
American Postal Workers Union, 117
Aoláin, Fionnuala Ní, 7–8, 10, 137, 145–146, 175
Appeal, 47–49, 69, 74–75, 89, 97, 99, 100, 150, 152, 154, 161
Application of emergency powers, 19, 129, 140
Arab Socialist List, 100–101
Arab-Israeli War of 1948, 114
Arato, Andrew, ix, 146, 172
Areas held by the Defence Army of Israel, 94, 160–161
Arendt, Hannah, 15, 172
Argentina, 137
Article 53 of the Geneva Convention, 87
Asia, 137, 176–177
Aslan v. Military Governor of Galilee, 155, 170

Association (*agudah*), 49, 58, 74, 97, 99, 152, 154, 157, 163, 165, 170, 171, 185
Association for Civil Rights in Israel (ACRI), 74, 157, 171
Attorney General, 28, 45–46, 61, 67, 79, 118, 130, 152, 157, 165–166
Attorney General's Guidelines, 67, 156
Australia, 43
Authorized agency, 87, 112
Authorized agents, 116, 119
Authorizing paragraph, 123, 126

B'Tselem, 160
Back to work, 116, 119–120, 171
Balance of payments (BOP), 122–123, 125, 176
Bank of Israel Law, 1954, 166
Bank of Israel, 126–127, 166, 179
Barak, Aharon, 40–41, 148–149, 151, 171, 179–180
Barzulai, Gad, 148
Basic Law, 30, 35–42, 49, 67–71, 73, 79, 100, 148, 151, 153, 156, 164, 165, 172, 181
Basic Law, Legislation, 30, 35, 39, 42, 151
Basic Law: Basic Human Rights, 39
Begin, Menahem, 34, 62, 74, 155
Beker v. the Food Supervisor, 161
Belgium, 30
Belligerent occupation, 54, 79, 86–87, 90–93
Ben-Gurion, David, 34, 145, 150, 155, 161
Benton, Lauren, 85, 87, 91, 98, 147, 173
Bergman v. Minister of Finance, 150
Bichler, Shimshon, 117, 180
Bilar precedent, 72, 172

Boer War, 57
Bracha, Baruch, 23, 54, 134, 173
Bretton Woods, 124
British colonial enactment, 56
British colonial legal tradition, 59
British colonial orders, 60
British Emergency Enactment (Security Matters) 1951, 63
British legal tradition, 29
British mandate, 3, 30, 32, 47, 62–63, 75, 81, 95, 112, 150
British Mandatory law, 31–32
British Mandatory legal system, 31
Budget, 42, 92, 122

Canada, 8
Canadian Charter, 151
Carrying and Presenting Identification Law of 1982, 77
Central Election Commission (CEC), 100
Chief of staff, 60–61, 75, 152, 170
Chile, 137
Citizens 1, 5, 21, 34, 90, 92, 96, 99, 126, 148, 161, 164, 180, 181
Civic participation, 99
Civil Defense Law, 77
Civil liberties, 34, 48, 151, 184
Civil settlements, 84, 90
Civil society, 49, 128, 141, 180, 183
Closed areas, 88, 97, 154–155,
Co-constitution [of Law and Emergency], 17, 102, 133, 138, 142
Co-constitutive model, 137–138, 140
Cohn, Haim, 101
Cohn, Margit, 54, 56, 69, 83, 147, 159, 164–166, 173
Cole, David, 8, 174
Colonial India, 94, 147
Colonialism, 15–16, 147, 176, 178, 183, 185

Colonization, 85, 181
Colonizers, 15–16, 85, 147,
Colony, 15–16, 179
Columbia, 137, 174
Commingling [of law and emergency], 8, 10, 25, 121, 129, 136–137, 140–141
Committee, 35, 36, 38, 44, 45, 61–63, 68, 82, 92, 97, 100, 155, 157, 159, 161, 170–171
Common emergency powers, 106
Communist party, 99, 162
Company (*khevrah*), 99, 120, 151, 162, 176
Complementary relationship, 5, 24, 56, 71, 83–87, 90, 103
Complex legal
  structure, 31, 53, 85, 135
  system, 3
Conflict, 20, 22, 81, 85, 117, 142, 148, 159, 173, 176, 181, 183
Constituent assembly, 29, 34–35, 42
  Eternal, 30, 135
Constituent body, 29, 34–35, 38
Constitution
  complete legislated, 28
  formal, 6, 41, 46–48
  making, 28, 30, 34–35, 62
  material, 28
Constitutional
  additions of 1992, 30
  amendments, 29, 39, 135
  arrangement, 54
  authority, 29
  court, 46, 50, 137
  drafting, 34–35
  engineering, 137
  expansion, 106
  extra-constitutional measures, 7
  extra-constitutional powers, 106, 111, 121

extra-constitutional responses, 106
fluidity, 37, 43, 108
framework, 6, 29, 43, 135
law, 8, 28–30, 35–36, 38, 42, 135, 174, 175, 181, 184
moment, 39, 41
order, 137, 139
powers, 6, 106, 111, 114, 121
reform, 28, 38, 39, 41, 45, 48
revolution, 38, 40–41, 172, 174–175, 182
sag, 106, 111
status of human rights, 40
Continental civil law, 33
Contra legem (contrary to the law), 44, 111
Control of Products and Services Law of 1957, 59, 75, 89, 112–113, 154
Control system, 23, 54, 177
Convoluted
  governing system, 24
  legal structures, 19, 22, 70, 82, 87
Cook v. the Minister of Defence, 60, 169
Correction to the Penal Law (State Security), 1957, 78
Count Bernadotte, 74
Crawling peg devaluation, 125
Criminal Jurisdiction and Legal Aid Law, 92, 160
Criminal law, 78, 141, 148, 158
Crisis
  economic, 106–107, 121, 127–128
  governability, 50, 135
  immediate, 1
  non-, 114
  profound, 121
  time of, 6, 107, 141
  violent, 10, 106, 175
Curfew, 4, 80

Currency, 2–3, 59, 89, 105, 107, 112, 114–115, 120–129, 134, 145, 154, 156, 166
  devaluation, 123–126
  exchange, 114, 124, 129, 134
  rates, 3, 105, 107, 114–115, 120–121, 123–128
  speculations, 125
Currency Supervision Law of 1978, 89, 112, 114, 122
Customary international law, 82, 146

Darian-Smith, Eve, 14, 141, 147, 174
Declaration of Independence (DOI), 13, 18, 29, 33–34, 74, 100, 148, 150
Declared SOE, 54, 56, 76, 113
Decree
  confinement, 116, 119–120, 166
  prevention, 117
Defence (Emergency) Regulations, 109, 173
Defence Regulations (Finance), 1941, 112
Defence Regulations (Food Supervision), 1942, 89, 112
Defence Regulations (Prevention of Price Expropriation), 1944, 112
Defence Regulations, 1939, 112
Defence Services Law, 1959, 160
Defensive democracy, 101, 164
Democracy,
  debate, 20, 175
  ethnic, 21, 174–175, 180, 184
  formal, 21
  liberal, 6, 8, 10, 11, 23, 43, 73, 105–106, 178
  Western liberal, 8, 23
Democratic rule, 1, 23, 43, 137
Demolition of houses, 59, 87

Derogation clause, 146
Derogation of the rule of law, 141
Despouy Report, 8, 137, 167
Development Authority, 162
Dictatorship
  extreme, 15
  Roman, 6
Discrete juridical order, 95, 102
Discriminatory
  colonizers, 15–16, 93
  policies, 101, 136
  politics, 136
Doctrine of two hats, 29–30
Dowty, Alan, 23, 54, 58, 71, 80, 134, 148, 158, 174
Due process, 16, 38, 67, 69, 89, 103, 111, 117, 130, 173
Duplicity of provisions, 84, 86
Dynamics of law, 3, 17–19, 24, 83, 103, 135, 139, 142
Dyzenhaus, David, 7, 146, 174

East Jerusalem, 61, 149
Economic
  change, 130
  ends, 103–104, 106, 110, 114, 129, 134, 140, 142
  liberalization, 130
  meltdown, 4, 107
  objectives, 103–105, 107, 110–111, 130
  outcomes, 1
  plan, 2
  policies, 22, 24, 43, 89, 106–107, 109, 111, 113, 127, 129, 134, 142, 156
  program, 2, 105, 125
  regulation, 11, 59, 104, 105, 108, 111, 113, 121,
  restructuring, 104, 125, 128
  stagnation, 122
  strategy, 2

Index

Economic emergency codex, 112
Economic-financial states of emergency (EFSE), 105–106
Economy
  capitalist, 106
  centralized, 107
  free market, 130, 185
  global, 124
Egypt, 75, 137, 159
Ehrlich, Simcha, 126
El Karbutli v. Minister of Defense, 155
El Salvador, 137
Election, 2, 21, 30, 34, 92, 99, 100–1, 149, 151, 156, 160, 170–171, 175
Electoral system, 30–31, 151, 173
Elef-Shilo, Michal, 43–44, 151, 174
Emergency
  apparatus, 20, 24, 53, 104, 140, 142,
  based, 99, 122, 137
  crisis, 5, 106, 145
  enactment, 16, 53–54, 56–58, 61, 63, 73, 83, 87, 88, 108, 118, 123, 128, 135, 166
  Jordanian's emergency powers, 80
  jurisprudence, 22–23, 25, 51, 101, 136, 138, 143
  legal mechanisms, 3, 19, 53, 55–56, 64–66, 71, 82, 84–85, 88, 91, 94, 135, 151
  legal state of, 53
  legislation, 64, 110, 114, 173
  measures, 2, 3, 8, 20, 25, 111, 118
  multiple emergency legal sources, 3, 24, 83
  national (emergencies), 137, 167, 180
  non-, 87, 111
  paradigm, 9, 12, 138
  permanent, 11, 23, 179
  regime, 4, 8, 16–17, 21–24, 80, 96, 101, 134, 141, 175
  rule, 9, 109
  special SOE, 20
  State of (SOE), 1, 4, 10, 23, 53, 65, 68, 134, 137, 145, 147, 157, 162, 182
  statutes, 6
  times of, 4–7, 9, 77, 138
Emergency (Absentees' Property) Regulation, 1949, 97
Emergency (Cancelation of the Services Import Tax and the Travel Tax Correction of the Value Added Tax Law) Regulation, 3, 166
Emergency (Compulsory Payments) Regulation, 123
Emergency (Essential Work Services) Regulations, 105, 114, 116–120
Emergency (Exploitation of Uncultivated Lands) Regulation, 1949, 97
Emergency (Foreign Currency Acquisition Tax) Regulations, 128
Emergency (Foreign Tourist Services Deposit) Regulations, 128
Emergency (Imported Services Tax) Regulations, 128
Emergency (Procedures Following Changes in Currency Rates—Import Tax) Regulations, 128
Emergency (Procedures Following Changes in Currency Rates) Regulation, 3, 105, 107, 114, 120–121, 123–127
Emergency (Products and Services Price Stability) Regulations, 129
Emergency (Security Zones) Regulation, 96, 171

Emergency (Shekel) Regulation, 128
Emergency (the Jurisdiction Constitution) Regulations of 1948, 152
Emergency Defense and Security Law, 1949, 155
Emergency Labor Services Law, 1967, 160
Emergency Power Act of 1973, 137
Emergency Powers (Defence of the Colonies) Order in Council of 1939, 57, 171
Emergency Powers (Detention) Law of 1979, 61, 64
Emergency Regulation (Areas held by the Defence Army of Israel–Criminal Jurisdiction and Legal Aid), 1967, 94
Emergency Regulation (Areas Held by the Defence Army of Israel—Service of Documentation), 1969, 161
Emergency Regulation (Compulsory Payments) of 1952, 112
Emergency Regulation (Continuance in Force of Validity of Provisions), 1951, 89, 159, 171
Emergency Regulation (Requisition of Property) 1948, 97
Emergency Regulation for the Prevention of Terrorism, 74
Emergency Regulations Extension (Registration of Equipment) Law, 1981, 160
Emergency State Search Authorities Law (Temporary Order), 1969, 75
Englishman's personal law, 93
Entrenched bill of human and civil rights, 21
Entrenched clause, 37, 40
Entrenchment, 29, 38, 41, 42, 91, 135, 164
Entry into Israel Law, 1952, 160
Eretz Yisrael, 32, 34, 150
Essential service, 65–66, 68, 110, 118, 166, 179
Essential work services, 105, 114–120
Ethnocracy, 21, 185
European Convention on Human Rights and Fundamental Freedoms of 1950, 146, 176
Evidence Ordinance, 77, 171
Executive
  action, 7
  branch, 43, 108, 130
  privilege, 108
ex post facto review, 7, 8
Exception
  legal, 102, 133, 140
  regimes of, 137, 177–178
Exceptional
  executive prerogatives, 7
  governing mechanisms, 4
  order of government, 9, 138
  times, 9
Exceptionalism, 23–24, 30, 47
Exchange rate system, 126
Exploitation of Uncultivated Lands regulation, 97
Export subsidies, 123–124
Extra-legal
  alternatives, 7
  measures, 6–7, 146
Extraterritorial, 48, 92
Extreme
  conditions, 107–108
  measures, 104, 119, 131

Ferejohn, John, 67, 146, 153, 174
First Gulf War, 20
First Lebanon War, 20
Fitzpatrick, Peter, 14, 141, 147, 174

Floating Rate, 125
Fluid
  dynamics of law, 24, 142
  environment, 43
  framework, 30, 103
    legal-political structure, 10, 24, 27, 107
    legal system, 19
    structure, 3, 19, 27, 38, 47, 50, 51, 85, 135
Foreign exchange
  controller, 112
  market, 2, 130, 179
Formal entrenchment, 29, 42
Formalist jurisprudence, 100
Foucault, 167
Foundations of Law, 33
Fourth Geneva Convention, 81, 158–159
Fraenkel, Ernst, 14–16, 18, 106, 129, 133, 174
Free speech, 33, 80
Freedom of
  association, 39
  conscience, 34
  demonstration, 39
  education and culture, 34
  from religion, 39
  language, 34
  movement, 39, 90
  press, 33
  religion, 34, 39
  speech, 21, 39
French civil code, 149
French weapons embargo, 117
Friedmann, Daniel, 50, 150, 153, 174

Gaza Strip, 20, 148, 152, 159–160
Gaza Withdrawal, 49
General Amnesty Ordinance of 1949, 78
General elections, 21, 34
General international law, 146
Goldstein, Michael, 54, 159, 175
Governability, 27, 43, 50, 135
Governance
  co-constitutive mode of, 2
  conventional tool of, 116
  dominant form of, 108
  Israel, 20–21, 104–105, 108
  method of, 11, 12, 141
  modes of, 4–5, 8–11, 15–16, 105, 141
  ordinary scheme of, 7
  proper forms of, 116, 121
  state, 15
  two modes of, 4, 8
Governing
  culture, 103, 130
  dynamics, 138
  flexibility, 19, 24, 27, 43, 50, 51, 86, 102–103, 107, 142
  legitimacy, 138
  methodology, 141
  modes of, 105
  party, 103
  techniques, 84
  tool, 23, 108, 130, 142
Government
  by law, 3, 15, 18, 22, 102, 136
  coalition, 29
  democratic forms of, 125, 130, 135
  enduring government composition, 17, 133
  "exceptional," 9, 138
  expenditure, 127
  involvement, 130, 131
  Labor, 113, 117, 124
  left-wing, 107
  Likud, 113, 128
  military, 16, 63, 78, 96, 98, 133, 147, 152, 161, 177

Government (*continued*)
  modes of, 15, 16, 141
  "normal" order of, 138
  order of, 9, 138
  political systems of, 12, 147
  provisional, 145
  right-wing, 107
  setting, 104
Government's Working Rules, 67, 157
Governmental
  apparatuses, 137
  branches, 28
  flexibility, 22, 140
Governmental flexibility, 22, 140
Green Line, 21, 23–24, 79, 86, 95, 109, 111, 134, 142–143, 148, 152, 183
Gross, Oren, 6–8, 10, 41, 137, 145–146, 173, 175
Grunis, Asher, 50
Guardian of Civil Liberties, 48
Gudridge, Patrick, 7, 184

H.S.A v. the Minister of Labor and Welfare, 159
Haifa district commissioner, 99, 163
Haifa district court, 99
Hamas, 20
Harrari Resolution, 29, 34–36, 39, 135
Hegemony, 13, 148, 178, 180
Herut party, 34, 64, 127, 171
Herzog, Chaim, 81
Hezbollah, 20
Hierarchy [legal], 28–29, 35, 37, 39, 42, 49, 54, 72, 135,
High Commissioner, 57
High Court of Justice (HCJ), 47–50, 60–61, 67, 69, 70, 72, 74, 82, 84, 88, 89, 97, 99, 113, 152–155, 162, 175, 178, 182–183
Histadrut (Israel's organization of trade unions), 117, 128
Hofnung, Menahem, 23, 54, 58–59, 71, 73, 77–78, 98, 134, 149, 152, 156–158, 160–161, 164, 176
Holocaust, 152
Horowitz, David, 21, 112
House arrest, 163
Human dignity, 37–40, 42, 156
Hussain, Nasser, 15–18, 93, 139, 147, 167, 176
Hybrid, 15, 30, 32–3, 45, 94–7, 96, 106, 181
Hyperlegality, 15, 17, 139, 147

Iberian Peninsula, 85, 91
Identity
  Israel's national, 21, 151, 164
  national, 27
  national-religious, 21
  political, 27
IDF commander of the West Bank, 81
IDF's chief military prosecutor, 152
Illegal, 18, 62, 91, 94, 163, 184
Implementation orders, 44, 111
Import tax, 3, 124, 128, 166
Imprisonment, 74–75, 120, 124
Income Tax Ordinance, 92
Income Tax—Amendment in 1980, 160
India, 93–94, 137, 147, 173, 177
Indian magistrates, 94
Inflation, 122–123, 125, 127
Institutionalized states of emergency, 137
Internal absentees, 162
International Covenant on Civil and Political Rights of 1966, 146

Iraq, 75
Irgun/Etzel *Irgun Tzavai Leumi*, 62, 74, 155
Israel
  coalition, 31
  constitutional framework, 29, 43, 135
  electoral system, 30
  emerging leadership, 111
  governing officials, 84, 136
  law books, 5, 7, 54, 61, 70, 73, 78, 155
Israeli
  authorities, 1–2, 14, 21, 24–25, 80, 84, 86, 90–93, 98, 100–101, 107, 121, 123, 128, 134, 160, 162
  citizens, 90, 92, 126, 150–151, 161, 164
  citizenship, 92, 150, 151
  constitutional framework, 29, 43, 135
  currency, 3, 122–123, 125
  economy, 107, 122, 127, 176, 181, 185
  financial institutions, 112
  government, 3, 30, 43–44, 59, 66, 74, 90, 104, 109, 111, 120–121, 135, 167, 182
  history, 1, 104
  Lira, 122–123, 126
  political structure, 29
  regime, 16, 20–22, 54, 90, 116, 133–134, 142, 160
  resident, 92, 126, 134

Jayasuriya, Kanishka, 106, 137, 176
Jefferson, 6, 12
Jellamy detainees, 62
Jewish
  control, 89, 96
  majority, 21–22, 134
  settlers, 49, 80, 91–94, 143, 160
  superiority, 21
  supremacy, 99, 142–143
  underground, 62
Jewish legal traditions, 33
Jiryis v. The Haifa District Commissioner, 163
Jordanian Arms and Ammunition Law, 81
Judea, 154–155, 160, 175
Judicial
  approach, 69, 98, 100, 153
  doctrine, 100–101
  formalistic, 69, 101
  mandate, 47
  philosophy, 98
  precedent, 46–47
  review, 5, 8, 35, 39, 41, 45, 49, 61, 69, 72, 77, 87–88, 93
Judicial bill of rights, 40, 46, 48
Judicial precedent, 46–47
June 5 1967, 80, 86
Juridical
  order, 95, 102, 139, 140
  complexity, 140, 142
  border, 140
  branch, 48
Jurisdictional complexity, 140, 142
Jurisdictions, 46, 66, 85, 87, 140
Juxta legem (according to law), 44, 111

Kahan, Rebecca, 106, 111, 114, 121, 164, 177
Kaplan, Eliezer, 112
Kelsen, Hans, 14, 177
Kimmerling, Baruch, 16, 21, 23, 54, 177
King-in-Council, 59, 149
Klinghoffer, Hans, 54, 66, 72, 88, 177–178

Klofer-Nave v. the Minister of Culture and Education (1984), 87, 171
Knesset
  committees, 45
  First, 34–34, 73
  review, 44, 135
  Second, 29, 35, 156
  seventeenth, eighteenth, and nineteenth, 49
  Speaker of the, 49
  statutes, 31
  supervision, 43
Knesset Election Law, 160
Kol Haham, 162
Kolsky, Elizabeth, 93, 147, 177
Korean War, 150
Korematsu v. United States, 146
Kretzmer, David, 21–22, 99, 160–161, 164, 177

Labor
  controlling, 106
  disputes, 25, 103–104, 107, 114, 118, 130, 156, 179
  market, 117, 121, 129–130, 134
  organized, 116–117
  unions, 117
Labor party, 31, 117, 150, 155
Land Expropriation, 84, 95–96, 98, 161
Landau, Moshe, 35, 41, 163, 164, 178
Law
  administration of, 16, 91–92, 133
  administrative, 46–47
  authority of the law, 2, 22, 88, 94, 109
  autonomy of, 14
  boundaries of, 18
  canon, 85, 151, 165
  case, 41, 48, 158
  civil, 33, 74, 145, 178, 185
  colonial, 15–16, 24, 60
  common, 33, 41, 100, 145, 149
  constitutional, 8, 28–30, 35, 36, 38, 42, 135, 174–175, 181, 184
  contract, 32
  curtailment of, 139
  dependent, 56, 71, 73–75, 157
  dynamics of the law, 2–3
  extension of, 17, 139, 147
  foreign colonial, 60
  generality of, 13
  government by, 3, 15, 18, 22, 102, 136
  Hebrew, 33
  hyperextension of, 17
  independent, 56, 71, 76, 78
  interaction of, 85
  international, 5, 47, 54, 80, 82, 86–87, 90–91, 146, 147, 152, 158, 175, 177, 180
  Jordanian, 80–81, 86–87, 93
  judge-made, 46
  liberal understanding of, 23
  local, 63, 85
  martial, 4, 58, 145
  modern, 31–32
  Muslim, 150
  natural, 98, 100–101, 180
  normative, 6, 9, 74, 77, 113, 129, 140
  ordinary, 6, 77, 145
  Ottoman, 31–33, 86, 150
  outside, 5, 7, 153
  personal status, 33
  personal, 16, 91–93
  positive, 101
  private, 32, 36, 47
  rational, 4–5, 14, 141
  regular, 35–38, 40, 72, 127, 149
  religious, 31, 85
  renewal, 56, 59, 62, 66–67, 71–73, 89, 154, 158, 160–161
  rule of, 4–13, 16, 17–18, 21, 43,

51, 73, 101, 108–109, 111, 121, 125, 134, 136–139, 140–142, 147, 172, 176, 179, 180, 182
  secular, 85
  sources of, 19
  special emergency, 6
  state, 91, 92
  statutory, 41, 46
  suspended, 147
  suspension of, 1, 140
  suspension of, 1, 140
  temporary, 72, 129
  territorial, 93
  traditional, 1
  Western, 15, 32, 177
  withdrawal of, 17, 147
Law against Racism, 36
Law and Administration Ordinance (Amendment No. 2) Law, 1952, 89
Law and Administration Ordinance, 1948, 11, 110, 153, 165
Law Concerning the Laws and Regulations, 81
Law for Stability of Products and Services Price (Temporary Order) of 1985, 129
Law for the Correction and the Extension of the Validity of Emergency Regulations (Judea, Samaria and the Gaza Strip, Criminal Jurisdiction and Legal Aid), 1977, 60
Law of Cities and Urban Development, 160
Law of Modification of Administrative Procedures in Palestine, 81
Law of Return, 1950, 35–36, 92, 150
Lawlessness, 21
Lazar, Nomi Claire, 7, 11, 136, 141, 178
Lebanon, 20, 75, 128, 147
Lechi underground / Stern Gang, 74

Legal
  activism, 49, 153
  annexation, 142
  apparatuses, 14, 104
  authority/ies, 20, 50, 83, 102, 104, 118, 135, 139, 140, 146
  borders, 45
  consultants, 45
  councilor, 32
  exceptions, 133, 140
  execution, 107
  fluidity, 102, 139, 142–143, 152
  formal legal procedure, 18
  formalism, 153
  foundation, 31, 73, 86–87, 86, 100, 135, 140
  hierarchy, 28, 35, 37, 39, 42, 54
  imperialism, 15, 84
  maneuver, 90
  manipulation, 83
  measures, 1, 6–7, 18, 145–146
  metaphor, 84, 94–95, 98, 136
  norm, 5, 153
  order, 14, 22, 84–85, 87, 103, 136, 146, 174
  patchwork, 31, 53, 71, 79, 83, 85, 88, 96, 97, 135
  pluralism, 85, 141, 142
  principles, 10, 16
  realm, 7, 18–19, 139, 153
  regime, 57, 85, 146, 173
  regular SOE, 20
  SOE, 1, 16, 20, 68, 109
  structural complexity, 15
  systems, 1, 28, 50, 80, 86, 89, 90, 94, 134
  tools, 5, 6, 13, 21, 103, 112, 133, 146
  traditions, 29, 31, 33, 46, 59, 135
Legal systems
  dual, 90
  unequal, 90
Legalism, 106

Legality, 5, 13, 19, 84, 91, 138
Legislation
　antiterrorism, 15, 17
　emergency, 64, 110, 114, 173
　formal act of, 45
　formal, 28, 67, 69
　ordinary, 6–7, 10, 108, 113
　primary, 2, 41, 43, 44, 48, 61, 62, 76, 89, 110–112, 121, 125, 129
　secondary, 28, 41, 43–45, 64, 72, 89, 108, 110–11, 113, 121, 174
Legislative
　authority, 57
　branch, 29, 34–35, 38, 40, 44, 111
　model, 6
　power, 54–56, 64, 70–71, 74, 77, 88, 113–114, 124
　process, 109–110
Legislature, 121, 130
Levi-Faur, David, 131, 165, 167, 177
Levon v. Gubernik, 60–61, 154, 169
lex posteriori derogat legi priori, 37
lex specialis derogat legi generali, 37
Liberal
　paradigm, 10
　positivism, 23
　theory, 23
　thinkers, 4
　perspective, 33, 49
Likud party, 2, 64, 75, 125, 127, 155
Limitation clause, 40–41
Lira (Israel first and old currency), 122–124, 126, 128
Locke, John, 4, 6, 12, 146, 178
Lord Gort, 58
Lustick, Ian, 21, 22, 148, 161, 178

Machiavelli, 6, 12
Maintenance of supplies, 65, 66, 68, 110
Majalla, 32, 150
Mandatory Defence (Finance) Regulation of 1941, 3
Mandatory Emergency (Defence) Regulations, 3, 57
Mandatory emergency defence regulations, 54, 109
Mandatory emergency regulation 111 (Detention), 61–62
Mandatory Emergency Regulation 84(1)b, 163
Mandatory emergency regulations (Regulation 119), 87
Mandatory Emergency Regulations, 3, 54–64, 66, 69–71, 73, 75–76, 78, 80–1, 85–90, 96–98, 110, 112, 163
Mandatory Regulation 125 (Closed Areas), 88, 155
Mandatory regulations, 57, 109, 154–156, 160
Mandatory tradition, 43, 47
Mapai party, 34, 62, 74, 150, 155, 161
Martial law, 4, 58, 145
Mdinovest v. the Health Ministry CEO, 159
Michaeli, Michael, 122–123, 127, 179
Michlin v. the Minister of Health (HC 70/50), 88, 170
Military
　government, 16, 63, 78, 88, 96, 98, 100, 133, 17, 152, 155, 161, 170, 177
　commander, 56, 60–61, 75–76, 81, 87, 90, 92, 96, 170
Military Government in Jerusalem (Confirmation of Acts) Ordinance of 1949, 78
Military governor of Galilee, 88, 155, 170
Military Order 224, 160
Military Order 378, 160

Military order 65, 160
Military order 783 (administering regional councils), 92
Military order 892 (administering local councils), 92
Military orders, 53, 90, 92–93, 97, 124
Military Service (Consolidated Version) Law of 1986, 77
Minister of
  communications, 119
  education, 87, 119, 171
  energy and infrastructure, 119, 156
  finance, 3, 64, 112, 119, 123–123, 126–127, 129, 150, 156, 170
  labor, 119, 156, 159
  transport, 156
Minister's voting records, 44
Ministry of Finance, 112, 126–127
Mironi, Mordechai, 104, 114, 116–120, 156, 164, 179
Models of accommodation, 4, 6, 9, 146
Monists, 7, 9
Multiple legal sources, 3, 28, 31, 86

National Insurance (Consolidated Version), 1968, 160
National unity government, 128
Natural law philosophy, 98, 100
Nazi regime, 14–15, 138
Neoliberal(ism), 130, 147
  deregulation, 130
  politics, 130
  reform, 107, 131
  transformation, 130
Neo-Roman model, 6
Neocleous, Mark, 6, 10–11, 136, 138, 147, 167, 179
Neumann, Franz, 13, 180
New Shekel, 128, 166

Nitzan, Johnathan, 117, 180
Nixon administration, 117
Nizame, 150
Niztan v. Shlomo Lahat, 159
Non-crisis powers, 106, 111, 114, 121
Nondemocratic systems of law, 32
Nonsecurity purposes, 140
Norm, 4–5, 36, 137, 147, 153, 167, 176, 185
Normal
  order of government, 138
  times, 9–11, 138
Normalcy, 4, 6, 9–10, 108, 139, 176
Normative
  assessment, 116
  channels, 108
  concepts, 6, 12
  hierarchy, 37, 49, 54
  laws, 6, 74, 77, 113
  superiority, 37, 42
Northern Ireland, 136–137

Obligatory international law, 152
Occupied land, 90
Occupied Palestinian Territories (OPT), xi, 21, 47, 84
Occupied population, 90, 158
Occupied territories, 48, 64, 124, 127, 159–160, 175, 178
Official Gazette, xi, 65, 155, 169
Ophir, Adi, 139, 148, 160, 167, 172, 180, 183
Order for the Extension of the Validity of Defence Regulations (Finance), 159
Original Israeli law, 58–59, 64, 154
Original legal system, 85, 139
Origins of Totalitarianism, 15, 172
Oslo Accord, 160
Ottoman Empire, 32, 162
Overcoming clause, 40, 151

Overlapping, 3, 19, 24, 53, 70, 82, 84–85, 87–88, 140

Pakistan, 137, 159, 172
Palestine (Defence) Order in Council of 1937, 57, 171
Palestine International Documents on Human Rights 1948–1972, 159
Palestine Order in Council, 1922, 32–33
Palestinian
  citizens, 99, 181
  faction, 98
  Nakba, 95
  nationalism, 163
  organization, 98
  refugee, 161
  residents, 48, 90
  villages, 88
Palmon, Yehoshua, 98
Paradox of neoliberal deregulation, 130
Parliamentary republic, 28
Parliamentary supremacy, 29
Pasquino, Pasquale, 6–7, 146, 153, 174
Patchwork system, 39, 45, 53, 58, 70, 71, 79, 83, 85, 88, 90, 96–97, 112, 135,
Penal Law of 1977, 78, 86, 158
Peres, Shimon, 98
PLO, 46, 75
Plural legal order, 85
Pluralist structure of Israeli law, 32
Pluralistic legal structure, 31
Policy
  discriminatory, 93, 136
  executing, 27, 108
  fiscal, 3
  foreign exchange rate, 129
  making, 101, 134, 141
  monetary, 25, 103, 107, 114, 128

Policymaker, 46, 50, 106, 108, 113, 126, 133, 162
Political
  abuse, 107, 134
  advantages, 84
  battle, 40
  benefits, 23, 83
  branches, 29, 50, 135
  culture, 130
  deadlock, 28, 128
  economy, 11, 140, 180
  environment, 16, 25, 138
  extreme political settings, 16
  flexibility, 28, 70, 98
  identity, 27
  management, 104
  myth, 10, 138, 167
  player, 14, 27
  pluralism, 141
  representation, 22, 84, 98–99, 134, 141
  spectrum, 49, 107, 118
  system, 12, 19, 23–24, 27–51, 133–135, 138–140, 147, 153
  transformation (1977), 113
  turmoil, 106
  upset, 2, 124
  voice, 101
Population in need, 25, 107, 114, 129
Population Register Law, 1965, 160
Population registration, 92
Poraz v. The State of Israel, 151, 159
Posner, Richard, 6–7, 28, 146–147, 179–180
Power
  arbitrary use of, 18
  arbitrary, 13, 106
  class, 13
  constitutive, 30
  constraining, 16
  executive, 107–108, 146
  illegitimate, 13

infinite, 139
naked, 17
non-crisis, 106, 111, 114, 121
occupying, 81
scope of, 17
separation of, 29, 31, 44, 111
serving, 16
sovereign, 19, 24, 27, 43, 81, 83, 84, 102–103, 135–136, 138–140
Praetor legem (outside of the law), 44, 111
Precarious, 1, 12, 39
Pre-crisis position, 126
Prerogative rule, 9
Present-absentees, 162
Press Ordinance, 78
Prevention authorities, 59
Prevention of Infiltration (Offences and Jurisdiction) Law of 1954, 75
Prevention of Terrorism Ordinance of 1948, 74, 156
Price freeze, 128
Primary emergency laws, 54, 112
Principle of
  democratic process of enactment, 111
  equality, 34, 108
  majority rule, 108
  participation, 108, 130
  publicity, 108
  sovereignty of the Knesset, 125
Principles
  civil democratic, 21
  democratic, 109
  soft, 48
Privy council, 57
Procedure 19B, 44
Promulgated, 57–57, 69, 88, 110, 113, 119, 126–127, 145, 169
Property, 75, 85, 95, 97–98, 140, 157, 161–162, 170,

Protected right, 40, 42
Protocols of the Knesset's committees, 38
Protocols of the ministers' committees, 44
Provisional Council of the State. 32, 145
Psychologist Law, 1968, 160
Public officials, 120, 146
Public order, 57, 78, 81, 141
Publicity, 5, 16, 43, 108, 111
Punishment authorities, 59

Qardosh v. The Registrar of Companies, 162
Quantitative restrictions, 123

Rabin, Yitzhak, 113, 124, 155, 170
Rabinovitz, Joshua, 124
Racism, 18, 36, 164
Radical legal formalism, 153
Ratio (rational law), 5
Rational, 4–5, 14–16, 99, 106, 141
Rationale, 16, 77, 108, 123, 147, 166
Raz-Krakotzkin, Amnon, 16, 181
Realists, 6–7
Reallocation of land, 95
Rebellion, 4, 57, 107, 116
Reception statute, 32
Referendum Law, 149
Reform of controls, 2
Regime
  authoritarian, 11
  British colonial, 93
  democratic, 10–11
  hybrid, 15
  liberal democratic, 11
  modern political, 17
  non-democratic, 143
  old, 85
  political, 9, 17, 102, 104, 136, 138, 141

Regular majority, 38
Regulation 86 of the Emergency
  (Defense) Regulations, 1945, 87
Religion, 21, 27, 33–34, 39, 64
Review committee, 97
Rights
  bill of, 21, 28, 40, 46, 48
  civil, 5, 12, 17–18, 21, 28, 36, 40,
    48, 74, 108, 157, 171
  highest, 5, 13
  human, 27, 29, 39–40, 42, 48,
    105, 135, 140, 146, 157, 159,
    172–173, 176, 180–181, 184
  public, 116
  secure civil, 21
  violation of human, 140
Rightwing coalitions, 49
Right-wing, 2, 38, 74, 107
Rivlin, Reuven, 49, 122–123,
  125–126, 181
Role of emergency powers, 104, 130,
  133, 139,
Rosen, Pinchas, 63, 149
Rossiter, Clinton, 6, 11, 181
Rouhana, Nadim, 22, 148, 181
Rousseau, 6, 12
Routine economic regulation, 104,
  121
Rubinstein, Amnon, 30, 38, 54, 151,
  181
Rule
  colonial, 64, 91, 93
  imperial, 15
  military, 14, 90
  political, 104, 106, 141
Rule of law
  perspective, 109, 111, 121
  principles, 5, 18, 108, 141

Saltman, Michael, 54, 58, 182
Samaria, 154–155, 160, 175
Sanctions, 78, 80, 120

Sapir, Gideon, 38, 41, 49, 151, 153,
  179, 182
Saudi Arabia, 75
Scandinavian states, 30
Scheuerman, William, 11, 105–106,
  136, 146, 165, 182
Schmitt, Carl, 5, 13, 139, 146–147,
  167, 174, 182
Secondary implementation order, 119
Secret appendix, 161
Section 46 of Basic Law, 36–37
Section 46 of the Control of Products
  and Services Law, 1957,
  113
Section 7A Basic Law, 164
Section 9(a) of the Law and
  Administration Ordinance
  1948, 68, 145
Security
  committee, 68
  elastic concept of, 21
  Fence, 91
  measure, 130, 134, 175
  national, 111, 176, 179
  necessities, 3, 22, 77–78, 158
  non-, 140
  physical, 1–2
  Zone, 96, 161, 170–171
Separate jurisdictions, 85, 140
Settlements, 84, 90–4, 98, 127, 175,
  183
Shamgar, Meir, 152
Shamir, Ronen, 16, 32, 152–153
Shapiro, Yonatan, 21, 183
Shari`ah Islamic law (Sharia), 150
Shekel, 128, 166
Shetreet, Shimon, 54, 71, 184
Shimshon, Yaakov, 63, 117, 180
Singapore, 137
Single house, 2, 29, 135
Single-house parliamentary system,
  2

Six Day War, 63
Skeptics, 5–7, 9–10, 138
Slavery, 18
Smirat Hadinim, 40
Smooha, Sami, 21, 184
Snap back, 106, 177
Social security, 78, 92, 158–159
Social Security Labor Union v. the Minister of Labor and Welfare, 159
Social Security Law (Consolidated Version), 1968, 78
South Africa, 57, 137
South American countries, 137
Southeast Asia/South Asian, 137
Sovereign,
  gaps, 167
  power, 19, 24, 27, 43, 81, 83–84, 102–103, 135, 136, 138–141
  prerogatives, 4, 9
  will, 5, 12, 19, 138, 140
Sovereignty
  Jordanian, 81
  juridical, 48
  manifestations of, 140
  Schmittian concept of, 139
  territorial, 48
Special Committee Report, 82
Special majority, 38, 39, 156
Special powers, 4
Special tribunals and commissions, 17, 147
Sri Lanka, 137
Stacked emergency legal mechanisms, 85
Stacked legal system, 85, 102, 135
State
  defence of, 65–66, 68
  developing, 136, 137
  dual, 14, 106, 174
  establishment of the, 24, 47, 58–59, 89, 112, 122, 156
  garrison, 148
  inception of the, 1, 23, 109, 111, 114
  Jewish, 34, 100, 176, 178, 180, 181
  liberal-democratic, 29
  normative, 14, 15, 91, 130
  of alert [or alarm], 4
  of internal war, 4
  of normality, 109
  of readiness, 4
  of siege, 4, 145, 167
  of urgency, 118
  prerogative, 14, 15, 106, 129, 184
  protection of, 24, 103, 108, 111
  security, 76, 78–79, 86
  state-of-no-law, 12
  totalitarian, 136
  well-being, 1, 107
  withdrawal of the, 130
State Comptroller Report, 161
State Economic Regularization Emergency Law of 1985—*Hok Hahesderim*, 104, 128
Statute, 6, 10, 14, 31–33, 35, 37, 39–40, 46, 48, 58, 63, 67, 71, 73, 79, 95, 100, 108, 171
Stoler, Ann, 167, 184
Strike (labor), 116–120, 166
Structural reform, 121
Structured ambiguity, 24, 28, 79, 82, 83, 93, 101–102,134, 139
Supervision over Commodities and Products Law, 113
Supply of Products and Services (Transitional Provision) Decree, 59
Suspension of guarantees, 4
Suspension of law, 1, 140
Symbolic capital, 29, 33
Syria, 75
System of control, 21–22

Tanzimat, 32, 149
Tariff, 123–124, 156
Tax, 3, 13, 65, 92, 112, 124, 126, 128, 166
Territorial enclaves, 93
Territorial Jurisdiction and Authorities Order, 1948, 149
Terror, 62
Terrorism, 8, 10, 15, 17, 74, 156, 157, 171, 184
Thatcher, Margaret, 117
The Association for Civil Rights in Israel v. Israel's Government and Knesset, 157, 171
The Criminal Law Ordinance of 1936, 78
The Custodian of Abandoned Property v. Sammara Al-Rabi, 162
The Ehrlich Liberalization, 126
The Jewish Bar Association of Palestine, 58, 154
The Jewish National Fund (JNF), 172
The Police Ordinance, 158
The Rhodes 1949 Armistice Agreements, 148
The Triangle, 96
Thompson, E. P., 12–13, 16, 184
Threat
    existential, 5
    external, 57
    imminent, 1, 18, 102, 107–100, 133
    internal, 57
    objective, 20, 107
Transactions in Foreign Currency Decree, 145, 166
Transition Law, 29, 34–35, 156
Transjordan Defense Law of 1935, 81
Travel tax, 3, 126, 166
Tribe, Laurence, 7, 96, 184

Turkey, 33
Tushnet, Mark, 7, 146, 180, 184

Underground, 62, 74
Unequal administration, 93, 102, 133
Unified legal methodology, 54
Unilateral actions, 45
United Nations (UN),
UN Doc. A/8089, 159
UN General Assembly, 159
United Nations General Assembly Resolution 181, 34
UN Security Council, 8
    Resolution 1368, 8
United Kingdom (UK), 8, 17, 43, 117, 147, 159, 177
United States (USA), 8, 11, 108, 117, 122, 124, 137, 167
Universal equality, 18
Universal standards, 13
Urban and infrastructure civil code, 93

Values, 27, 51, 100, 148, 151, 179
    security-military, 21
Veil of legality, 19, 84, 136
Victim, 47
Violence, 14, 17, 75
voluntas (sovereign will), 5

War of 1948, 81, 97, 111, 114
War on terror, 11, 104–104, 138, 140
Wartime conditions, 140
Wartime, 2, 140, 180, 184
Weber, Max, 13, 15, 184–185
Weberian rational authority, 15
Weimar Republic, 11
Welfare state, 127, 175
West Bank, 80–81, 91, 148, 152, 159–160, 171, 173, 175, 183

Whigs and Hunters: The Origins of the Black Act, 13
Women Equality (1951), 35
World War II, 57

Yardor, 100–101, 164, 170
Yemen, 75
Yiftachel, Oren, 16, 21, 185

Yishuv, 30, 58, 149, 154
Ylakut ha-Pirsomim, 163
Yoo, John, 6, 146, 185
Young Turk Revolution, 33

Zamora, Moshe, 149
Zosman, Yoel, 101